Hitler's Shattered Dreams of Empire

Hitler's Shattered Dreams of Empire

Crucial Battles of the Eastern and Western Front 1941–1944

Rex Bashford

Pen & Sword
MILITARY

First published in Great Britain in 2023 by
Pen & Sword Military
An imprint of Pen & Sword Books Limited
Yorkshire – Philadelphia

ISBN 978 1 39907 031 7

Typeset by Mac Style
Printed in the UK by CPI Group (UK) Ltd, Croydon, CR0 4YY.

Pen & Sword Books Limited incorporates the imprints of After the Battle, Atlas,
Archaeology, Aviation, Discovery, Family History, Fiction, History, Maritime,
Military, Military Classics, Politics, Select, Transport, True Crime, Air World,
Frontline Publishing, Leo Cooper, Remember When, Seaforth Publishing, The
Praetorian Press, Wharncliffe Local History, Wharncliffe Transport, Wharncliffe
True Crime and White Owl.

For a complete list of Pen & Sword titles please contact

PEN & SWORD BOOKS LIMITED
47 Church Street, Barnsley, South Yorkshire, S70 2AS, England
E-mail: enquiries@pen-and-sword.co.uk
Website: www.pen-and-sword.co.uk
or
PEN AND SWORD BOOKS
1950 Lawrence Rd, Havertown, PA 19083, USA
E-mail: uspen-and-sword@casematepublishers.com
Website: www.penandswordbooks.com

*This book is dedicated to my dear children
Alisdair, and Louise, with much love.*

Contents

Glossary of Terms and Abbreviations

Abwehr   The German military intelligence and secret service. The head of the service was Admiral Canaris, who was opposed to the Nazi regime. Canaris came into conflict with Reichsfuhrer-SS Himmler, who suspected him of playing a double game with the enemy Western powers, which he convinced Hitler was true. The Abwehr was abolished in February 1944 and its operations subsumed with those of the SS intelligence services. After the attempt on Hitler's life on 20 July 1944, Canaris was arrested by the Gestapo and, although there was no direct evidence against him, was executed on 9 April 1945.

AGp   Army Group. In the German context, usually a group of three corps of three or four divisions each. However, these groupings could be much larger; for example, Army Group Centre on the Eastern Front comprised over seventy divisions for Operation *Typhoon*, the attack on Moscow in October 1941.

JG   Abbreviation of Jagdgeschwader. A wing of single-engine fighters, which was three fighter Gruppen. Each Gruppe consisted of three or four squadrons, so a Jagdeschwader would usually contain between nine and twelve fighter squadrons.

Luftflotte   The largest command grouping of the Luftwaffe for major campaigns. For the *Eagle Day* attack on South-East England in August 1940, Luftflotte 3 – under the command of Field Marshal Sperrle – comprised three air corps with approximately 1,000 aircraft.

Nazi Party   National Socialist German Workers' Party (or NSDAP, Nationalsozialistische Deutsche Arbeiterpartei).

ObdH   Oberfehlshaber des Heeres, the Commander-in-Chief of the Army.

OB West   Oberbefehlshaber West, the Commander-in-Chief of the western group of armies in France, the Netherlands and Belgium.

OKH   Oberkommando des Heeres, the High Command of the Army.

OKL   Oberkommando der Luftwaffe, the High Command of the Luftwaffe.

OKM   Oberkommando der Kriegsmarine, the High Command of the Navy.

OKW   Oberkommando der Wehrmacht, the Supreme Command of the Armed Forces. Hitler's personal military staff.

PzKpfw   Abbreviation of the German term for tank types, Panzerkampfwagen.

SA   The Sturmabteilung, the semi-military arm of the Nazi Party, formed by Hitler to guard speakers at their meetings and to disrupt the meetings of other political parties. At its height in 1933, it had an estimated membership of 2 million, which made it potentially more powerful than the German Army, which was limited to 100,000 troops by the Versailles Treaty. Hitler accused the leadership of the SA of plotting to overthrow the government, and on 30 June 1934 ('The Night of The Long Knives') used the SS (Schutzstaffel) to murder the leadership of the SA, even though it was comprised of some of his longest-standing and most devoted followers.

Waffen-SS The military branch of the SS. It did not have any duties guarding concentration camps. Its units were used in conjunction with normal Army units on the field and were under the direction of the Army's commanders when they were used in battle. However, they were not under the jurisdiction of the Army command in any other respect, but remained under the control of Reichsfuhrer-SS Heinrich Himmler. The divisions of the SS conducted themselves very brutally on the battlefield, frequently not taking prisoners or murdering enemy soldiers on the battlefield when they had surrendered. There are well-evidenced accounts of this occurring on the Eastern and Western Fronts, which frequently led to the opposing forces using the same tactics in retaliation.

Wehrmacht The name given by Hitler to the armed forces of Nazi Germany. It encompassed the four branches, which were the Army, Air Force, Navy and Waffen-SS.

Introduction

Hitler's dream of creating a Germanic Empire in the East was the longest-meditated and most-fundamental of his aims. The 'logic' behind his dream was that it was the only way[1] to solve the problem of '*lebensraum*'[2] for the German *Volk* and to enable his people's ultimate development as the master race. Hitler – the political master of the Greater German Reich – mobilized the nation's resources so that he, as Supreme Commander of the Wehrmacht, could ensure the achievement of this dream. To do so, he had to defeat his enemies. The campaigns of 1940 convinced him of the invincibility of the Third Reich's military forces under his command. After disposing of his Western enemies, he was free to concentrate on the war he really wanted: the one to destroy communism and its incarnation, the USSR, which would also enable him to create his new empire from its territories. If his Western enemies continued their fruitless resistance, then they too would be '*aushloschen*'.[3]

The campaigns analysed in this and the other volumes in this three-part series reflect my view of those which illustrate how Hitler went about achieving his aim with the greatest clarity. Operation *Barbarossa* against the USSR was the single most important campaign of the Second World War, followed by the invasion of France, and these are dealt with in detail in the first two volumes. This does not mean that campaigns which are not included were not important, but in my view they do not reveal any changes in Hitler's strategic approach or his methods of command in dealing with the problems of decision which arose as Supreme Commander of the Wehrmacht and especially as the operational Commander-in-Chief of the Army. I have included in this volume the Ardennes offensive because it was the last and only German offensive on any scale that occurred on the Western Front following the defeat in Normandy, and clearly shows how Hitler intended to deal with the disastrous situation which, ironically, he had created. Because it was the last of the major offensives the Germans made in the Second World War, it also allows a comparison with Hitler's strategy and methods in earlier campaigns.

Nazi Germany presents the clearest example in the modern era of a major state reflecting the beliefs and idiosyncrasies of a single human being. Hitler stamped his authority on the Nazi state to such a degree that by 1939, nothing of any consequence occurred unless it was exactly in accordance with his wishes.[4] An attempt to dress up this mania for control was made through the Nazi doctrine of the '*Fuhrerprinzip*',[5] under which, because Hitler had absolute authority and responsibility for making decisions, no-one had the ability to question them. This had been Hitler's method of running the Nazi Party since 1921 and became the way that the German state was run once President Hindenburg died in 1934 and Hitler (unconstitutionally) created the new office of Fuhrer and Chancellor for himself.

In such a state, it was only to be expected that this doctrine of unquestioning obedience would be inflicted on the military from the highest levels to the lowest. It may be thought that this was the norm for the military, but the German military tradition had been to develop strategy at the highest levels in a collegiate manner, promoting initiative at the operational level so that commanders could, within reason, react to situations as they developed with the benefit of information that their higher leaders did not have because they weren't 'on the spot'. Hitler strove to reverse this situation from the first day that he became the Supreme Commander of the Wehrmacht in 1934 until he committed suicide in the Berlin Chancellery in 1945.[6] He viewed almost any difference of opinion as obstruction, defeatism or worse, and unless coming from one of an extremely small group of favoured officers, he would brook no alternatives.

The result of this 'leadership' was predictable in that almost all initiative at the operational level of command was stifled, and very few higher-level commanders were able to work constructively with Hitler. The fact that he had three Chiefs of the General Staff during the war, and that none of them had any doubt that he was totally unfit to be the operational head of the German Army, speaks for itself, especially as he picked them as being suitable for that role himself. His approach to planning operations was extremely amateurish, with no testing of his plans carried out in critical operations such as the 1942 offensive leading to the disaster at Stalingrad, the Ardennes offensive or any other of the operations he 'masterminded'. His sacking of army group commanders once these operations developed contrary to his plan is evidence of his ignorance of the limitations which force, space, time and logistics place on military operations.

Hitler's conduct of the invasion of the USSR in 1941 clearly shows all the characteristics of his method of command. His directives changing the emphasis of the invasion plan developed by OKH, so that Army Group Centre's armour was split and sent to the wings of the theatre of operations in attempts to take Leningrad and Kharkov at the same time, imposed totally unrealistic expectations on them and limited the time for any subsequent attempt to take the pre-eminent prize: Moscow. These changes meant that the chance to obtain strategic victory in 1941 was lost (if indeed it was ever possible). Moreover, the objectives of these diversions of effort were primarily political and economic in nature, and were not directed at the critical military objective of the campaign, which was to destroy the Red Army in front of Moscow. Because of these misguided changes, the Wehrmacht was condemned to fight a desperate winter campaign in circumstances so disadvantageous that it never fully recovered.

It was during the 1941 winter campaign that Hitler found his version of military strategy – unyielding defence in all circumstances, regardless of the tactical situation. His best generals – including Manstein, Rundstedt, Kluge, Halder, Guderian, Zeitzler and Kleist – tried to convince him that elastic defence was best suited to the strengths of the German Army and would conserve its power to the greatest degree possible. This formidable array of professional military ability was unable to change his mind, and his credo of unyielding static defence became Hitler's obsession; in keeping, no doubt, with his mania for absolute control.

A typical example of this approach was Hitler's first sacking of Field Marshal von Rundstedt on 30 November 1941, which resulted from a difference of opinion over withdrawing German forces from Rostov. Rundstedt told Hitler that Rostov could not be held with his overextended forces, but Hitler ordered it be held anyway. When Rundstedt stated that if Hitler did not have confidence in his judgement then he should get someone else, Hitler replaced him with Reichenau. The result was that the Germans were forced to retreat from Rostov the very next day to the position that Rundstedt had indicated, but at the cost of additional losses because of Hitler's refusal to accept the reality of the situation.

The campaign of 1942 in the USSR saw an almost identical re-run of the errors committed in 1941, the main elements being underestimation of the enemy, dispersal of the attacking force across too many objectives – resulting in insufficient power to attain any of them – and incessant chopping and changing by Hitler of the deployment and objectives of those attacking forces. Once again, the objectives of the campaign were not selected with a view to destroying the Red Army, but to deprive the USSR of economic assets. It is a matter of record that Halder, Zeitzler and other senior commanders warned Hitler of the dangers represented by the weak and exposed flank north-west of Stalingrad, through which the Red Army eventually attacked. They implored him to withdraw the German forces to a new front before the beginning of the Soviet offensive which cut off Stalingrad, but were ignored.

The sacking of Halder as Chief of Staff of the Army High Command (OKH) occurred at virtually the same time that Hitler had a serious falling out with Jodl and Keitel, caused by Hitler's view that the failure of the attack in the Caucasus was due to Field Marshal List not obeying his orders. This was not correct, and Jodl said that this was the case. A furious Hitler decided to sack both Jodl and Keitel, as well as List, but the events surrounding the Stalingrad disaster intervened so although List was sacked, Jodl and Keitel remained. Halder represented the traditions of the German General Staff and did not shrink from giving his view on matters needing a decision, which did not ingratiate him with Hitler, who eventually could not abide his continued proximity due to his willingness to voice a contrary opinion. An attempt to relieve Stalingrad had no realistic chance of success with the forces available, as was pointed out to Hitler by Manstein and Zeitzler, but once again they were ignored. Goering's assurance that the Luftwaffe could supply the Sixth Army in situ was transparently reckless, but Hitler chose to accept the word of the Reichsmarschall while doing nothing to determine whether it was possible.[7] Disaster on a huge scale was the result, all of it being Hitler's work.

It was primarily due to Zeitzler's repeated importuning of Hitler that the order to evacuate Army Group A in the Caucasus was given, thus saving the German forces there from certain encirclement, and an irreversible even greater catastrophe in 1942 was averted.

Field Marshal Manstein's defensive battles after Stalingrad and the ripostes delivered at Kharkov and Belgorod in early 1943 should have been evidence enough to Hitler that the techniques of manoeuvre and the tactics employed within the overall strategy of elastic defence were successful and could be used to inflict very high losses on the Red Army, while also conserving German forces. However, the Fuhrer chose to ignore or did not understand the reason for these successful ripostes.

Neither of the alternative plans postulated by Manstein to Hitler in February 1943 advocated the attack which Hitler developed, and which eventually became Operation *Citadel* in July at Kursk. Critically, Manstein's plan was predicated on any attack occurring before the Red Army had regained its balance and was reinforced after the German counterattacks earlier that year. Not only was the plan of attack adopted a very obvious one, and correctly predicted by the Soviet High Command, but Hitler repeatedly delayed its commencement in the hope that by adding more forces to give more weight it would have a greater chance of success. He was warned that this would not be the case, for the simple reasons that the Soviets would be able to make their defences even more formidable during the interval and were out-producing the Germans in war materiel; any additional German power would be more than offset by the lost time and extra Soviet production. He also ignored this advice. The fact that some of the generals were in favour of the operation should not be allowed to disguise the fact that Field Marshal Model – who was to command one of the attacking armies – and others senior commanders were not. As Hitler had assumed operational command of the German Army, he cannot escape the responsibility for the failure of *Citadel*. This defeat sounded the death knell of the German Army in the east, and marked the irrevocable move of the initiative from the Germans to the Red Army where it stayed for the rest of the war. Total defeat could now only be avoided if a completely different approach to strategy and tactics was adopted. Manstein suggested changes to Hitler[8] and was not only ignored but sacked, although he had again shown his brilliance by largely containing the Red Army offensives against Army Group South from July 1943 until his removal from office on 30 March 1944.

These reverses on the Eastern Front did not occur in a vacuum. Germany suffered a significant defeat in Tunisia in 1943. After the British victory at El Alamein, Hitler insisted on clinging to the remnants of the Italian-African Empire and reinforced it with more German troops and materiel, despite Axis troops in North Africa now facing the enemy on two fronts following the launch of Operation *Torch* by the Western Allies. Nevertheless, the inevitable defeat occurred, with 157,000 German prisoners being taken.[9] This was a pointless and gratuitous gift to the Allies which Germany could ill afford, one which could have been avoided if the Fuhrer had listened to the advice of his operational commanders and evacuated the troops in a timely manner.

Hitler had stated on numerous occasions that if the invasion of France succeeded, Germany would lose the war.[10] On 6 June 1944, the Allies did indeed invade, coming ashore in Normandy, and German defences in France were overwhelmed before the end of August. Hitler's orders prevented the nineteen divisions of the Fifteenth Army from being committed to the battle in Normandy until it was too late to affect the result. Some of its divisions were close to the Normandy battlefield, and had they been released early enough, there is little doubt that the Allies' situation would have been made much more difficult,[11] despite the dominating presence of the British and America tactical air forces. Similarly, Hitler overrode Rommel's deployment of forces that were in Normandy prior to and during the invasion, and in almost every instance this was to the prejudice of the defence. These suggested redeployments are set out in a remarkable memorandum from Rommel to Hitler of 3 July 1944, which is summarized in this volume and makes astonishing reading (see page 210). Once again, Hitler's mantra of inflexible defence was his sole strategy, but it achieved nothing and led to a catastrophic defeat which ended in the killing ground around Falaise. Between June and September 1944, the Germans lost sixty divisions in France, including some of their best formations, with 265,000 men killed or wounded and a further 350,000 taken prisoner.[12] This ranked amongst the greatest, if not the greatest, defeats suffered by Germany in the Second World War, even taking into account those on the Eastern Front.

Once the remnants of the German forces in the West had retreated almost to the frontiers of their homeland, they were only saved from even heavier losses when the Allies outran their supply lines and had to restrict their operations. In a bid to break the stalemate and end the war before Christmas 1944, Field Marshal Montgomery initiated Operation *Market Garden*, which attempted to outflank the Germans by seizing the Rhine bridges in the Netherlands and encircling German forces in northern Germany. By a combination of pure good fortune and Allied errors, the Germans were able to frustrate the aims of the operation.

Meanwhile, the Red Army attack on 22 June 1944 – the third anniversary of the German invasion of Russia – was the largest operation of the war on the Eastern Front so far. Operation *Bagration* was co-ordinated with the Russians' Western Allies to cause the utmost difficulty for Hitler, the attacks annihilating Army Group Centre and causing the loss of thirty German divisions.[13] A Russian offensive at Leningrad also led to its release from an encirclement lasting 1,000 days and the isolation of Army Group North, which was cut off in the Courland pocket. Despite the pleas of Guderian and others, Hitler would not sanction the withdrawal of these forces, even though they would have been a significant reinforcement to the German defences in the East, which were by now stretched to the limit. When they eventually surrendered to the Red Army in May 1945, they had provided no practical assistance to the defence of Germany.

Hitler made one last desperate gamble to avoid defeat in the West. Between the defeat in Normandy and December 1944, he had scraped together as many of the latest models of tanks and other weapons as Germany could produce to create fresh forces or re-equip others to attack the US 12th Army Group through the Ardennes, with the objective of separating it from the British 21st Army Group to the north and retaking the vital port of Antwerp. What almost immediately became known as the Battle of the Bulge once again exhibited all the characteristics of the Fuhrer's limited understanding of strategy. There was never any realistic chance of the Ardennes offensive succeeding, apart from in Hitler's delusions and in the fanciful writings of some journalists in the Western press. Its only purpose was to prolong Hitler's hold on power.

The only logical conclusion one can arrive at from the examples given in Volumes 1 and 2 of this work is that Hitler was utterly unsuited to higher military command. Although he and his acolytes greatly esteemed his abilities in the field, the results of his command of the Wehrmacht – and particularly of the German Army – were catastrophic. It is true that he contributed to the early victories of the war; his choice of the Manstein Plan for the attack in the West in 1940 was the best decision he made during the entire war. However, the rapid victories in the Polish, Norwegian and French campaigns apparently convinced him that he was a military genius, reinforcing his overweening arrogance, which he exhibited daily when dealing with the Army General Staff and leading to his taking operational control of the whole German Army. Had he been satisfied to remain as the titular Supreme Commander of the Wehrmacht and appointed one of the many far more capable commanders as Commander-in-Chief of the Army, they could hardly have failed to make more rational decisions relating to its operational employment. They may even have been able to achieve victory in the East in 1941 or to secure a stalemate in 1942/43, possibly providing a diplomatic solution with Stalin for Nazi Germany. This, of course, is unknowable. However, what can be said with some conviction is that none of his commanders could have achieved a worse result for Germany than did Hitler.

Comparison of Equivalent Senior Ranks in Armies During the Second World War

UK	Germany	USA	USSR	France
No equivalent	Reichsmarschall (this rank was created to make Hermann Goering the most senior member of the armed forces on 19 July 1940)		No equivalent	No equivalent
Field Marshal	Generalfeldmarschall	General of the Army ☆☆☆☆☆	Marshal of the Soviet Union	Marechal de France
No equivalent	Colonel General	No equivalent	Army General ☆☆☆☆	General d'Armee
General	General of Artillery, Panzer Troops, Infantry (and others according to specialization)	General ☆☆☆☆	General ☆☆☆	General de Corps
Lieutenant General	Lieutenant General	Lieutenant General ☆☆☆	Lieutenant General ☆☆	General de Division
Major General	Major General	Major General ☆☆	Major General ☆	No equivalent
Brigadier	No equivalent	Brigadier General ☆	No equivalent	General de Brigade

Chapter 1

Operation *Barbarossa*

Hitler's decision to invade the USSR

The Nazi invasion of the USSR began the greatest military campaign in history in terms of the forces involved, its duration and the casualties suffered. Because of the overwhelming Soviet victory that ensued and its pivotal role in the utter destruction of Nazi Germany, it is easy to assume that Hitler's decision to attack the USSR was militarily stupid, or evidence that he was, in fact, insane. Whether or not these conclusions are correct, however, considerations were applied, which shows that the decision was not without some foundation in logic from the Fuhrer's viewpoint. These considerations can be summarized as follows:

1. Germany defeated Russia in the First World War while also engaged in the fearsome struggle with the Western Allies. In 1941, France had already been defeated, and there was no prospect of Britain returning to Europe for the foreseeable future, if ever. Consequently, Hitler rationalized that he was not embarking on a two-front war, and there would be enough time to overwhelm the USSR in a blitzkrieg campaign of the kind which had previously been successful against his other enemies, before a final reckoning was required with Britain.

2. Stalin's drastic purge of the Soviet military in 1937 had significantly weakened its power, and this factor would not last much longer at the same level of advantage to Germany. Virtually all the senior officer corps in the Soviet Army were either liquidated or imprisoned, and the effect of this drastic action had severely lowered its efficiency. The opportunity to strike while the Red Army was recovering from this self-inflicted calamity would not last forever.

3. The performance of Soviet forces during their war with Finland was exceptionally poor, indicating that they would not be able to withstand an attack by the Wehrmacht. Hitler believed there could not be better evidence that the Soviet Army would not be a difficult opponent. And given what the Finns had already done, it was reasonable to assume the Germans could do as well, or even better.

4. In the campaigns before the invasion of the USSR, the Wehrmacht had demonstrated that it was a finely tuned instrument of power; not to take advantage of this capability would be a mistake. The performance of the German Army and Luftwaffe in Poland, Norway, France, Yugoslavia, North Africa and Greece had been exemplary. They employed the most modern technology and had attained a degree of strategic and tactical flexibility never previously achieved, along with an aura of invincibility not seen since Napoleon's Grande Armée. However, their weapons and aircraft had been designed before the outbreak of the war, and the same level of technological and operational advantage could not be expected to be maintained indefinitely. Therefore, he felt it would be better to strike as soon as favourable circumstances presented themselves.

5. Hitler believed that Britain's position was militarily hopeless and that its continued resistance could only be explained on the basis that it was expecting the USSR to join the war on its side. Destroying the USSR would thus force Britain to sue for peace or enable Germany to end the war victoriously. Therefore, the sooner that the USSR was eliminated the better.

6. If there was to be war with the USA, as in the First World War, it would be better to deal with the USSR before this occurred. It took until 1917 for the USA to become involved in the First World War, and it was well-known that most Americans wanted to stay out of any European conflict, even though they did not view Hitler or the Nazis positively. In June 1941, the Fuhrer had no reason to suspect that the USA would become involved in the current war, so attacking the USSR while the USA remained neutral was far preferable to waiting until later, when the USA might be involved and the circumstances would be less favourable for Germany.

For all these reasons, Hitler could justify to himself his decision to attack, and without any counterbalancing institutions or advisors to inhibit him, his view was final in Nazi Germany.

Hitler's irrational dogma

Nevertheless, the mere rational balancing of positive and negative factors was never Hitler's way. Among other similar declarations, he stated:[1]

'I go the way that Providence dictates for me with all the assurance of a sleepwalker.'

Obviously, the Fuhrer trusted his instinct more than any rational considerations.

The long-standing reasons behind Hitler's attack on the USSR had little to do with rational balancing of the military factors involved. These reasons were associated with his racial and ideological dogma, which were anything but logical and rational. They are well known and included his visceral hatred of communism, which in his twisted view he saw as part of the 'Jewish world conspiracy'; his classification of all Slavic peoples as *'untermensch'* (sub-humans); and his belief that Germans were the 'master race' destined to rule the world. Consequent to these beliefs was the entitlement of the German *volk* to a greater share of *'lebensraum'* (living space) than Europe could offer the master race, which could only be obtained in the East, as he clearly stated many years prior to the war in his autobiographical manifesto *Mein Kampf*:[2]

'The demand for the reestablishment of the frontiers of the year 1914 is political nonsense of such a degree and consequence as to look like a crime... The frontiers of the year 1914 signify nothing at all for the future of the German nation... They would lead to an additional bleeding of our national body... As opposed to this we National Socialists must cling unflinchingly to our foreign policy aims, that is, to guarantee the German nation the soil and territory to which it is entitled on this earth.

'We terminate the endless German drive to the South and West of Europe and direct our drive to the land of the East. We finally terminate the colonial and trade policy of the pre-war period and proceed to the territorial policy of the future. But if we talk about new soil and territory in Europe today we can think primarily only of Russia and its vassal border states.'

There could hardly be a clearer statement, and Hitler was far from being alone in these beliefs. There were many in power in Germany in the First World War and afterwards who shared this view, as well as many in the German Nationalist parties during the period of the Weimar Republic. These views were also commonplace in the Austro-Hungarian Empire at the time that Hitler grew up, especially in Vienna. Anyone who studies the terms of the Treaty of Brest-Litovsk, which the Germans forced on the infant USSR in February 1918 to end the First World War in the East, will see these very ideas in operation. Under the terms of that treaty, the former Russian Empire lost 34 per cent of its population, 54 per cent of its industrial land, 89 per cent of its coalfields and 26 per cent of its railways. The USSR was also fined 300 million gold Marks. According to historian Spencer Tucker, the German General Staff had formulated such extraordinarily harsh terms that they shocked even the German negotiators.[3] Hitler is on record as praising the terms of the treaty for providing the 'land and soil' needed to sustain the German people.[4] Viewed against the terms of Brest-Litovsk, those of the Versailles Treaty, which Germany was required to sign by the victorious Allies at the end of the First World War, and about which Hitler and his followers complained so much and so volubly, were mild indeed.

Any thought that Hitler's views may have changed in the interval between writing *Mein Kampf* in 1923–25 and the invasion of the USSR are dealt with by a quote from Hugh Trevor-Roper's *Hitler's Table Talk*, which has a verbatim record taken by stenographers of Hitler's informal conversations at his various headquarters, compiled on the orders of the Fuhrer's secretary, Martin Bormann.[5] Hitler's remarks at midday on 25 September 1941 included the following:[6]

'Asia, what a disquieting reservoir of men! The safety of Europe will not be assured until we have driven Asia back behind the Urals. **No organised Russian state must be allowed to exist west of that line. They are brutes, and neither Bolshevism or Tsarism makes any difference – they are brutes in a state of nature [Author's emphasis].** The danger would be still greater if this space were to be mongolised. Suddenly a wave comes foaming from Asia and surprises a Europe benumbed by civilisation and deceived by the illusion of collective security!

'Since there is no natural protection against such a flood, we must meet it with a living wall. **A permanent state of war [Author's emphasis]** on the Eastern Front will help to form a sound race of men, and will prevent us from relapsing into the softness of a Europe thrown back upon itself.'

There is thus absolutely no doubt that Hitler's views were the same in 1941 as when he wrote *Mein Kampf* in the mid-1920s.

It is also important to appreciate that the destruction of communism was central to Hitler's entire political worldview. His thoughts on this were recorded in remarks he made on the night of 5/6 July 1941, as reported in Trevor-Roper's invaluable book:[7]

'To those who ask me whether it will be enough to reach the Urals as a frontier, I reply that for the present it is enough for the frontier to be drawn back as far as that. **What matters is that Bolshevism must be exterminated [Author's emphasis].** In case of necessity, we shall renew our advance wherever a new centre of resistance is formed. Moscow, as the centre of the doctrine, must disappear from the earth's surface, as soon as its riches have been brought to shelter. There's no question of our collaborating with the Muscovite proletariat.'

Once again, Hitler's intentions are here made absolutely clear.

The Nazi–Soviet Non-Aggression Pact

Hitler's non-aggression treaty with the USSR was a political masterstroke which he believed would seal the fate of Poland and render valueless the guarantee of support from Britain and France. His Foreign Minister, Joachim von Ribbentrop, went to Moscow to finalize the treaty as quickly as possible, and Abert Speer – the Fuhrer's chief architect and future Reich Minister of Armaments and War Production – happened to be with him when he heard of the Soviet government's agreement:[8]

> '[T]hree weeks later, on August 21, 1939, we heard that the German Foreign Minister was in Moscow for some negotiations. During supper a note was handed to Hitler. He scanned it, stared into space for a moment, flushed deeply, then banged on the table so hard that the glasses rattled, and then exclaimed in a voice breaking with excitement: "I have them! I have them!" Seconds later he had already regained control of himself. No one dared ask any question, and the meal continued.
>
> 'After supper Hitler called his entourage together. "We are going to conclude a non-aggression pact with Russia. Here, read this. A telegram from Stalin."…To see the names of Hitler and Stalin linked in friendship on a piece of paper was the most staggering, the most exciting turn of events I could possibly have imagined.'

Hitler, however, only ever regarded the pact as a temporary expedient to neutralize the Soviets militarily while he dealt with Poland. There is much evidence that he thought that Stalin could not be trusted and was only waiting for favourable conditions to attack Germany, no doubt reflecting his own view of how to comply with treaties, as is set out in Chapter 3 of Volume 1 of this work, 'Hitler Rolls the Dice for War'. This view was clearly recorded in the diary of the Chief of the General Staff of the Army, Colonel General Franz Halder, after a meeting on 13 July 1940:[9]

> 'The Fuhrer is greatly puzzled by Britain's persisting unwillingness to make peace. He sees the answer (as we do) in Britain's hope on Russia, and therefore counts on having to compel her by main force to agree to peace. Actually that is much against his grain. The reason is that a military defeat of Britain will bring about the disintegration of the British Empire. This would not be of any benefit to Germany. German blood would be shed to accomplish something that would benefit only Japan, the United States, and others.'

Just over a week later, Halder wrote on 22 July:[10]

> 'Stalin is flirting with Britain to keep her in the war and tie us down, with a view to gain time and take what he wants, knowing he could not get it once peace breaks out. He has an interest in not letting Germany become too strong, **but there are no indications of any Russian aggressiveness against us [Author's emphasis].**'

He added on 31 July:[11]

> 'Britain's last hope lies in Russia and the United States. If Russia drops out of the picture, America, too is lost for Britain, because elimination of Russia would tremendously increase Japan's power in the Far East.'

Whether this appreciation of the USSR's likely course is correct is not important – what is important is that it shows Hitler's perception of their likely course. The evidence of Stalin's intentions at the time shows that he definitely wished to keep well away from any war with Germany.

During the trial of the major war criminals at Nuremberg following the defeat of Germany, General Jodl gave the following evidence under examination of when he first heard from Hitler of his intention to attack the USSR:[12]

> 'DR. EXNER: Now, when did you first hear of the Fuhrer's fears that Russia might prove hostile to us?
> 'JODL: For the first time, on 29 July 1940, at the Berghof near Berchtesgaden.
> 'DR. EXNER: In what connection?
> 'JODL: The Fuhrer kept me back alone after a discussion on the situation and said to me, most unexpectedly, that he was worried that Russia might occupy still more territory in Romania before the winter and that the Romanian oil region, which was the condition sine qua non for our war strategy, would thus be taken from us. He asked me whether we could not deploy our troops immediately, so that we would be ready by autumn to oppose with strong forces any such Russian intention. These are almost the exact words which he used, and all other versions are false.'

There was no evidence that the Soviets were intending any operation of this kind. This evidence does show, however, that the Fuhrer was concerned about Soviet intentions seriously enough to consider attacking them in 1940, but was this due to a rational view regarding their intentions or was it a reflection of his long-held and deep-seated hatred of the USSR as the 'cradle of communism' and his wish to crush it?

Von Schulenberg, the German Ambassador to the USSR, tried to promote the Nazi–Soviet relationship to a more permanent level, sending a memo to Hitler in May 1941 on the implications of Stalin's appointment as Chairman of the People's Council of Commissars, making him the executive head of the Soviet government while retaining the leadership of the Communist Party:[13]

'He was convinced that Stalin will use his new position in order to take part personally in the maintenance and development of good relations between the Soviets and Germany.'

Stalin also showed some personal warmth toward the German Ambassador, which he rarely did with anyone. When the Japanese diplomat Matsuoka was leaving Moscow after the signing of the Tripartite Agreement in April 1941, Stalin sought out Schulenberg and embraced him, saying:[14]

'We must remain friends and you must do everything to that end.'

These actions by Stalin were quite out of the ordinary, and while not conclusive in itself, certainly indicate that he wished to stay as close as possible to Germany, which had, after all, just shown the power of the Wehrmacht with the campaign in France, something that certainly did not go unnoticed by Stalin.

The German military attaché in Moscow, General Ernst Kostring, travelled throughout the USSR during May 1941 and could find 'no signs of an offensive intention'.[15] This was duly reported back to Berlin, but seemingly made no impression on the Fuhrer.

It should also be remembered that Britain and France had come very close to being at war with the USSR during its recent conflict with Finland and were instrumental in expelling the USSR from the League of Nations in December 1939 because of that war. Relations between the Soviets and Britain were thus extremely cool, remaining so until Operation *Barbarossa* commenced.

Stalin was very conscious that Russia had been invaded by foreign powers five times during the prior 200 years (France in 1812, Japan in 1905, Germany in 1914, international intervention following the birth of the USSR itself in 1918 and most recently the war with Poland in 1921). He also believed that the Czar's mobilization order in 1914 had been premature and had led to the German declaration of war and the ultimate defeat of Russia in the First World War. His preoccupation with the security of the USSR is therefore understandable. Additionally, many of the independent states on the borders of the USSR had been part of the Czarist empire when it collapsed, including Poland, Estonia, Latvia, Lithuania and Finland, and sections of that empire's territory had been taken by other countries during the Soviet Civil War in the 1920s. It is to some degree understandable that Stalin looked upon these territories as rightfully belonging to the USSR, even if they had changed ownership many times in the past.

Soviet provocations?

There is also no doubt that the actions of the Soviet government after the signing of the 1939 non-aggression pact, and following the German campaigns in Poland and the West, aggravated Hitler's mistrust of their motives, making the decision to attack Russia more likely. The Soviets moved quickly to take advantage of the secret territorial provisions of the pact and gain every advantage they could from it, leading to the war with Finland and the virtual annexation of Lithuania, Estonia and Latvia. No doubt they saw their actions as merely implementing the provisions of the pact. But in Hitler's eyes, the Soviets had gone much further than they were entitled to; he did not equate their actions with what he meant by including these territories in the Soviet 'sphere of influence'. Probably the most concerning of the provocations to Hitler was when the Soviets sent an ultimatum to Romania requiring the cession of Bessarabia and Bukovina as recompense for alterations made to the USSR's borders during the civil war. Although the Fuhrer advised the Romanians to accept these changes, their effect was to bring the Soviet Air Force within striking distance of the only external German source of oil, the Romanian Ploesti oilfields. This was a grave matter to Hitler.

Field Marshal Wilhelm Keitel, Chief of the OKW (Oberkommando der Wehrmacht, the Supreme Command of the German armed forces) from 1938–45, noted in his memoirs:[16]

> 'The Soviet Union's demeanour throughout our Polish campaign was of especial interest and particularly edifying. After we had launched our attack, Hitler had, of course, arranged for Stalin's immediate intervention in the campaign to be requested through diplomatic channels; we had a vested interest in this, because we particularly wanted the quickest possible conclusion of the campaign – we wanted a lightning war – in view of our western frontiers' vulnerability. Stalin, on the other hand, intended to reap his reward in the division of Poland with as little [Russian] bloodshed as possible, and he informed the Fuhrer that he

could not be ready to attack before three weeks at the earliest, as his forces were neither prepared or mobilised. …

'But, just as we were crossing the River San in the south and Warsaw was within our operational grasp, the Red Army – despite their alleged "total unreadiness" – was suddenly marching into Poland, overrunning the last of the Polish troops as they fell back and taking them into captivity, while they deflected a large part of the others into Roumania.'

Keitel's clear implication is that Stalin had misrepresented the state of readiness of the Red Army, as rather than taking three weeks to be ready to invade Poland they took only sixteen days. This accentuated Hitler's suspicion that the Soviets had concealed their true state of mobilization from the Germans, and that they thus represented a clear danger.

However, Speer noted after the Polish campaign had been concluded that there had been evidence that the Red Army was not actually ready for war:[17]

'In October, Hanke told me something which had been learned when the German troops met Soviet troops on the demarcation line in Poland: that Soviet equipment appeared extremely deficient, in fact, wretched. Hanke had reported this to Hitler. Army officers confirmed this point; Hitler must have listened to this piece of intelligence with the keenest interest, for thereafter he repeatedly cited this report as evidence that the Russians were weak and poorly organized. Soon afterward, the failure of the Soviet offensive against Finland confirmed him in this view.'

Hanke was Goebbels' deputy at the Propaganda Ministry and was often with Hitler and the inner circle of his court, although not part of it. His report obviously fed Hitler's chronic tendency to underestimate the power of his enemies.

Hitler's meeting with Molotov

Relations between Germany and the USSR deteriorated to such a degree that Foreign Minister Molotov was sent by Stalin to meet Hitler in Berlin on 12 and 13 November 1940, to 'clarify the position' regarding the two states. Molotov was a rigid, difficult person who had come up the hard way through the Soviet system, and was as much the opposite of Hitler's style and methods of government and personality as it was possible to be. It is interesting to read Paul Schmidt's record of this meeting in his book *Hitler's Interpreter*. Schmidt was Hitler's preferred interpreter and was present at almost all the important meetings Hitler had during the war, but did not interpret at this meeting, being there merely to take notes. He recollected:[18]

'Little time was wasted on formalities. The talks began soon after the Russians arrived, first Molotov and Ribbentrop, then Hitler and Molotov. There was no cordiality, and at the end of those two fateful days the relationship between the two countries was left severely strained.'

According to Schmidt, Molotov asked Hitler:[19]

"Does the German–Soviet Agreement of 1939 still apply to Finland? What does the New Order in Europe and in Asia amount to, and what part is the USSR to play in it? What is the position with respect to Bulgaria, Romania and Turkey, and how do matters stand with regard to the safeguarding of Russian interests in the Balkans and the Black Sea? May I be given information about the boundaries of the so-called Greater Asia area? How does the Tripartite Pact stand with regard to it?"

'The questions hailed down upon Hitler. No foreign visitor had ever spoken to him in this way in my presence.'

Molotov continued:[20]

"The Soviet government considers it to be its duty to make a final settlement of the Finnish question. No new agreement was necessary for this purpose since the existing Russo–German agreement had quite clearly assigned Finland to the Russian sphere of influence."

"We must have peace in Finland because of their nickel and timber!" [said] Hitler [who] was now getting cross. "A conflict in the Baltic would put a severe strain on Russo–German relations, with unpredictable consequences."

"It's not a question of the Baltic, but of Finland," Molotov snapped back.

"No war with Finland," Hitler repeated.

"Then you are departing from our agreement of last year," Molotov answered obstinately.

'This exchange never became violent but the debate was conducted by both sides with singular tenacity. Even Ribbentrop felt himself called upon to intervene soothingly.'

Later, Molotov raised the German–Romanian guarantee which Romania had requested from Germany in November 1940:[21]

"You have given a guarantee to Romania, which displeases us. guarantee also valid against Russia?"

"It applies to anyone who attacks Romania," Hitler declared flatly, but added immediately, "This should nevertheless not become acute in your case. You have just made an agreement with Romania yourselves."

"What would you say," Molotov enquired, "if we gave a guarantee to Bulgaria similar to the one granted to Romania and on the same terms, that is, with the despatch of a strong military mission?" Bulgaria, he said, was an independent country lying very near the Dardanelles, and therefore important to Russia.

"If you want to give a guarantee on the same terms as we did to Romania," Hitler remarked, "then I must first ask you whether the Bulgarians have asked you for a guarantee as the Romanians did from us?"

'Molotov's reply was in the negative but he expressed the view that "Russia could certainly reach agreement with Bulgaria", and emphasised that they had no intention of interfering in that country's internal affairs. He would be grateful if Hitler would reply to his question.

"I must talk it over with the Duce [Mussolini]," Hitler replied evasively.'

These exchanges obviously did nothing to allay Hitler's suspicions regarding the motives and actions of the USSR or to facilitate continued accord with Stalin. Another interpretation of the Soviet attitude is to expect just such a consequence from the pact that the two countries had only recently signed. It is only to be anticipated that there would be a period of change in the areas covered by the terms of the treaty which could only be managed through close accord between the partners. Such accord never existed, as Hitler entered into the pact for short-term personal gains which had nothing to do with the security of the USSR.

Hitler's Army Adjutant from 1938–43 was Major Gerhard Engel (later a lieutenant general), who kept a diary which was published in 1974 as *At the Heart of the Reich*. It contains the following entry for 15 November 1940:[22]

'F. [Fuhrer] spoke at length about Molotov visit. Said that he had not expected much to come from it. Talks had shown the direction the Russian plans were taking. M. [Molotov] had let the cat out of the bag. **He [F.] was really relieved: this would not even remain a marriage of convenience [Author's emphasis].** To let Russia into Europe would be the end of Central Europe: even the Balkans and Finland were dangerous flanks. In this connection Schmundt [Hitler's Chief Adjutant] and I to

F. In whatever case field headquarters were to be constructed with all haste, and primarily South, Centre and North. F. wants a permanent headquarters in East Prussia: he left it at that and will explore everything else with Minister Todt [Author's emphasis].'

Hitler's true intentions are reflected in his Directive No. 18, dealing with 'Strategy in the Immediate Future', issued to his military commanders on the same date as the meetings with Molotov. This stated:[23]

'Political discussions for the purpose of clarifying the attitude of Russia in the immediate future have already begun. **Regardless of the outcome of these conversations all preparations for the East for which verbal orders have already been given will be continued [Author's emphasis].** Further directives will follow on the subject as soon as the basic operational plan of the Army has been submitted to me and approved.'

This leaves little room for doubt that Hitler had made up his mind before meeting with Molotov that Germany would invade the USSR.

In evidence at Nuremberg, Reichsmarschall Herman Goering – the Commander-in-Chief of the Luftwaffe and Hitler's designated successor in the event of his death – stated that when he heard of the Fuhrer's intention to invade the USSR, he advised him not to attack at the proposed time because to do so would involve Germany in a two-front war, especially for the Luftwaffe.[24] He suggested the attack be postponed until Britain was defeated. Goering also said that Hitler was very suspicious of the USSR and that the overthrow of the pro-German government in Yugoslavia by a pro-British regime headed by General Simovic, and its immediate recognition by Moscow, was an important factor in Hitler's view of the situation. Goering testified before the war crimes tribunal:[25]

'The new Yugoslav Government quite obviously and beyond doubt, stood visibly in closest relationship with the enemies we had at that time, that is to say, England and, in this connection, with our enemy to be Russia.

'**The Simovic affair was definitely the final and decisive factor which dispelled the very last scruples which the Fuhrer had in regard to Russia's attitude, and caused him to take preventative measures in that direction under all circumstances [Author's emphasis].** Before this Simovic incident it is probable that, although preparations had been undertaken, doubts as to the inevitable necessity of an attack against Soviet Russia might have been pushed into the background. These clear relations between Moscow and Belgrade, however, dispelled the Fuhrer's very last doubts.'

While Goering's evidence is very clear, it seems incredible that Hitler believed this to be the position.

Negative lessons from history

From Hitler's standpoint, the factors mentioned above made the decision to attack the USSR both logical and rational, although utterly unscrupulous and unprincipled. Yet in reaching his decision, he completely ignored the negative lessons of history regarding the problems of attacking the USSR, which were practically the same in 1941 as had applied to Napoleon in 1812 and Charles XII of Sweden in 1708–09; but then again, they had also ignored these problems. The difficulties were very significant and can be conveniently categorized as problems relating to geography, time and weather, all of which are inter-related.

The geographic problems are self-evident to anyone who peruses a map of the USSR from 1941. It is simply immense, and an attacker from the West must travel considerable distances before reaching any objectives crucial to the Soviet continuation of the war. The main objectives are obviously Moscow, Leningrad and the economically strategic areas of the Ukraine and the oil-producing trans-Caucasus. These objectives are considerable distances from the western border of the USSR, in some cases over 1,500km. In all of Hitler's previous blitzkrieg campaigns, none of the crucial objectives were so far from the starting point, so the complexities caused by these distances had never before been present for German forces. In addition to the shorter distances involved, in the campaigns in the West, the Wehrmacht had been able to use extensive road and rail networks in the modern, developed countries it passed through, something that hardly existed in the USSR. These new factors aggravated supply problems and made it imperative that the military defeat of Soviet forces be accomplished as close to the German starting point as possible.

Another consequence of the geography through which the attacker must proceed is that the front line becomes longer the further east he goes. The effect of achieving victories and moving further east is that the attacker loses the concentration of force which is so vital to maintaining the momentum essential to overall victory. Any loss of concentration also emphasizes any disparity in numbers, making it easier for the attacker's front to be infiltrated and disrupted by irregular or partisan forces.

The impact of time on the invasion was also crucial, because unless victory was obtained in the blitzkrieg campaign as planned – that is, within five or six months – Germany did not have the economic resources to maintain the pressure at the level necessary to achieve final victory. Hitler himself stated this, stressing the importance of a quick victory to the commanders of the armed forces and those chosen to lead the various armies in the field.

Once these first two factors are combined with the difficulties of weather during autumn, and especially during winter, it can be seen how they all interact. Distance imposes restrictions on supply and other vital operational matters, which consequently impacts on the time taken to achieve victory, which then leads to complications caused by the weather. The weather in European Russia is unpredictable, except for one element, the winter: the question is not whether the winter will be severe, but how severe it will be. The Germans had recent knowledge of this from their campaigns in the East in the First World War, but in taking approximately four years to defeat Czarist Russia they were able to supply their armies with the required clothing to lessen winter's effect. With catastrophic consequences, Hitler did not sufficiently take the harshness of the Russian winter into his calculations for the 1941 invasion, with no adequate attempt to supply winter clothing early enough in the campaign.

Hitler also ignored the obvious fact that Nazi Germany had only just negotiated a very favourable trade relationship with the USSR, under which many raw materials necessary for the German economy were accessible, and that terminating this agreement would have significant effects if the invasion was not successful within the planned timeframe.

It is thus clear that from the military point of view, although there were factors that show the decision to attack the USSR was not without some rational foundation, there were also negative considerations which Hitler either ignored completely or he did not give sufficient weight to.

When did Hitler decide to attack?

It is important to note that the decision to invade the USSR was taken by Hitler some time before 1941. The evidence shows that he wanted to attack as soon as possible after the victory in France in 1940, but he was convinced by others that it was simply not operationally possible then. This is borne out by a conversation between Keitel, Jodl and Hitler on 29 June 1940 that was heard by Speer and later recorded in his book *Inside the Third Reich*:[26]

'[A]s I approached the group I heard a snatch of the conversation. "Now we have shown what we are capable of," Hitler was saying, "believe me, Keitel, a campaign against Russia would be like a child's game in a sandbox by comparison."'

This quote clearly shows Hitler's disdain of Soviet fighting potential, which deluded him into underrating the difficulties of a campaign in the East.

Another important factor is that the decision to attack the USSR occurred after the astonishing run of success that had attended virtually all of the Fuhrer's previous undertakings. Consequently, he considered himself to have far better judgement than any of his advisors, including his senior military commanders. From the decision to re-enter the Rhineland to the annexation of Austria (the Anschluss), the grabbing of the Sudetenland, the subsequent takeover of the rest of Czechoslovakia, the invasions of Poland, Denmark and Norway and the campaign in the West, Hitler had overruled his military advisors' objections in many respects and was proven right in almost every case. In making the decision to attack in the East, therefore, he did not take the objections of his armed forces chiefs seriously; it is reasonable to believe that many of them had been so dazzled by his successes that they did not object to the invasion of the USSR with the same conviction they had previously objecting to other of his undertakings, having thereby suffered from his displeasure. It is also true that some of the senior military commanders admired Hitler's successes, especially those whom he kept close to him at the OKW, such as Field Marshal Keitel and General Jodl. In July 1940, the Fuhrer promoted eleven of his senior commanders to the rank of field marshal and appointed Goering as Reichsmarschall, the most senior military officer in the Wehrmacht; this could not have failed to affect the view some of them had of Hitler and his next proposed attack.

The view of the senior military commanders

One of the few German commanders whom Hitler respected, despite his expressing contrary views directly to him throughout the course of the war, was Field Marshal Gerd von Rundstedt. Widely viewed as one of the best German commanders during the Second World War, Rundstedt had spent two years on the Russian Front during the First World War and was fully aware of the conditions likely to affect an Eastern campaign. Lieutenant General Guenther Blumentritt, Rundstedt's Chief of Staff, wrote in his biography *Von Rundstedt: the Soldier and the Man*:[27]

'Rundstedt was bitterly opposed to the campaign from the beginning. From the First World War he had obtained considerable knowledge of the east – the country, the Russian soldier, the difficulties on account of the climate, the illimitable distances and bad roads. He therefore asked Hitler whether he realized what risks he was taking upon himself by attacking Russia. Like Rundstedt, the Commander-in-Chief of the Army, Brauchitsch, and the Chief of the General Staff, Halder, also had grave doubts.'

These factors were the very ones that determined the course of the campaign, but Hitler ignored Rundstedt's opinion, as he did those of everyone else if they differed from his own. In his testimony before the International Military Tribunal at Nuremberg after the war, the Commander-in-Chief of the Army from 1937–42, Field Marshal Walther von Brauchitsch, described how the Fuhrer 'discussed' the proposed invasion with his most senior military leaders on 3 February 1941:[28]

'According to the statement made by Hitler in the case of Russia, we were concerned with the fact that if a war were to break out at all, **it was to be a preventive war [Author's emphasis].** In the conference I limited myself to the purely military misgivings. General Halder and I reported on three points. One was the size of the Russian area which even today cannot be bridged by motor vehicles alone. The second point was the number of the population, and therewith the large number of picked reserves which were available, and the quite different level of education and enlightenment of the Russian population as compared with the years 1914–1918, matters which I could see for myself when I was a guest of the Red Army in the year 1931. And the third point was the high armament potential of Russia. According to our estimate, **Russia at that time had at her command approximately 10,000 tanks [Author's emphasis].** Hitler must have given some thought to these problems, for he answered immediately and refuted the first two points; namely, **by saying that the domination of the Soviets was so much in disfavour by the Russian population, that the system would collapse. Everything would depend on the decisiveness of the first successes [Author's emphasis].** As far as the third point was concerned, the point of armament, he mentioned, on the basis of detailed figures that he had, as always, at his finger tips, that the armament of Russia could not be at the level we imagined it to be. Exact proof, however, we did not have at our disposal.'

When questioned whether Hitler listened to any of the misgivings that he had, Brauchitsch replied:

'He would not enter into any further discussion [Author's emphasis].'

On the question of whether the Soviets were preparing to invade Germany, Rundstedt said when interviewed by Basil Liddell Hart for his book *The Other Side of the Hill*:[29]

'Hitler insisted we must strike before Russia became too strong, and that she was much nearer striking than we imagined. He provided us with information that she was planning to launch an invasion herself that same summer, of 1941. **For my part, I was very doubtful about this – and I found little sign of it when we crossed the frontline [Author's emphasis].** ...

'In the first place, the Russians appeared to be taken by surprise when we crossed the frontier. **On my front, we found no signs of offensive preparations in the forward zone [Author's emphasis]**, though there were some further back. They had twenty-five divisions in the Carpathian sector, facing the Hungarian frontier, and I had expected that they would swing round and strike at my right flank as it advanced. Instead, they retreated. I deduced from this that they were not in a state of readiness for offensive operations, and hence that the Russian command had not been intending to launch an offensive at an early date.'

Field Marshal Ewald von Kleist, a panzer group commander at the outset of Operation *Barbarossa*, also told Liddell Hart:[30]

'It was the same with the other high commanders. **We were told the Russian armies were about to take the offensive [Author's emphasis]**, and it was essential for Germany to remove the menace. It was explained to us that the Fuhrer could not proceed with other plans while this threat loomed close, as too large a part of the German forces would be pinned down in the east keeping guard. It was argued that attack was the only way to remove the risks of a Russian attack.

'We did not underrate the Red Army, as is commonly imagined. The last German military attache in Moscow, General Kostring – a very able man – had kept us well informed about the state of the Russian army. But **Hitler refused to credit his information [Author's emphasis]**.

In his book *Lost Victories*, Field Marshal Erich von Manstein commented on the deployment of the Soviet forces when his panzer corps advanced through the USSR at the start of the invasion:[31]

'[It was] a deployment against every contingency. On 22nd June 1941, undoubtedly, **they could then have been used only in a defensive role [Author's emphasis]**.'

On the available evidence, it therefore seems obvious that Hitler distorted the true situation and that what he told his commanders suited his ideological and political purpose rather than reflecting reality.

Halder noted some of his concerns in an entry to his diary dated 28 January 1941:[32]

'BARBAROSSA: Purpose is not clear. We do not hit the British that way. Our economic potential will not be substantially improved. Risk in the west must not be underestimated. It is possible that Italy might collapse after the loss of her colonies, and we get into a southern front in Spain, Italy and Greece. **If we are then tied up in Russia, a bad situation will be made worse [Author's emphasis]**.'

These were prophetic words indeed.

Nevertheless, Hitler clearly thought his own evaluation of the military position was superior to that of his military experts.

Field Marshal Keitel commented in his memoirs on Hitler's decision to invade the USSR:[33]

'I requested a brief interview with the Fuhrer, intending to ask him to his face what reasons he had for his ominous interpretation of Russia's intentions. His reply, in brief, was that **he had never lost sight of the inevitability of a clash between the world's two most diametrically opposed ideologies, that he did not believe it could be evaded, and that being the case it was better for him to shoulder the grave burden now, in addition to the others, than for him to bequeath it to his successor [Author's emphasis]**.'

This meeting had taken place on 11 August 1940. It can hardly be doubted that the political considerations mentioned by Keitel and in *Mein Kampf* were the most significant elements in Hitler's decision to invade.

Field Marshal Erhard Milch of the Luftwaffe discussed the attack on the USSR with his commander, Goering. He gave evidence of these discussions at the Nuremberg trials as follows:[34]

'On 22 May, on one of my tours, I again came into contact with the Commander-in-Chief for the first time after a long interval. It was in Veldenstein where Goering was at the time. **There I discussed the question with him and I told him that, in my opinion, it would be a great historical task for him to prevent this war since it could only end with the annihilation of Germany. I reminded him that we should not voluntarily burden ourselves with a two-front war, et cetera. The Reich Marshal told me that he also had brought forward all these arguments, but that it was absolutely impossible to dissuade Hitler from this war [Author's emphasis].** My offer to try to speak to Hitler once more was declared by the Reich Marshal to be absolutely hopeless. We had to resign ourselves; nothing could be done about it. From these words it was quite clear that he was against this war, and that under no circumstances did he want this war but that also for him, in his position, there was no possibility of dissuading Hitler from this project.'

It is obvious from this testimony that Hitler had irrevocably made up his mind to attack the USSR; according to Goering, no arguments could dissuade him from doing so.

The reasons for the decision to invade Russia therefore included a mix of what was from Hitler's point of view militarily logical, together with illogical conclusions, idealistically based irrational dogma and ignorant opinions stemming from his lack of education.

Alternative projects for Hitler to pursue were suggested to him at the time. Perhaps the best of these would have been to conclude the conflict with the British Empire, which in the spring of 1941 was just about at its weakest ebb of the whole war, with major setbacks in North Africa, Greece and Crete. This could have been achieved through using existing Italian bases to eject Britain from the Mediterranean and the strategically important oil countries of the Middle East. Part of this process may also have included co-operating with the Spanish to take or neutralize Gibraltar, thus securing the Axis hold of the Mediterranean. Another alternative would have been to adopt a largely defensive strategy, consolidating the economies of the countries Germany had conquered while dramatically expanding the Luftwaffe and Kriegsmarine to intensify the war against Britain. In all these scenarios, the forces necessary would not have been anywhere near as significant as those committed to *Barbarossa* and would have enabled Nazi Germany to defend itself against the Western Allies almost indefinitely. However, such projects did not interest Hitler; his aim had always been to establish a German empire in the territories of the USSR, as set out years beforehand in *Mein Kampf.*

Hitler's decision to head east was therefore an enormous gamble, which he took knowing the grave doubts of his own military experts and in which everything depended upon how quickly the Germans could achieve the strategic defeat of the Red Army.

THE DEVELOPMENT OF OPERATION *BARBAROSSA*

The German plan to invade the USSR – Plan *Otto* meets Operation *Barbarossa*

Probably the single most important document to become available relating to the operation of the German High Command during the Second World War is the diary of the Chief of the General Staff from 1938–42, Colonel General Franz Halder, published as *The Halder War Diary*.[35] It has an almost daily record of events during his tenure in that role, including his comments on the operations undertaken and, by default, the role Hitler played as Supreme Commander of the Wehrmacht and operational Commander-in-Chief of the Heer (army) after he sacked Field Marshal von Brauchitsch on 19 December 1941. The diary contains many entries relating to the planning for and conduct of the German operations in Russia until Halder was himself dismissed on 24 September 1942.

The first entry referring to a discussion with Hitler concerning invading the USSR is that of 13 July 1940. The first reference relating to the strategy of that campaign was written a few days later on 22 July, summarizing Hitler's intentions as follows:[36]

'Our attention must be turned to tackling the Russian problem and prepare planning. The Fuhrer has been given the following information:

'a. German assembly will take at least four to six weeks.

'b. Object: To crush the Russian army or at least to take as much Russian territory as is necessary to bar enemy air raids on Berlin and Silesian industries. It is desirable to penetrate far enough to enable our air force to smash Russia's strategic areas.

'c. Political aims: Ukrainian state, federation of Baltic states, White Russia–Finland, Baltic states as "a thorn in the flesh".

'd. Strength required: Eighty to one hundred divisions. Russia has fifty to seventy-five good divisions. If we attack Russia this fall, pressure of the air war on Britain will be relieved. United States could supply both Britain and Russia.

'e. Operations: What operational objective should be attained? What strength have we available? Timing and area of assembly? Gateways of attack: Baltic states, Finland, Ukraine. Protect Berlin and Silesian industrial area. Protection of Romanian oil fields. (Check with Op. Sec.).'

The next entry is on 26 July, when Halder reviewed the position with his intelligence staff:[37]

'Kinzel (OQaIV): Reviews enemy intelligence relating to an operation against Russia. **The best chances of success lie in an operation in direction of Moscow [Author's emphasis]** with flank on the Baltic Sea, which, subsequently, by a drive from the North, compels Russian concentrations in the Ukraine and the Black Sea to accept battle with an inverted front.'

There is then an entry on 29 July:[38]

'General Marcks (Chief of Staff of 18th Army), on special assignment to OKH, is briefed on particulars of his work. (Stays to luncheon).'

Then on 31 July, after a Fuhrer conference, Halder wrote:[39]

'With Russia smashed, Britain's last hope would be shattered. Germany then master of Europe and the Balkans.

'Decision: Russia's destruction must therefore be made a part of this struggle. Spring 1941.

'The sooner Russia is crushed the better. Attack achieves its purpose only if Russian state can be shattered to its roots with one blow. Holding part of the country alone will not do. Standing still for the following winter would be perilous. So it is better to wait a little longer, but with the resolute determination to eliminate Russia. This is necessary also because of contiguity on the Baltic. It would be awkward to have another major power there. **If we start in May 1941, we would have five months to finish the job [Author's emphasis]**. Tackling it this year would have been best, but unified action would be impossible at this time.

'Object is the destruction of Russian manpower. Operation will be divided into three actions:

'First thrust: Kiev and securing flank protection on the Dnieper. Air force will destroy river crossings. Odessa.

'Second thrust: Baltic states and drive on Moscow.

'Finally: Linkup of northern and southern prongs.

'Successively: Limited drive on Baku oil fields.

'It will be seen later to what extent Finland and Turkey should be brought in.

'Ultimately: Ukraine, White Sea, Baltic states to us. Finland extended to White Sea.'

This is the first indication of Hitler's thinking regarding the strategy to achieve the military destruction of the USSR, and the first note in Halder's diary which confirms the Fuhrer's decision to invade the USSR and the territorial aims involved. The entry also includes a table of the strength of the German Army at the time, showing that of a total of 180 divisions, 120 would be committed to the invasion of the USSR.

The planning of the invasion was assigned by Halder to Major General Erich Marcks, Chief of Staff at Eighteenth Army (later killed in Normandy), which explains the cryptic entry referring to him on 29 July reproduced above. Marcks was one of the most able and intelligent of the junior members of the General Staff. The Marcks plan, Fall *Otto*, was presented to Halder on 1 August 1940. Halder's entry relating to it stated:[40]

'I point out that (a) Operational Group Kiev, based on Romanian territory, is treading very insecure political ground; and (b) that **the extension of the operations of the Moscow group to the Baltic states should be treated as a subsidiary action which must not detract from the main thrust on Moscow [Author's emphasis].**'

This entry makes it absolutely clear that in the view of the OKH, the main operation from its inception was to be the thrust on Moscow, with the other operations being treated as 'subsidiary'. The emphasis of the plan was to destroy the Russian forces as far west as possible (which had also been Napoleon's strategy for the invasion of 1812).

General Walter Warlimont was Chief of the National Defence Section of the OKW and reported to Colonel General Jodl, the OKW's Chief of Operations. Warlimont's book *Inside Hitler's Headquarters 1939–45* provides an unparalleled insight into the operations of Hitler's OKW during virtually the whole duration of the war. In it, he commented on the planning of the invasion of the USSR:[41]

'The working out of the entire plan of campaign together with the move forward and initial objectives was left completely in the hands of OKH; they included the Luftwaffe and Navy in their planning at the appropriate time. The operations staff of Supreme Headquarters was entirely on the sideline. General Jodl was never once invited either as a visitor or an observer to the large-scale war games which the Army Staff held in the autumn of 1940, nor, as far as one knows, did he make any attempt to play any important part in the planning, as he should have done in view of his job and position.

'The only exception of any significance was the fact that in the summer of 1940 he ordered Section L [Warlimont's section – Author's note] to work out on their own the basic factors governing an operation against Soviet Russia, but this was, as he admitted, merely to familiarise him with the geographical and other military conditions before the Army leaders presented their proposals to Hitler.'

In September 1940, toward the end of the planning process but before the plan had been tested by simulated war games or other processes, another person became involved on behalf of OKH. This was Lieutenant General Frederick Paulus, who had just been appointed Deputy Chief of the General Staff (at Hitler's insistence); he was later to achieve notoriety as the commander of the doomed Sixth Army at Stalingrad. Paulus directed that a series of war game simulations should be staged to test the Marcks plan, and these were duly held during late November and early December 1940. These war games led the Germans to believe that the first stage of the campaign would likely be to reach a line from Leningrad to Smolensk and on to the Dnieper River. Once that line was reached, there would need to be another plan for further exploitation. The simulations also indicated possible supply problems, assuming the armies kept to the timetable beyond two thirds of the way to the Leningrad–Smolensk–Dnieper line. The draft OKH plan proposed by Paulus following this testing involved 120 divisions. The emphasis was on Moscow as the primary objective, and it was estimated that the Soviet capital could be taken by the central army group in the sixth or seventh week of the campaign. Halder then revised the plan and on 5 December presented the final draft to Hitler, which called for 137 divisions – including thirty-two armoured and motorized divisions – in three army groups, two of which were north of the Pripet Marshes. The final OKH plan firmly established Moscow as the primary objective of the campaign, with all dispositions and supply arrangements predicated on this basis.[42]

The operational intent of the OKH plan was stated as follows:[43]

'The German Army is to defeat the portion of the Russian Army positioned in Northern Russia with its main forces and take Moscow [Author's emphasis]. To this end, the main effort will advance from the line Brest–Insterberg against the line Rogachev–Vitebsk. Weaker forces south of the Pripjet Marshes will prevent an advance of the enemy's southern group in the direction of Rumania by attacking from the line Jassy–Przemysl–Hrubiszow in the direction of Kiev and the middle Dnjepr [Dnieper]. They will also prepare the way for a later combined effort with the main forces east of the Dnjepr.

'The concept: Destroying the bulk of the Soviet northern group while still west of Moscow by advancing directly on Moscow; turning to the south after taking Northern Russia and Moscow; conquering the Ukraine in conjunction with southern group; taking the desired line of Astrakan–Gorki–Archangelsk as final objective.'

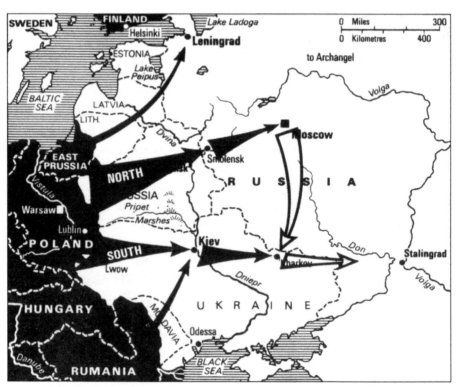

Map 1: The Marcks Plan.
It can readily be seen that the emphasis of the Marcks plan was to threaten Moscow, thereby forcing the Red Army to defend it and provide the opportunity to destroy it and achieve a strategic victory. The plan was revised by Halder who increased the number of divisions committed but kept the major effort in Army Group Centre. Hitler approved the revised plan on 5 December 1940.

With such a clear statement in the first sentence, OKH obviously felt that there could be little room for doubt as to how the campaign would be conducted. As will be obvious from Map 1, the intention of the campaign is absolutely clear, the aim of the attack is to take Moscow to precipitate the strategic defeat of the Red Army.

Why Moscow?

It is important to look at the reasons why the OKH plan stressed Moscow as the primary objective of the campaign. In 1941, Moscow and its industrial area was an essential part of the war-making potential of the USSR in at least three major respects. It was a focus of manufacturing industry, especially optical and electrical components; it was the seat of government; and perhaps most important of all from the military point of view, it was the central hub of the national rail transport system. If Moscow was to be taken, the ability of the Soviet High Command to move troops and supplies to different parts of the (very long) war fronts would be severely compromised. Such a development would significantly increase the distances and times that troops and supplies had to be transported, potentially entirely dislocating the Soviet war machine. These factors, quite apart from the political considerations pertaining to the taking of Moscow, meant that it was logical to expect that the Soviets would have to defend their capital if it was threatened, which would give the Germans the opportunity to destroy the enemy on their way to, or at the gates of, Moscow. The OKH plan's primary objective was thus based on the purely military objective of destroying the enemy's armed forces, not on any economic or political aspect which may have accrued as an additional benefit of taking Moscow. These considerations can be distilled to the proposition that in 1941, the German generals knew that the Russians had to defend Moscow or suffer unacceptable consequences through losing it, and therefore they also knew where to find the major Soviet forces in order to inflict on them a decisive strategic defeat. In this respect, it seems impossible to find any fault with the reasoning of the plan as envisaged by the OKH.

Another important factor in developing the strategy was the characteristics of the weather in Russia. Simply put, winter arrives earlier in the areas around Moscow and Leningrad, which are further north, than it does in the Ukraine, and consequently there was less time available to take the more northerly objectives than those in the southern area of operations. This was a factor of extreme importance in determining what could be achieved within the campaign's timeframe.

On 5 December 1940, Halder presented the plan to Hitler. Warlimont, who was present at their meeting, stated:[44]

'When the Army leaders presented the results of their detailed studies in broad terms to Hitler on 5 December, he initially gave their plan his unconditional approval, although he made certain comments which gave some indication of the lines on which he was later to interfere. He gave instructions that: "preparations were to proceed at full swing on the basis of the planning so far carried out."'

Hitler interferes with the strategic plan for *Barbarossa*

A draft of the plan was then issued and presented to Hitler on 17 December, but according to Warlimont, Hitler ordered 'a considerable alteration' to be made. Warlimont recalled: [45]

'OKH had from the outset considered that the crucial factor for the entire campaign was that the main weight of the campaign should be directed towards Moscow because in all probability this was the best method of ensuring that the main enemy forces would be brought to battle and defeated. Hitler however, now gave orders that, as soon as the Soviet Armies in White Russia had been broken, Army Group Centre was to divert a considerable proportion of its mobile forces northwards "in order, in co-operation with Army Group North, to annihilate enemy forces in the Baltic area"; the advance towards Moscow was to be continued only when Leningrad and Kronstadt had been captured. The reasons which led him to this decision are typical; as so often before and even more later, he disregarded the invariable first principle of all strategy, the destruction of the enemy forces, and instead went chasing after less important objectives.... . **So with the stroke of a pen a new concept of the main lines of the campaign against Russia was substituted for that which the OKH had worked out as the result of months of painstaking examination and cross-checking by the best military minds available [Author's emphasis].** Any idea that the study carried out by Section L had anything to do with this decision is wide of the mark for the very good reason that, as always, our study had been agreed beforehand with the Operations Section of OKH. The idea is further disproved by the fact that when, as will be shown later, similar differences of opinion arose in the summer of 1941, Section L wrote two appreciations emphatically supporting the Army point of view.'

Warlimont continued:[46]

'Thus was produced the patched-up document which set the Wehrmacht off on the fatal road to the east [Author's emphasis].'

Warlimont could hardly have been more caustic. He obviously regarded Hitler's interference as a completely negative development which upset the balance of the operational plan and reduced its chances of success; and he was not the only senior German general to have this view. Hitler's variant is set out in Map 2, and the difference in emphasis of the two plans is immediately obvious.

Halder's diary on 28 January[47] made the following comments about the purpose of *Barbarossa* and the essentials required for success after a conference with Brauchitsch, Chief of the Reserve Army General Friedrich Fromm and Chief of Army Ordnance General Emil Leeb:

'b. Crush Russia in a rapid campaign.
'4. Execution should evidence the following characteristics:
'a. Great space to the Dnieper = Luxembourg – mouth of the Loire.
'b. **Speed. No stop! No waiting for the railroad [Author's emphasis].** Depend on motor transport.
'c. Increased motorisation (as opposed to 1940): thirty-three motorised units, motorized artillery, engineer, signal etc.'

It is obvious from this entry that the OKH was aware that the outcome of the campaign would depend on the speedy exploitation of the opportunities which arose from its implementation. The crucial importance of Hitler's changes to the operational implementation to this vital element of the plan of campaign is highlighted later in this chapter.

At the Nuremberg trials after the war, the United States counsel tendered US Exhibit Number 134,[48] a summary of a conference held on 3 February 1941, attended by Hitler, Keitel, Jodl, Brauchitsch and Halder. It included among its conclusions:

'1. Barbarossa.
'a. The Fuhrer on the whole is in agreement with the operational plan. When it is being carried **out it must be remembered that the main aim is to gain possession of the Baltic States and Leningrad [Author's emphasis].**
'b. The Fuhrer desires that the operation map and the plan of the deployment of forces be sent to him as soon as possible.'

This document shows that there was a fundamental difference between the concept of the OKH plan and Hitler's subsequent view, which led to confusion regarding the aims of the whole campaign and significantly lessened the chance of its successful execution.

It is widely accepted that Field Marshal von Manstein was among the best – if not the best – of the German military leaders of the Second World War. As detailed in Volume 1 of this work, he was responsible for the creation of the strategy behind the 1940 campaign in France, which had been the greatest German military victory in history. It is thus remarkable that he was not involved at all in the planning of the Eastern campaign. Perhaps this was an example of the German General Staff machinery working in its normal manner, but it might also be evidence of professional jealousy, with his seniors getting revenge for showing them up through his plan being used in the French campaign. Whatever the case, given his high standing and record of success, Manstein's view on *Barbarossa* is very relevant. In his book *Lost Victories*,[49] he pointed out a number of major faults in the thinking behind the operation and the implementation of the plan. He opined:

> 'The first mistake committed by Hitler, if no one else, [was] of underrating the resources of the Soviet Union and the fighting qualities of the Red Army. In consequence he based everything on the assumption that the **Soviet Union could be overthrown by military means in one campaign [Author's emphasis].**'

He continued:[50]

> 'The second factor was **the failure to achieve a uniform strategic policy at the summit – i.e., between Hitler and OKH [Author's emphasis].** This applied both to the planning of the overall operation and to its execution in the campaign of 1941.
>
> 'Hitler's strategic aims were based primarily on political and economic considerations [Author's emphasis]. These were: (a) the capture of Leningrad (a city he regarded as the cradle of Bolshevism), by which he proposed to join up with the Finns and dominate the Baltic, and (b) possession of the raw-material regions of the Ukraine, the armaments centres of the Donetz Basin, and later the Caucasus oilfields. By seizing these territories he hoped to cripple the Soviet war economy completely.
>
> 'OKH, on the other hand, rightly contended that the conquest and retention of these undoubtedly important strategic areas depended on first defeating the Red Army [Author's emphasis]. The main body of

the latter, they argued, would be met on the road to Moscow, since that city, as the focal point of Soviet power, was one whose loss the regime dare not risk.

'It was on this divergence of basic strategy that the German conduct of operations ultimately foundered. **Although Hitler agreed to the distribution of forces proposed by OKH, according to which the bulk of the Army was to be committed in two army groups north and only one in the area south of the Pripet Marshes, the tug-of-war over strategic objectives continued throughout this campaign. The inevitable consequence was that Hitler not only failed to attain his aims, which were too far flung anyway, but also confused the issue for OKH [Author's emphasis].'**

There can be no doubt that this view, coming from Manstein, is most persuasive and reflects the problems that actually occurred during the campaign, as will become evident below. Hitler's alteration of the emphasis of the campaign may not have been a problem had the necessary changes been made to the operational plan which he was determined to enforce on the German Army's leaders, reflecting his concept of the required strategy at the time the plan was finalized. This could have been achieved through either Hitler insisting on the changes or the OKH forcing a final resolution of the issue in its favour. But because these changes were not made, the distribution of the forces that OKH made had to be adapted midway through the execution of the plan by transferring units from Army Group Centre to the wings of the theatre of operations. This was ultimately a major problem because of the time wasted in arguments between Hitler and the OKH relating to this strategic misalignment, and in the movement of units to conform to Hitler's strategy. This loss of time was aggravated by the reduction in mobility caused by mud during autumn in European Russia and the onset of winter, which meant that a decisive strategic victory over the Soviet forces could not be achieved within the available time. Nevertheless, the basic misalignment of strategy was the prime reason for the failure of the offensive in the East.

As noted previously, Rundstedt had been on the Eastern Front for much of the First World War, and therefore had intimate knowledge of the problems fighting in the USSR would involve. His view of the correct strategy to follow was quite different to that advocated by Manstein, but he agreed with him that the intention to knock out Russia in one campaign was a basic flaw in the plan of Operation *Barbarossa*. In *Von Rundstedt: the Soldier and the Man*, Blumentritt wrote of Rundstedt's views regarding an Eastern campaign:[51]

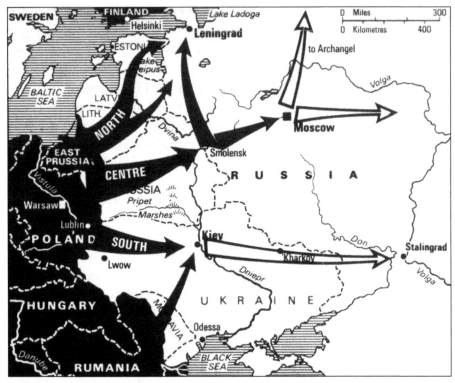

Map 2: Final Plan *Barbarossa*.
Hitler's changes meant that the concentration of the OKH plan on Moscow was altered so
that the main effort was intended to be to the North, in taking Leningrad. However, this did
not occur and the campaign was changed in practice so that the offensive resulted in the Battle
of Kiev on the Southern extremity of the front, where over 600,000 Soviet prisoners were
taken. The time taken in this operation meant that there was not enough time left in the 1941
campaign to achieve a strategic victory.

'He was of the opinion that from a purely military point of view the
centre of gravity should lie in the north, that is, with Army Group
"North" (Ritter von Leeb). He regarded Leningrad as the first objective.
In the second place, this political-economic military thrust would at the
same time forge an immediate link with the gallant Finns. Furthermore,
a thrust towards Leningrad would have the advantage of cutting off
the Russians from the Baltic completely. As the second phase of the
operation, Rundstedt envisaged a main attack from the Leningrad area
towards the south-east in the direction of Moscow.

'... it was clear to him that a campaign against Russia meant an
indefinite undertaking. Such a colossus could not be brought down in
a blitzkrieg of a few months, but only in the course of time. A war with
Russia might last for years.'

It is worth noting that Army Group North was not under Rundstedt's command, so there can be no question that these comments represent his completely impartial view. One of the obvious operational advantages of Rundstedt's strategy was that Leningrad was the closest of the main objectives in the USSR, so concentrating on it made sense, whilst the ability to send supplies to Leningrad by ship would also have eased the supply problems the Germans suffered, so there were clear positives to Rundstedt's preferred course of action. Once Leningrad was taken, it may have been possible to push on to Moscow, had all the available forces then been concentrated to achieve that objective. However, this would not necessarily have yielded the strategic defeat of the USSR which *Barbarossa* envisaged.

The views of Manstein and Rundstedt regarding the strategy to be adopted in the East would have been very difficult to resist if they had been allowed to contribute to discussions with Hitler about the planning of *Barbarossa*. But Hitler did not seek their opinions, and the reliance on knocking the USSR out of the war in a single blitzkrieg campaign led to decisions being made to keep to a timetable which would not have been necessary if a longer timeframe had been envisaged. The OKH's plan was governed by the instructions it received from Hitler, so planning for a campaign over more than the duration he imposed was out of the question.

On 5 April 1941, Halder made the following prophetic diary entry relating to a meeting with Brauchitsch, who had just spoken with Hitler regarding the campaign in Yugoslavia which became necessary following the coup, and which installed a pro-British government opposed to Germany:[52]

'Overall position: The conduct of the campaign (Yugoslavia) once more comes under the dictate of political considerations and, what is more, considerations of purely transitory nature. **This precludes any planning with clear goals and harbors the danger of dissipating our strength in a series of isolated operations. Good nerves are the only antidote [Author's emphasis].**'

This entry encapsulates the problems that the Army High Command was to experience with Hitler to an extreme degree during *Barbarossa*.

German forces committed to *Barbarossa*

The German forces deployed for the attack on the Soviet Union, as set out in the final OKH plan, consisted of three army groups:

- Army Group North commanded by Field Marshal Ritter von Leeb, comprising twenty-one infantry divisions, three panzer divisions, two army motorized infantry divisions, one Waffen-SS motorized infantry division and four security divisions. The army group had 619 tanks, 557 armoured cars, 3,980 artillery pieces and approximately 125,000 transport vehicles, and was supported by the 1st Air Fleet commanded by Colonel General Karl Koller.
- Army Group Centre commanded by Field Marshal Fedor von Bock, comprising thirty-three infantry divisions, nine panzer divisions, five army motorized infantry divisions, one Waffen-SS motorised infantry division, one cavalry division and three security divisions. These units included 2,241 tanks, 1,370 armoured cars, 7,746 artillery pieces and 240,800 transport vehicles, and were supported by the 2nd Air Fleet commanded by Field Marshal Albert Kesselring.
- Army Group South commanded by Field Marshal von Rundstedt, comprising eighteen German infantry divisions, five panzer divisions, two motorized divisions, one Waffen-SS motorized division, one mountain division, four light infantry divisions, fourteen Romanian divisions and two Hungarian divisions. The army group had 821 tanks, 489 armoured cars, 5,658 artillery pieces and 171,800 transport vehicles, with the 4th Air Fleet under Colonel General Alexander Lohr providing aerial support.

The OKH reserve for the Eastern Front comprised two panzer divisions, two motorized divisions, two SS divisions, eleven infantry divisions and one mountain division.[53]

The total number of aircraft deployed by the Luftwaffe was 1,945, some 61 per cent of its strength on 22 June. The number of serviceable aircraft were as follows: 510 bombers, 290 dive-bombers, 440 single-engined fighters, forty twin-engined fighters and 120 reconnaissance aircraft.[54]

The total number of personnel committed to *Barbarossa* in the three army groups and the Luftwaffe air groups was approximately 3,359,000.

The Soviet forces opposing the German invasion comprised 170 divisions.[55] From north to south, these were organized in the Leningrad Military District, Baltic Military District, Western Military District and Kiev Military District. The strongest concentration was in the Kiev Military District, which opposed the German Army Group South, as the Soviet High Command believed that any invasion would be directed there first.

The OKH calculated the relative strengths of the German army groups compared to the opposing Soviet forces in each of the theatres of operations as being equal for Army Group North, heavily in German favour for Army Group Centre and weaker for Army Group South.

It will be noted that the number of panzer divisions had increased markedly in comparison to the ten used in the 1940 campaign in the West, with seventeen armoured divisions available for use in *Barbarossa* on 22 June 1941. However, the increase did not mean a corresponding rise in the number of tanks available to the Germans, as tank warfare expert General Heinz Guderian explained in his memoirs:[56]

'On the basis of experience gained during the Western Campaign, Hitler ordered a tank production of 800 to 1,000 units per month. However, the Army Ordnance Office reckoned that the cost of this programme would be about two milliards of marks [two billion marks], and that it would involve the employment of 100,000 skilled workers and specialists. In view of these heavy expenses Hitler unfortunately agreed to the abandonment of this plan for the time being.

'... After the campaign Hitler ordered a considerable increase in the number of panzer and motorised divisions. The number of panzer divisions was soon doubled, though this involved a halving of the tank strength of each division. The German Army, though doubling its nominal strength in armoured divisions, did not acquire double the number of tanks, which is after all what counted. The simultaneous doubling of the motorised infantry divisions placed such a terrific burden on the motor vehicle industry that Hitler's orders could only be carried out by making full use of all available supplies, including the material captured in the countries of Western Europe. These captured vehicles were markedly inferior in quality to the German ones and were particularly ill-suited for any employment that might be foreseen in eastern or African theatres.'

'These changes to the panzer divisions were very important. Firstly, by reducing the number of tanks by half, the firepower of the divisions was reduced. There was some compensation for this though in the fact that the percentage of the Mark IV tanks was increased, and these had considerably higher firepower than the earlier marks. Secondly, the changes meant that of the 17,000 men comprising each division, only 2,600 were tank crews and that of the 3,000 vehicles the vast majority of them were wheeled, not tracked. Thus, the mobility of the divisions was reduced because wheeled vehicles cannot easily travel cross country whereas tracked vehicles can. This was a major defect in the German panzer divisions because it meant that the infantry was nowhere near as mobile as the tanks, and therefore could not keep easily up with them in any attacks being made. Additionally, as pointed out by Guderian, the increase in number of the panzer divisions could only be accomplished by using trucks taken after the armistice from the French and their reliability and capabilities were not adequate for the campaign in the USSR. These problems were the result of the low output of tracked vehicles by German industry. Thus, the panzer divisions based on the new model were more in the nature of a reinforced mobile infantry division than the fully mobile concept of the armoured division.[57]

The types of vehicle comprising the armoured divisions had not been a concern in the campaign in the West because, as noted previously, there were many high-quality roads in the countries the offensive was going through, where wheeled vehicles could easily be used. But in the USSR there were very few roads and therefore the mobility of armoured divisions was significantly impaired. This was evident even before there were any complications caused to the Germans by the weather conditions in the USSR. This impairment of mobility meant that every manoeuvre that the Germans needed to carry out for their invasion took more time than they had expected, making it more difficult to carry out encircling attacks of the Soviet armies, which frequently were able to partially escape from the German encirclements. The problem for the Germans was to ensure that their campaign could be successfully completed despite the reduction in their mobility caused by the lack of developed roads in the USSR. This should have been a factor taken into account by Hitler when he was setting the strategy for the German armies so that they would be required to move only as far as was absolutely necessary to achieve the aim of the campaign. However, the Fuhrer's requirements did exactly the opposite, requiring the armies to be committed to the wings of the theatre of operations, significantly increasing the distances they had to travel. The different origin and configuration of the vehicles used also meant that servicing them became increasingly difficult, those taken from the defeated armies in the West having inadequate stores of spare parts, causing delays in them being available. This was a fundamental problem with the German armoured units, and occurred because German industrial production could not provide the same level of motor vehicles as the Western Allies. The British and American armoured divisions had no such problems, their troop transport vehicles being tracked like the tanks, meaning that the infantry and tanks could be deployed together.

The composition of the *Barbarossa* armoured divisions reflected Hitler's requirement for rapid expansion, the percentages and types of tanks involved in the offensive being as follows:[58]

- PzKpfw I   8 per cent
- PzKpfw III   49 per cent
- PzKpfw IV   13 per cent
- Stug III   7 per cent;
- Model 35t   4 per cent;
- Model 38t   19 per cent

It can therefore be seen that of the armoured divisions, 23 per cent (Model 35t/38t) were of Czechoslovakian manufacture. Only the PzKpfw IV was armed with a 75mm gun that was effective against the Soviet T34 and KV1 tanks. Thankfully for the Germans, these Russian tanks were in very short supply in June 1941, but they did cause real difficulties when they were encountered.

In addition to the difficulties caused by the lack of tracked vehicles, the Germans had problems with rail transport. During the campaign in the West, the Germans had been able to easily supply their forces by rail, but there were far fewer railway lines available in the USSR and they were of a different gauge. Consequently, because of the distances involved and the difficulties in using road transport, the supply position of the German forces was much worse than it had been during their earlier campaigns.

The decision not to increase the manufacture of panzers was typical of the short-sighted nature of Hitler's methods. He made no provision for the possibility that *Barbarossa* might not work out as planned, so expansion of tank production did not occur until it was too late to enable the Wehrmacht to achieve his aims.

The involvement of Germany's allies

Although the Italians and Romanians contributed armies to *Barbarossa* from the beginning of the invasion, when it was being planned there was no considered attempt to involve Japan opening another front against the Soviets, although doing so would undoubtedly have made the achievement of *Barbarossa*'s aims more likely. This lack of co-ordination is one of the most marked contrasts between the Axis and Allied powers in the Second World War. The Axis nations did not act in concert on any meaningful basis or develop a common strategy to win the war, whereas the Allied powers co-operated closely and on a continuing basis to assist each other toward the achievement of their common strategy. On every major occasion in the war, the Axis partners failed to act together to achieve their goals, which were never even defined or properly agreed between them. Italy had stayed out of the campaign in the West until

Mussolini thought the French were beaten, then Mussolini did not advise Hitler until the last minute with respect to the Italian invasion of Greece. Likewise, Hitler did not alert Mussolini until the last possible moment about matters relating to *Barbarossa*. Most pointedly, the Japanese only heard about the details of *Barbarossa* after the event, as happened with Germany and Italy after the Japanese attack on Pearl Harbor.

Hitler's decision not to act in concert with the Japanese in defeating the USSR from the beginning of *Barbarossa* resulted in a major problem for the Germans. This occurred because the Soviet High Command was able to transfer a substantial part of its Far Eastern Army to the front around Moscow. These forces became a major part of the armies used by Zhukov in the counterattack commencing on the night of 5/6 December 1941, which finally eliminated any possibility of Hitler's invasion succeeding as set out in his *Barbarossa* directive of 18 December 1940. Had the Japanese exerted pressure in the Soviet Far Eastern territories, or even acted as a 'threat in being' by keeping the Soviets guessing as to their strategy, there is little doubt that the Far Eastern Army would not have been available, even in part, to be transferred to the Moscow Front. The Soviets became aware that the Japanese were going to pursue a southern offensive and not attack them through the efforts of one of the greatest spies of all time, Richard Sorge.[59] Working as a Soviet spy, Sorge was attached to the German Embassy in Tokyo, where he had a very close relationship with the German Ambassador, Major General Ott. He was told through his sources in the Japanese government on 4 July 1941 that two days previously the Japanese Cabinet had met with Emperor Hirohito, who had sanctioned a southern strategy, and that the Japanese would not be attacking the USSR. However, the detail of the exact strategy the Japanese would be following was not learned by Sorge. As it turned out, their southern strategy called for the Japanese attack on US naval assets at Pearl Harbor and expansion in the Pacific, as opposed to attacking Soviet forces to take Siberia and the Far Eastern territories of the USSR. However, Stalin did not act on Sorge's information straight away, but waited to see what would happen. Once it became clear that the spy's information was correct, the partial transfer of the Soviet Far Eastern Army – which consisted in total of twenty-five infantry divisions and nine armoured brigades – was commenced. The forces actually transferred totalled eighteen infantry divisions and 1,700 tanks. Without these high-grade reinforcements, the defence of Moscow would have been much more problematic for the Soviets. Had Hitler chosen to include the Japanese in the plans for *Barbarossa* and assigned them a definite role to perform in holding the Soviet Far Eastern forces while the Germans dealt with the armies in European Russia, *Barbarossa*'s outcome may have been very different. There were highly placed generals in the Japanese Army in Manchuria who were thirsting for revenge against the Soviets after two recent border wars in which they had been defeated, and they would willingly have co-operated in almost any plan to expand into Soviet territories in the Far East.

Warlimont commented on Hitler's attitude to their Japanese allies as follows:[60]

'Even after the opening of the campaign against Russia little thought was given to the possibility of direct Japanese assistance as proved by the fact, that after a period of disillusionment, the old confidence in the imminent collapse of the Soviets revived in the autumn of 1941. The overweening self-assurance in German headquarters was illustrated by the phrase coined when Japan was thought to have made an offer of assistance: **"we don't need anyone just to strip the corpses"**! [**Author's emphasis**].'

Warlimont provided further evidence of Hitler's attitude to the Japanese:[61]

'Hitler: You mustn't believe what the Japanese say. I don't believe a word of it.

'…

'Hitler: They lie to beat the band; everything they say has always got some background motive of deception.'

Whether or not his view of the Japanese government at the time was correct, it hardly spoke of an attitude that would promote co-operation and trust between the so-called Axis partners. It is quite apparent that from the beginning of the campaign against the USSR, Hitler did not want his allies to become involved in any meaningful way, an attitude that recoiled to his detriment.

Conclusions

In order that *Barbarossa* achieve its aim, which was the defeat of the USSR in a single blitzkrieg campaign lasting approximately six months, the following five elements had to combine in favour of the Germans:

1. they had to achieve at least initial tactical surprise over the Russian ground forces;
2. they had to achieve air superiority;
3. they had to overcome the supply problems which the plan testing had shown to exist;

4. the weather, and especially the winter, had to hold off long enough so that it wasn't a complication to the supply or manoeuvrability of the armies; and

5. the Germans had to destroy the Soviet forces far enough west to prevent them crossing the Dnieper River or before they were able to retire into their eastern territories and continue to conduct the war from there.

In other words, absolutely everything had to fall in favour of the Germans. Such expectations are not often fulfilled in military operations or any other spheres of human endeavour.

In staking everything on the gamble that all these factors would work out in his favour, Hitler ignored the advice of his generals, including the most senior officers of the Luftwaffe.

He also declined to involve his 'ally' Japan in keeping the Soviet Far Eastern Army in place while *Barbarossa* was underway, materially lessening the chances of its success.

The decision to attack the USSR was therefore based on extremely optimistic assumptions and were further complicated by the problems foreshadowed by Manstein and Rundstedt and the basic misalignment of strategy that existed between Hitler and the High Command of the Army. These factors proved to be fatal to *Barbarossa*'s successful execution, with existential consequences for the Nazi regime. But such was the authority that Hitler had gained over his generals that the campaign nevertheless went ahead as he wished.

Chapter 2

The Failure of Operation *Barbarossa*

My intention in this chapter is not to show the day-by-day progress of all aspects of *Barbarossa*, but to highlight how Hitler, the OKH and the commanders in the field viewed and attempted to overcome the problems and exploit the main opportunities that presented themselves as the campaign developed. I will also show how the decisions made by Hitler determined the course of the campaign. As the operations of Army Group South and Army Group North were regarded as being subsidiary to the main effort, I will mainly deal with the events pertaining to operations in Army Group Centre, and particularly the attempt to take Moscow, as these were the most important for the achievement of the aims of the campaign. I have taken the end point of *Barbarossa* as the commencement of the Soviet offensive before Moscow of 5–6 December 1941, as by that time it was clear that the operation as envisaged by Hitler's Directive No. 21 of 18 December 1940, 'Case *Barbarossa*', could not succeed.

The important terms of Directive No. 21 were as follows:

'The German Wehrmacht must be prepared to crush Soviet Russia in a quick campaign (Operation Barbarossa) even before the conclusion of the war against England.

'I. General Purpose:
'The mass of the Russian Army in western Russia is to be destroyed in daring operations, by driving forward deep armoured wedges, and the retreat of units capable of combat into the vastness of Russian territory is to be prevented.

'In quick pursuit a line is then to be reached from which the Russian Air Force will no longer be able to attack the territory of the German Reich. The ultimate objective of the operation is to establish a cover against Asiatic Russia from the general line Volga–Archangel. Then, in case of necessity, the last industrial area left to Russia in the Urals can be eliminated by the Luftwaffe.'

The aim was thus the elimination of the USSR as a power in Europe and the Baltic region. On 3 February 1941, when he saw the final draft of *Barbarossa*, Hitler said that when it began, 'the world would hold its breath and make no comment'.[1]

German forces launched the invasion of the USSR at 3.30 am on 22 June 1941. They achieved complete tactical surprise along virtually the whole invasion front, destroying much of the Soviet Air Force on the ground, even though Stalin's government knew of the German build-up on its borders and had specific information given to it by Britain that Germany was going to attack, including the strength of the forces involved and the planned date of the invasion.

This is confirmed by the diary of the USSR Ambassador in Britain, Ivan Maisky, published as *The Maisky Diaries*.[2] During the early part of 1941, there are numerous references in his diary to information in the British press and directly from UK government sources that Germany was going to invade his homeland. An important warning was given to him by the British Foreign Secretary, Sir Anthony Eden, at a meeting on 13 June:[3]

'(1) Eden informed me on behalf of the prime minister that the concentration of German troops on the Soviet borders has intensified, particularly in the last 48 hours. The aim of the concentration: war or war of nerves? In case it turned out to be war, the British Government wished to bring it to the notice of the Soviet Government that if Germany attacked, the British Government will be prepared to offer assistance using its air force units in the Middle East, to send to Moscow a military mission to share the experience gained during the war, and to develop economic cooperation in every possible way (through the Persian Gulf and Vladivostok).'

After a meeting on 18 June with Sir Stafford Cripps, the British Ambassador to the USSR who was in London at the time, Maisky noted:[4]

'Cripps is absolutely convinced of the inevitability of a German attack on us and is certain it will happen very soon.

"If this does not happen before the middle of July," he noted, "I'll be greatly surprised."

'Cripps added that, according to the British Government's information, Hitler has amassed 147 divisions on the Soviet borders.'

These warnings culminate in an entry on 21 June:[5]

'After lunch, I was hastily summoned to London at Cripps's request. He came to see me at 4.30 pm.

'He again spoke of the inevitability of a German attack on the USSR. Very soon.

'"To tell the truth," he said, "I expected the attack to occur this 'weekend', tomorrow, the 22nd."'

The responsibility for not acting on this priceless knowledge rests directly with Stalin, who profoundly distrusted the information because he believed that the Western powers were trying to generate suspicion between the USSR and Germany to provoke war between them, which the Western powers would observe from the sidelines while the two totalitarian states fought it out. But while he did not issue orders to alert the Red Army to ready itself in time for the German attack, Stalin had authorized a limited mobilization, which had been issued by General Zhukov on 26 April.[6] Stalin also authorized the redeployment of thirty-three divisions to the western areas of the USSR, although of these only four had been moved before the start of the German invasion, and on 1 June 793,500 conscripts were called up.[7] While these steps were belated, the process set in motion meant that the Soviets had just enough troops available during the rest of 1941 to blunt the German attack, and with the help of the reinforcements from the Far East, to thwart the essential aim of *Barbarossa*, which was to defeat the USSR in six months.

The primary strategy of the OKH plan for Operation *Barbarossa* was to concentrate the main forces and power of the Army and Luftwaffe in Army Group Centre, operating north of the Pripet Marshes and approximately halfway to the Baltic States, enabling a vast scale blitzkrieg campaign that would drive straight for Moscow. This was intended to force the Soviets to concentrate their main forces at or on the road to Moscow, creating the opportunity for the decisive strategic defeat of the Red Army there. It was essential to the achievement of this plan that the momentum of the blitzkrieg be maintained, with the Soviet forces continuously disrupted and unable to establish cohesive defence lines, and crucially so that the campaign could be concluded as quickly as possible, or at least before the winter became a factor.

Creating and maintaining the momentum needed to achieve victory in *Barbarossa* was no easy task for the German forces, due to limitations imposed by the composition of the German Army caused by industrial capacity and the timing of the war, which was well before when the armed forces had been told by Hitler to expect that conflict with the USSR would occur. Although the Germans had achieved great successes in the recent blitzkrieg campaigns in Europe, the distances covered in them were small when compared to those involved in reaching the objectives set for *Barbarossa*. Crucially, German infantry divisions – which made up approximately 80 per cent of the formations involved – were not motorized, relying almost entirely on horse-drawn transport as they had in the First World War. This meant that the infantry had to march all the way to their objectives and that all their equipment, including artillery, was horse-drawn, unless it was possible to use rail transport as had been the case in the recent campaigns in Europe. The roads in the USSR were virtually non-existent when compared to those in Western Europe, which meant that the infantry and horses had to walk through deep mud that the weather created, worsening supply problems, maintenance issues and their mobility. Furthermore, the disparity in mobility between the infantry, panzer and motorized divisions meant that the large distances involved in reaching their objectives in the USSR accentuated the gaps created between the different types of units as they advanced. This in turn led to significant problems in closing the arms of encircling movements, resulting in Soviet forces escaping from entrapment manoeuvres and the panzer formations being held back to assist the infantry in this task.

Lieutenant General Blumentritt was appointed Chief of Staff of Army Group Centre's Fourth Army, which was commanded by Field Marshal Guenther von Kluge. The Fourth Army was at the forefront of the offensive from the beginning of *Barbarossa* to the final attempt to take Moscow, so Blumentritt could hardly have been in a better place to know the circumstances surrounding the offensive. He wrote a treatise about this stage of *Barbarossa*, published as part of the book *The Fatal Decisions*, a collection of first-hand accounts by German commanders.[8] In it, he commented on the situation of the infantry divisions as follows:[9]

> 'The infantry had a hard time keeping up. Marches of twenty-five miles in the course of a day were by no means exceptional, and that over the most atrocious roads. A vivid picture which remains of these weeks is the great clouds of yellow dust kicked up by the Russian columns attempting to retreat and by our infantry hastening in pursuit. The heat was tremendous, though interspersed with sudden showers which quickly turned the roads to mud before the sun reappeared and quickly baked them into crumbling clay once again.'

Although 25 miles per day was about the limit that could be expected in short spells from a non-motorized infantry division, troops could not keep up this pace for any extended period while also fighting. The distances to the *Barbarossa* objectives, however, meant they would have to do so if the aims of the campaign were to be achieved. For example, Moscow is over 1,000km from Brest-Litovsk, where the Fourth Army started the campaign. In comparison, Liege to Amiens in France is less than 300km, the distance from the German starting positions to their main objective in the 1940 French campaign.

On 3 July, approximately two weeks after the start of the campaign, Halder, the Chief of the General Staff, wrote in his diary:[10]

'On the whole, then, it may be said even now that the objective to shatter the bulk of the Russian army this side of the Dvina and Dnieper has been accomplished. I do not doubt the statement of the captured Russian corps CG [Commanding General] that east of the Dvina and Dnieper we would encounter nothing more than partial forces, not strong enough to hinder realization of German operational plans. It is thus probably no overstatement to say that the Russian Campaign has been won in the space of two weeks. Of course, this does not yet mean that it is closed. The sheer geographical vastness of the country and the stubbornness of the resistance, which is carried on with all means, will claim our efforts for many more weeks to come.'

Halder's appraisal may seem ridiculous given subsequent events, but it must be stressed that he was commenting in the light of German intelligence assessments of Soviet forces as they were then identified, and critically was also assuming that subsequent operations would be carried out as planned by the OKH; in this he was to be frustrated.

Warlimont commented in his book on this phase of the campaign – the first three weeks – as being 'marked by an unusual measure of accord between OKW and OKH',[11] undoubtedly because the operations were implemented as envisaged by the OKH plan and were very successful. He noted further:[12]

'Hitler himself stated to his immediate entourage on 4 July: "to all intents and purposes the Russians have lost the war" and congratulated himself on what a good thing it was "that we smashed the Russian armour and air forces right at the beginning". The Russians, he went on "can never replace them." His appreciation of the situation therefore agreed generally with that of the Army. Accordingly during these early weeks he did not meddle with the conduct of operations in the East apart from certain pressure and nagging at OKH to get them to close the great "pocket" [at Bialystok–Minsk] more rapidly and securely, and later, just as in the West, being beset by "fear" for the flanks of the armoured thrusts which had driven far ahead.'

In similar vein, Halder's diary recorded the following for 8 July:[13]

'11.00 Kinzel [OKH intelligence office]: review of enemy situation:

'Of 164 identified rifle divisions, **89 have been totally or largely eliminated [Author's emphasis].**

'... Of twenty-nine identified armored divisions, twenty have been totally or largely eliminated; nine still have full fighting strength.

'The enemy is no longer in a position to organize a continuous front, not even behind strong terrain features. At the moment the apparent plan of the Red Army High Command is to check the German advance as far to the west as possible by draining our strength with incessant counterattacking with all available reserves. In pursuing this policy they evidently have grossly overestimated German losses.'

All of these early developments seemed to confirm the Fuhrer's prediction to Field Marshal von Rundstedt prior to the commencement of the campaign:[14]

'You have only to kick in the door, and the whole rotten structure will come crashing down.'

Warlimont gave an overview of the state of the invasion during early July:[15]

'The campaign seemed to be going quickly and successfully, and so in this case also there was little opportunity for the Supreme Commander or his staff to do any real job of overall direction.'

Nevertheless, there were early signs that the Eastern campaign was going to be different from anything the Germans had experienced before. The Red Army was resisting as strongly as it could, even though its efforts were unco-ordinated and piecemeal. In his book *Barbarossa*, Alan Clark describes the fighting between the Germans and the Soviets at this stage:[16]

'Like some prehistoric monster caught in a net, the Red Army struggled desparately [*sic*] and, as reflexes gradually activated the remoter parts of its body, with mounting effect. Until that day the Germans had always found that bodies of surrounded enemy laid down and died. There would be a contracting of perimeters, a drawing in of "flanks," perhaps some perfunctory efforts to break out or counterattack, and then – surrender. The speed and depth of the Panzer thrust; the tireless ubiquity of the Luftwaffe; and above all, the brilliant coordination of all arms, had given the Germans an aura of invincibility that had not been enjoyed by any army since Napoleon. Yet the Russians seemed as ignorant of this as they were of the rules of the military textbook.

'The reaction of the surrounded formations was in every case vigorous and aggressive. Their very lack of co-ordination bewildered the Germans and hampered the plans for containing the various pockets. Whole divisions would assemble and move straight into the attack, "marching to the sound of the guns".'

Blumentritt commented on the defence put up by the Soviet troops compared to those whom the Germans had previously fought:[17]

'The conduct of the Russian troops, even in this first battle, was in striking contrast to the behaviour of the Poles and of the Western allies in defeat. Even when encircled, the Russians stood their ground and fought. The vast extent of the country, with its forests and swamps, helped them in this. There were not enough German troops available completely to seal off a huge encirclement such as Bialystok–Slonim. Our motorized forces fought on or near to the roads: in the great trackless spaces between them the Russians were left largely unmolested. This was why the Russians were able not infrequently to break out of our encirclements, whole columns moving by night through the forests that stretched away eastwards. They always attempted to break out to the east, so that the eastern side of each encirclement had to be held by our strongest troops, usually panzer troops. Nevertheless, our encirclements were seldom ever entirely successful.'

Halder's diary note for 15 July painted a similar picture:[18]

'Enemy situation. The overall impression is that the enemy, responding to the commanders and probably British efforts, is doing all he can to prevent being pushed back any farther to the east. The Russian troops now, as ever, are fighting back with savage determination and with enormous human sacrifices.'

During the campaign the problems associated with the new divisional establishment of the panzers rapidly became apparent. The situation in Army Group South was:

'Things had reached such a stage that when Halder visited HQ Army Group South, now housed in a Russian military school at Stara Konstantinov, on 20 July, he noted that 11th Panzer Division had been forced to leave all its wheeled transport in the rear, because of the state of the roads, and was advancing with just tracked vehicles and peasant carts. Indeed, by now half of von Rundstedt's motor transport was out of action and there was a serious ammunition shortage. The situation was aggravated by the fact that the allied contingents had very little motor transport of their own and leant heavily on the Germans for it. Rundstedt himself recalled just after the war:

'Transport difficulties were the most serious, even in the summer, or at any rate where I was, owing to the mud. I remember one thing, how a "Panzerdivision" covered 7km in 12 hours one day. If it begins raining, then that's the end, you simply cannot get out.'

Another problem:

'The maps we got were wrong. There was not one road marked nice and red and thick on the map. There were railways on the map which simply didn't exist.'[19]

The previously mentioned increase in the number of German panzer divisions and dilution in tank strength aggravated this problem by increasing the percentage of wheeled vehicles in the armoured divisions, meaning a reduction in their off-road capabilities. They had more vehicles, but less tracked ones.

As noted in the previous section of this chapter, there were significant differences between the concepts of the strategy to be pursued in the campaign advocated by Hitler and the OKH. The Army High Command envisaged the main emphasis being to concentrate the strongest forces of the Army to take Moscow, their rationale being that creating a threat to capture the capital would precipitate a battle with the main Soviet forces and lead to a strategic victory from which the USSR would be unable to recover. Such an outcome would also cripple the Soviet rail transport system and the industries around Moscow – such as those producing optical and electrical components for the armed forces – which could not readily be replaced. As Moscow was the administrative and governmental capital of the Soviet Union, the OKH also believed that the Soviet regime simply could not afford for Moscow to be taken. This meant that the Soviet High Command must concentrate its forces for the defence of Moscow, which would set the scene for the Germans to achieve a strategically decisive victory there. Hitler, on the other hand, wished to place the emphasis on taking Leningrad first, then possibly the Ukraine or Moscow, his view being that there were political and economic imperatives for taking the objectives on the wings of the geographical theatre of operations that were more important than Moscow. He particularly regarded Leningrad as being of prime importance because it was the birthplace of communism. However, these objectives at the extremities of the theatre of operations involved transferring forces from Army Group Centre to each of the wings, a move that the OKH did not agree because they would take precious time to achieve, disperse the forces involved in the offensive and – crucially – disrupt its momentum, which Halder had stated was absolutely critical to the success of the campaign. The Germans could not allow the Soviet forces time to consolidate a defensive line and had to continue attacking constantly to achieve victory before winter could intervene. It must also be noted that the distances involved to the objectives on the wings of the theatre of operations were very large, meaning further strain on the maintenance of vehicles as well as losses in combat which would have to be repaired or replaced, increasing the time required for the redeployment of units for subsequent operations.

The diary of Field Marshal von Bock, Commander-in-Chief of Army Group Centre, stressed this very point. In his entry of 13 July 1941, he commented:[20]

'The enemy is only really beaten at one place on the Eastern Front – opposite Army Group Center. If the armoured groups now fly apart to the south, east and north **it means foregoing the exploitation of our success [Author's emphasis]**. The enemy brought fresh forces up to the Dnieper. These were caught by the panzer army's attack while massing and have been hit hard frontally. What matters now is to completely smash this foe and make it impossible for him to establish another new front before Moscow. To do so it is necessary to tightly concentrate all armoured forces and with them drive quickly to the east until I can report that the enemy is offering no more resistance in front of Moscow! I consider diverting elements of Panzer Group Hoth to the north while elements continue to march to the east to be futile. Because of the tremendous wear and tear on their equipment, the panzer groups are only still an effective striking force if employed in unison. I consider employing individual panzer corps to operate alone pointless, [as] their fighting strength has become too low.'

Once the initial phase of the campaign had been achieved, this question of strategic priorities became urgently important and had to be resolved, which only the Fuhrer could do.

However, disagreements relating to this issue continued. Warlimont noted:[21]

'The first OKW directive of the Eastern Campaign (No. 33) was issued on 19 July and appeared to be more or less in consonance with the proposals which the Army leaders had made verbally to Hitler a few days previously. Before the resulting movements had begun however, the Supreme Commander, without further consultation with OKH, issued a "supplement to Directive No. 33" dated 23 July, intended to ensure finally that his wishes were executed. The objectives in the south were now to be, not only Kiev, but Kharkov and the lower Don, Caucasia and the Crimea; as soon as Army Group North had reached its objectives, which it was expected to do soon, OKH was to order it to send "considerable forces, including Armoured Group 3 back to Germany"! Similarly as soon as action in the Smolensk area was completed, the Luftwaffe was ordered to send a number of dive bomber groups to Finland to assist Dietl's corps in the area of North Cape. This flight of strategic fancy continued: "this will also reduce the temptation for England to intervene in the fighting along the Arctic coast". The directive also ordered air attacks on Moscow; these had nothing to do with the objectives of the campaign but were regarded as reprisals for Russian bombing of Bucharest and Helsinki.'

It seems unnecessary to stress how unrealistic these orders were. Hitler's total unsuitability as Supreme Commander of the Wehrmacht is perfectly encapsulated in them. He had conceived a picture of the campaign which did not correspond to reality, holding onto it despite any and all evidence to the contrary.

At the same time, according to Warlimont, Halder opined:[22]

'He [Hitler] has decided on his objectives and sticks to them without considering what the enemy may do or taking into account any other points of view. This means that **von Bock will have to give up his armoured groups and advance on Moscow with infantry alone [Author's emphasis]**. In any case the Fuehrer takes no interest in Moscow at the moment, only Leningrad.'

On 25 July, Bock made the following entry in his diary:[23]

'Generalfeldmarschall Keitel arrived in the morning for a briefing on the "hole at Smolensk". Then he related the Fuhrer's ideas on the subject, the gist of which was that for the moment we should encircle the Russians tactically wherever we meet them, rather than with strategic movements, and then destroy them in small pockets. This would be faster and more effective than the previously-used method. Unfortunately, I consider this to be a mistake and am convinced that it will take us longer to reach our objective this way.'

Halder's diary entry the following day was on a similar theme:[24]

'The Fuhrer's analysis, which at many points is unjustly critical of the field commands, indicates a complete break with the strategy of large operational conceptions. You cannot beat the Russians with operational successes, he argues, because they simply do not know when they are defeated. On that account it will be necessary to destroy them bit by bit, in small encircling actions of a purely tactical character.

'Of course, there is something in these ideas as regards the Russians. But following such a course implies letting the enemy dictate our policy, and **reduces our operations to a tempo which will not permit us to reach our goal, the Volga [Author's emphasis]**. We must remember that the Russians have plenty of manpower, and it is very unlikely that we could pursue the new policy to the point where the enemy cracks and the way is clear again for operations on a big scale.

'To me, **these arguments mark the beginning of the decline of our initial strategy of imaginative operations, and a willingness to throw away the opportunities offered us by the impetus of our infantry and armor [Author's emphasis]**.

'It remains to be seen whether this radical change in strategic conception, which at first will also come as a surprise to the enemy, will bring the desired success. My representations regarding the importance of Moscow are brushed aside without any valid counterevidence.'

This intervention by Hitler is extremely important because it shows his view of how his forces could win, his underlying 'understanding' of strategy and his appreciation of the abilities of the German Army as compared to the Red Army. The irony of his view is that if it was employed, this so-called strategy would result in the Germans discarding their greatest asset against the Soviet forces: the tactical and strategic flexibility attained as a result of the victorious campaigns they had so recently carried out. At this time, no other country's forces came close to the integration and flexibility of all the elements of their armed forces which the Germans had achieved, for which they were trained and at which they excelled. This flexibility was partially due to the superior technology available to the Germans, which was extremely important in defeating the more numerous Soviet tank forces. To voluntarily renounce the most effective method of exercising their advantage through large strategic manoeuvres, in which these very advantages were employed, was contrary to all logic. Halder's comment regarding the speed of the advance is also extremely important: the Germans simply had to maintain the tempo to ensure that the Red Army could not recover from the defeats already inflicted upon it and build new defensive positions or reorganize its forces to offer more effective opposition before the onset of winter.

Bock's comments in his diary for 26 July reflect how many senior German commanders felt:[25]

'If Guderian is turned south as sharply as planned, the gap between the later southern group and the elements of the army group going east will become ever larger. The attack by this group will get stuck with its right wing, for there are strong enemy forces at Rogachev. I continue to support a powerful, concentrated drive to the east by the entire army group, to destroy Timoshenko's badly-battered armies. Securing the attack's southern flank would, for the most part, be a matter for Army Group South. From all I have heard, however, I doubt that the Supreme Command will be talked into it.'

Blumentritt also commented on this situation in *The Fatal Decisions*:[26]

'In late July and early August precious weeks were largely wasted while our High Command debated what strategy we should now pursue. Hitler was anxious to secure the great economic prizes, the Ukraine, the Donetz Basin and finally the Caucasus. These, however, all lay within the sector of Army Group South. His second objective had been Leningrad, which at this stage of the campaign seemed about to fall, and which probably would have fallen had Hitler not repeated his blunder of the previous year at Dunkirk and ordered Field Marshal von Leeb to stop his tanks immediately outside the city.

'He was much less interested in Moscow. Indeed his original plan was to halt Army Group Centre along the line of the Desna and to the north, transfer a sizeable portion of its forces to Army Group South, and make no further attempt to advance on Moscow this year.

'With this in view, Fourth Panzer Army was dissolved. Field Marshal von Kluge's staff was [*sic*] withdrawn into the reserve and the two Panzer

Groups received their orders direct from Army Group Centre. It was proposed that Kluge now be given a command to control Guderian's Panzer Corps and a new infantry army. This force was to advance south-eastwards into the sector of Army Group South, and to destroy the very strong enemy forces massed there.

'The Commander-in-Chief, Field Marshal von Brauchitsch, and his Chief of the General Staff, General Halder, were both strongly opposed to this plan. Brauchitsch would have preferred to see Army Group Centre go on straight for Moscow, which he regarded as the prime objective of the whole campaign. Field Marshal von Bock and the staff of Army Group Centre shared this point of view. Field Marshal von Kluge, on the other hand, was inclined to prefer Hitler's strategic concept. There were sharp exchanges of opinion and weeks passed before a decision was reached.'

These comments show that it really didn't matter what the generals thought; Hitler's view was the only important one, and his ideas for the development of operations were the ones that were undertaken.

Warlimont quoted a discussion on 28 July between Halder and Brauchitsch in which Halder inveighed against:[27]

'the absurdity of the operations now ordered, which will result in a dispersal of our forces and bring the decisive operation against Moscow to a standstill.'

Field Marshal Keitel mentioned in his memoirs[28] the conflict of opinion between the OKH and the Fuhrer soon after the first victorious battles in Russia:

'Hitler's strategy called for a variation of that propounded by the War Office (OKH): while the latter had advocated that Army Group Centre should punch its way through with the aim of taking Moscow and capturing the Validai heights to the north, thereby severing communications between Leningrad and the capital, Hitler wanted to hold back along a general line running from Odessa to Lake Peipus through Orel and Smolensk: having done that he would draw off some of the strength from Army Group Centre (by far the most formidable and heavily armoured of the Army Groups) and use a reinforced Army Group South to deprive the enemy of the whole Donets Basin, and of the Maikop and Kransador oil fields: then he would seize Leningrad using a similarly reinforced Army Group North and link up with Finland.'

He went on to say:[29]

> 'Hitler visualised these targets on the flanks as being of great economic value in the case of the Donets Basin, and political and naval value in the case of Finland and the Baltic.'

Keitel was in daily intimate contact with Hitler in his role as Chief of the Armed Forces High Command (OKW), and his recollection of events is therefore very important. There could hardly be a clearer statement regarding the position, leaving no reasonable doubt that Hitler's objectives were based on the economic and political importance of these areas and not of the overriding need to defeat the Soviet Army, which was the basis of the OKH's plan.

During these weeks of indecision and delay, the Red Army and the citizens of Moscow were frantically creating new defences around the capital that would have to be taken once a new German offensive began in this sector, whether before or after the Kiev operation to the south. This inactivity and the respite it gave the Red Army was exactly the problem of most concern to Brauchitsch, Halder and Bock. By diverting the armour from Army Group Centre to the flanks, the impetus generated by the army group was dissipated and the opportunity of concluding the campaign by achieving the strategic defeat of the Red Army before winter encroached (whether it came early or not) was imperilled.

On 4 August, Halder made clear the conflict surrounding what their strategic objectives should be in his diary entry:[30]

> 'Our command function is exhausted in details, which are really the responsibility of army group HQ, where we should be giving them clear-cut missions and the material means for independent action. In order to remedy this situation, it would be necessary for ourselves to have a clear idea of what the political command regards as the prime objectives of the campaign. **What, in fact, is our chief object: to capture the Ukraine and the Caucasus as quickly as possible for economic ends, or else to defeat the enemy decisively? [Author's emphasis]**. If it is the former, we should have full liberty in the use of our resources, without that constant interference from the top level. OKH's objective for this year is the area around Moscow, leaving the gaining of more ground to the development of the situation. Under these circumstances, naturally we could not expect to reach the Caucasus before onset of this winter. For the former alternative, we would need strong forces for an invasion of the oil region, and then we would have to go all the way to Baku.'

If the Chief of the General Staff did not know what the strategic objectives of the campaign were, then there was no chance for its success.

Major (later Lieutenant General) Gerhard Engle, Hitler's Army Adjutant from 1938–43, wrote a diary covering the time he spent at Hitler's headquarters. Later published as *At the Heart of The Reich*, it is an invaluable source of his contemporaneous observations. He noted on 8 August 1941:[31]

> 'One sees clearly how indecisive F (Fuhrer) is regarding the continuation of the operation. **Ideas and objectives keep on changing [Author's emphasis]**. One emerges from the situation conferences as nonplussed as one went in. In the train of the situation conference this evening it seems that the following is the course of events. Leningrad come what may: this must be political and strategic, all the more so since Field Marshal von Leeb has declared that he can do it with artillery and the Luftwaffe. In the Centre: shift to the defensive. Everything mobile to head south: Ukraine, Donetz Basin and Rostov. **At the moment F. sees the economic defeat of the Russians as the more important goal [Author's emphasis]**, all the more so since he is being advised from the front and by OKH that the enemy has taken such a beating that the prospect of his being able to mount an offensive in the foreseeable future, particularly this year, no longer need to be taken into consideration.'

This confusion of aims, where not even the most senior officers of OKH knew what the objectives of the campaign were, could not have been more prejudicial to the successful outcome of *Barbarossa*. What was urgently required was clarity, and this Hitler did not provide. It should be noted that it is fundamental that in order to take and hold any objectives, economic or otherwise, it is necessary to first defeat the armed forces of the enemy.

On 11 August, Halder noted the scale of the problem then facing German commanders:[32]

> 'What we are now doing is the last desperate attempt to prevent our front line from becoming frozen in position warfare. The High Command is greatly handicapped in its capability for modifying the situation, as the Army Groups are separated by natural obstacles (marshes). Our last reserves have been committed. Any regrouping now is merely a shifting of forces on the baseline within individual army group sectors. This takes time and consumes the energy of men and machines. The upshot is impatience and irritation on the part of the High Command and an increasing tendency to interfere in trivial details.

'**The whole situation makes it increasingly plain that we have underestimated the Russian colossus [Author's emphasis]**, who consistently prepared for war with that utterly ruthless determination so characteristic of totalitarian states. This applies to organizational and economic resources, as well as the communications system and, most of all, to the strictly military potential. At the outset of the war, we reckoned with about 200 enemy divisions. Now we have already counted 360. These divisions indeed are not armed and equipped according to our standards, and their tactical leadership is often poor. But there they are, and if we smash a dozen of them, the Russians simply put up another dozen. **The time factor favors them [Author's emphasis]**, as they are near their own resources, while we are moving farther and farther away from ours. And so our troops, sprawled over an immense front line, without any depth, are subject to incessant attacks of the enemy. Sometimes these are successful, because too many gaps must be left in these enormous spaces.'

It is more than a little ironic that Halder's remarks seem not to recognize that Nazi Germany was an authoritarian regime too. However, his remarks do raise two matters directly relating to Hitler's decision to attack the USSR. The first is that the Germans did not know the strength of the Soviet Army when they planned *Barbarossa*, a matter Hitler was warned about by the long-term German military attaché in Moscow, General Kostring, whose advice he chose to ignore (along with that of everyone else). The second matter reflects the advice given to Hitler by Rundstedt and others that the distances involved before reaching critical objectives in Russia were very problematic when the lack of transport infrastructure was taken into account.

The consequence of Hitler ignoring these two factors was that the destruction of the Red Army before winter became more problematic as the time available lessened. Consequently, the Soviets would have the chance to revive their armies if they survived the first campaigning season. It had always to be borne in mind by the invaders that the USSR had a substantially larger population than Germany, and no other enemies to detract from the effort they could devote to fighting the Nazis, in contrast to the situation facing the Germans.

However, despite these problems, Hitler continued to underestimate the Soviet Army and its potential, as Keitel noted in his *Memoirs*:[33]

'As early as the end of July Hitler was already believing not only that the Red Army in the field had been beaten, but that the nucleus of their defences had been so gravely afflicted that it would be impossible for them to recover their enormous material losses before the country was overwhelmed by total defeat. For this reason – and this is of high historic interest – **he was at the end of July or early August already ordering considerable sections of the Army munitions industry (apart from tank construction) to be switched over to munitions production for the Navy (submarines) and the Air Force (aircraft and anti-aircraft batteries) in anticipation of the war with Britain, while on the Eastern Front the Army was to keep the defeated enemy in check using the weapons on hand, but with twice the armoured strike capacity [Author's emphasis].'**

It is one thing to underestimate an enemy, but quite another to be foolhardy in the provisions made for future developments. These decisions relating to the reduction of ammunition and transfer of resources had to be reversed later when it became apparent even to the Fuhrer that the Soviets were not defeated. This chopping and changing of manufacturing priorities was another indication of Hitler's unsuitability for high command and (understandably) disrupted the most important armament programs and the whole German war effort.

Despite all these critical factors, which meant that the speedy destruction of the Red Army was paramount to *Barbarossa*'s chance of success, the dispute continued between Hitler and the OKH regarding the strategy to be pursued. On 21 August, Engel, Hitler's Adjutant, entered in his diary:[34]

'Most serious conflict between C-in-C [Commander-in-Chief], Chief of the General Staff and F. The former two restate their objectives: capture Moscow and its industry. They are convinced that Soviets will have to plan for decisive battle before capital. F of exactly contrary view: to capture the capital will not decide the war. Alluded to Napoleon. He needed Russian vital arteries: oil, cereals, coal. With the panzers will, as previously, wipe out forces in south Russian region. Sensed disagreement amongst army commanders and chiefs of staff. C-in-C and Chief (of the General Staff) resigned to it and gave in. A black day for the Army. Outspoken personal attacks on Brauchitsch and Halder by F. Mood similar to November 1939. Schmundt and I see the C-in-C's days as numbered. But what then?'

Despite Hitler's comments regarding Napoleon, the position of Moscow in 1941 compared to 1812 differed in many significant respects, which meant that it was far more important in 1941. Firstly, in 1812, Moscow was not the capital of Russia; St Petersburg (Leningrad) was the Imperial capital. Secondly, because of technological advances, Moscow had become one of the most important concentrations of industry in the USSR, especially with respect to optical and electronic products for the armed forces. Thirdly, once again because of industrialization and technical advances, Moscow had become the country's most important railway hub. Losing it would enormously complicate the movement of troops and supplies around the whole country and thereby reduce the ability of the armed forces to defend the whole of the USSR, not just Moscow and the region around it. Hitler's argument that Moscow was not the most important military objective in the USSR was therefore invalid, and the OKH's planned concentration on taking the capital as the key to the *Barbarossa* campaign was not just a case of generals 'vying for the spires' for their own glorification. Virtually all the most senior German commanders saw Moscow as the single most important objective in the whole of the USSR, but Hitler could not be brought to this realization.

On 22 August, Halder made the following diary entry, which is probably the most trenchant that is contained in his writings:[35]

'I regard the situation created by the Fuhrer's interference unendurable for OKH. **No other but the Fuhrer himself is to blame for the zigzag course caused by his successive orders, nor can the present OKH, which now is in its fourth victorious campaign, tarnish its good name with these latest orders [Author's emphasis]**. Moreover, the way in which ObdH [Brauchitsch] is being treated is absolutely outrageous. I have proposed to ObdH to request his relief together with mine. ObdH refuses on the grounds that the resignations would not be accepted and so nothing would be changed.'

Halder's diary is overwhelmingly characterized by a restrained, dignified and logical tone, so he could only have written this entry when absolutely at his wits' end. There has been a great deal of criticism levelled at Brauchitsch and Halder by commentators and historians on the basis that they should have stood up to Hitler to a far greater degree. This criticism ignores that the history of their relations shows Hitler was not concerned with any criticism that Brauchitsch, Halder or anyone else may have had of his plans or decisions. Based on all the experience that the generals and other senior members of the hierarchy had dealing with the Fuhrer, it is extremely unlikely that any change to his decisions or views would have been achieved by further remonstrances from Brauchitsch, Halder or any other senior general. Hitler even ignored Goering's advice, so it was absolutely clear that no-one could have changed his view with respect to the timing of the attack on Moscow. Further evidence of this is the extensive list of generals whom Hitler sacked, which included Brauchitsch, Halder, Rundstedt, List, Leeb, Bock, Hoepner, Beck and Fritsch, together with some eighty others who were either executed or persuaded to take their own lives, such as Rommel, Kluge and Witzleben. Hitler was not interested in a debating society, just in getting his orders carried out, and whether the generals – singly or as a group – disagreed with them or not was of no concern to him. In his memoirs, Keitel discussed this aspect of Hitler and gave an illustration of how he reacted to resistance from Brauchitsch and Halder at the time of the Czechoslovakian crisis in 1938:[36]

'As Halder was writing out the orders, I could only ask Brauchitsch: "Why do you fight with him, when you know that the battle is lost before it's begun? Nobody thinks there is going to be any war over this, so the whole thing wasn't worth all that bitter rearguard action. You are throwing down your trumps in quite futile gestures and in the end you only have to give in just the same; and then when it really is a matter of life and death your opposition will lack the necessary authority to be effective."

'I have described this episode in detail only because it illustrates in one characteristic example (a controversy that was not even of the first order) the symptoms of the conditions under which we had to work with Hitler. **If he once got an idea into his head, no man on earth could ever shake him out of it; he always had his way, whether it was approved or disapproved by his advisers [Author's emphasis].**'

Keitel's recollection is supported by many other instances relating to Hitler's generals and advisors.

General Heinz Guderian is regarded by many as the foremost expert on armoured warfare in the Second World War, and as was set out in *Volume 1* of the series, *Hitler's Imperfect Victories: Campaigns in Western Europe*, his involvement in the exploitation of the breakthrough at Sedan was vital to its success. In *Barbarossa*, Guderian was in command of Panzer Group 2 in Army Group Centre and was involved in most of the major breakthroughs and battles of encirclement from the beginning of the campaign. He later became Chief of the General Staff after the 20 July 1944 failed attempt on Hitler's life. In his book *Panzer Leader*, published shortly after the war and remaining in print ever since, he mentioned a meeting with Hitler on 4 August 1941 to discuss the future course of *Barbarossa*, which included a passage concerning the maintenance of the panzer forces:[37]

'I stressed the fact that our tank engines had become very worn as a result of the appalling dust; in consequence they must be replaced with all urgency if any more large scale tank operations were to be carried out during the current year. It was also essential that replacements be provided for our tank casualties from current production. After a certain amount of humming and hawing **Hitler promised to supply 300 new tank engines for the whole Eastern Front, a figure which I described as totally inadequate. As for new tanks, we were not to get any, since Hitler intended to retain them all at home for the equipping of newly set-up formations [Author's emphasis].** In the ensuing argument I stated that we could only cope with the Russians' great numerical superiority in tanks if our tank losses were rapidly made good again. Hitler then said: **"If I had known that the figures for Russian tank strength which you gave in your book were in fact the true ones, I would not – I believe – ever have started this war."** [The figure for Soviet tank strength which Guderian had given in his book *Achtung Panzer* was 10,000 in 1938.]'

It seems almost impossible to assign any logic to this bizarre ruling by Hitler. One can only imagine the additional anxiety inflicted on field commanders who had to try to overcome the problems associated with wear and tear on the AFVs under their command and defeat the Red Army while at the same time dealing with the limitations imposed by this nonsensical order. The loss in power and efficiency this decision caused to the German armoured formations is not hard to imagine. Indeed, the wonder is that they achieved as much as they did.

Guderian also referred to a conference held on 23 August where the Chief of the General Staff, Halder, and Field Marshal von Bock (C-in-C Army Group Centre) were present. Halder informed the participants that Hitler had decided that the main effort of the German Army would be diverted to the Ukraine and that taking Leningrad or Moscow would be decided upon after the completion of the operation in the south. He noted that Halder 'seemed deeply upset' and continued:[38]

'**[We were] all agreed that this new plan to move on Kiev must result in a winter campaign [Author's emphasis]:** this in turn would lead to all those difficulties which the OKH had very good reasons for wishing to avoid.'

These difficulties included:[39]

'The road and supply problems which must arise if the tanks were to be sent south; I also expressed doubts as to the ability of our armoured equipment to perform these heavy new tasks as well as the subsequent winter advance on Moscow. I went on to draw attention to the condition of XXIV Panzer Corps, which had not had one single day for rest and maintenance since the opening of the Russian Campaign.'

After much further discussion, it was finally agreed that Guderian, as a front-line commander, would present these matters to Hitler in a further attempt to induce him to change his mind regarding the strategic priorities of the campaign. He flew that afternoon to the Fuhrer's headquarters at Rastenburg in East Prussia, where he reported to Field Marshal Brauchitsch:[40]

'[He] greeted me with the following words: "I forbid you to mention the question of Moscow to the Fuhrer. The operation to the south has been ordered. The problem now is simply how it is to be carried out. Discussion is pointless." I therefore asked permission to fly back to my Panzer Group, since in these circumstances the discussion I might have had with Hitler would simply be a waste of time. But Field-Marshal von Brauchitsch would not agree to this. He ordered that I see Hitler and report to him on the state of my Panzer Group, "but without mentioning Moscow!"'

Guderian made his report to Hitler, who was attended by Keitel, Jodl, Schmundt and other OKW representatives, but no-one from the OKH. Hitler listened and asked:[41]

'"In view of their past performance, do you consider that the troops are capable of making another great effort?"
   'I replied: "If the troops are given a major objective, the importance of which is apparent to every soldier, yes."
   'Hitler then said: "You mean, of course, Moscow?"
   'I answered: "Yes. Since you have broached the subject, let me give you reasons for my opinions."'

Guderian then repeated the reasons previously discussed with Halder and Bock. He said that Hitler let him speak and did not interrupt. At the end of his reasoning, Hitler put forward his reasons for the action in the south:[42]

'[F]or the first time I heard him use the phrase "my generals know nothing about the economic aspects of war [Author's emphasis]." Hitler's words all led up to this: he had given strict orders that the attack on Kiev was to be the immediate strategic object and all actions were to be carried out with that in mind. **I here saw for the first time a spectacle with which I was later to become very familiar: all those present nodded in agreement with every sentence Hitler uttered, while I was left with my point of view [Author's emphasis].**'

The crucial matter, the importance of which cannot be overstated, is that Hitler knew from his senior commanders that changing the priorities of the campaign to undertake the Kiev operation would mean that the final offensive to take Moscow could not now be finalized before the onset of winter. This was a major departure from the original intention of *Barbarossa*, which was to defeat the Soviet Army in six months during the 1941 campaign from June to November. By insisting on the Kiev operation, Hitler was leaving little room for errors or delays which may impact the time available for subsequent operations to take Moscow or Leningrad.

The encirclement battle resulting from Hitler's diversion of the panzer groups from Moscow to the Ukraine, known as the Kiev *Kesselschlacht* (cauldron battle), ended with the greatest German victory thus far in the war, with 670,000 prisoners and an enormous haul of equipment being taken.

Guderian commented on this victory in *Panzer Leader*:[43]

'The Battle of Kiev was undoubtedly a great tactical victory. But whether great strategic advantages were to be garnered from this tactical success remained questionable. **It all depended on this: would the German Army, before the onset of the winter and, indeed, before the autumnal mud set in, still be capable of achieving decisive results? [Author's emphasis].** It is true that the planned assault on Leningrad had already had to be abandoned in favour of a tight investment. But the OKH believed that the enemy was no longer capable of creating a firm defensive front or of offering serious resistance in the area of Army Group South. The OKH wanted this Army Group to capture the Donetz Basin and reach the River Don before winter.

'But the main blow was to be dealt by the reinforced Army Group Centre, with objective Moscow. Was there still sufficient time for this to succeed?'

The Kiev encirclement was hard-fought and continued from 23 August until 26 September, which left little time for redeploying the necessary forces to continue the drive on Moscow – which Hitler now authorized – before the autumnal mud or the winter freeze intervened. So while the southern diversion was a great tactical victory, it was not the decisive strategic victory that taking Moscow would probably have involved and which the OKH plan had been directed towards achieving. Furthermore, the forces necessary for the offensive to take Moscow now had to move back from the southern army group to Army Group Centre. While the Kiev operation was underway, the Soviets had been frantically preparing the defence of Moscow and transporting troops to create a reserve being formed around the capital for its defence. These troops were also to be used for a counteroffensive being planned by General Georgy Zhukov, who had been in command of the Soviet forces in the Far East when they defeated the Japanese, and more recently those at Leningrad when the Germans were stopped. Had the German victory been achieved on the road to Moscow instead of around Kiev some 200km to the south, the Red Army would have not had forces in place to oppose a German drive on the capital. However, there were now significant forces defending Moscow to forestall any German attack towards it.

Rundstedt was of the opinion that his army, at least could not go further. On 3rd November, Brauchitsch was visiting Army Group South and in discussion with von Rundstedt who stated:[44]

> 'that a halt be called and the offensive continued in the spring, citing the increasing supply problems. Von Brauchitsch answered that these were well understood, but it was vital that Voronezh, Stalingrad and Maikop, just north of the Caucasus Mountains, be reached. These objectives represented a distance of up to 300 miles form Army Group South's positions and von Rundstedt later recalled 'we laughed aloud when we heard that.'

The German offensive to take Moscow eventually started on 2 October, codenamed Operation *Typhoon*. Army Group Centre had been reinforced to seventy divisions, including almost all the armoured divisions the Germans had, the force under Field Marshal von Bock being more than half the total of the Army on the Eastern Front. The plan, in brief outline, was that Soviet forces would be split into two groups, one around Vyazma and the other around Bryansk. These would then be enveloped and the troops in them destroyed or taken prisoner as the Germans pushed on to Moscow. Halder's diary entry for 2 October 1941 noted:[45]

'Center: Favored by sparkling fall weather, army group opened the TYPHOON offensive today at 05.30. Whereas Guderian has been gaining despite the handicap of his lagging right wing, the attacks of the other armies and armored groups by noon had carried the advances only between 6 to 12km. In some sectors, the enemy is retreating in great disorder.'

Guderian, in command of Panzer Group 2, recalled:[46]

'On October 2nd the attack was resumed with violence. A complete break-through was achieved and the Russian Thirteenth Army was thrown back to the north-east. I visited the 10th (Motorised) Infantry Division and its Infantry Regiment 41, commanded by Colonel Traut. Our casualties during these days were happily light. But if the figures for total casualties since the start of the campaign were examined it was a grave and tragic total. These troops had received a number of replacements, but although these were keen and eager men they yet lacked the combat experience and toughness of the older men.

'4th Panzer Division took Kromy and thus reached the metalled road that led to Orel.

'The whole of Army Group Centre had been attacking successfully along its entire front since early morning and was much helped by the good weather.'

On 3 October, Halder entered in his diary:[47]

'The TYPHOON front is making cheering progress. Guderian has reached Orel. Enemy resistance has been broken on the entire front, except in the sector of Second Army. The armored divisions have carried their penetrations as far as 50km, the infantry theirs as far as 40km into enemy territory. The enemy is hanging on and defending himself as well as he can. Even reserves have been brought forward to the front. Nowhere are there any signs of deliberate disengagement. The southern assault group has broken through the enemy positions, while the northern group has overrun the advance positions and is now approaching the big continuous line of enemy positions.'

On 4 October, Halder was almost exultant:[48]

'Operation TYPHOON is developing on a truly classic pattern. Guderian has reached Orel and is now pushing into completely empty space. Hoepner has broken through the enemy positions and has reached Mozhaysk. Hoth has pushed to Kholm (on the upper Dnieper) and has gained elbow room to the north as far as Byelyi. The enemy is holding all parts of the front not under direct attack, a policy that bodes well for the encirclement of pockets.'

When Guderian entered Orel, the trams were still running and the component parts of some factories being prepared to be sent east were at the rail station, such was the degree of surprise that the penetration by the panzers had achieved.[49]

Halder's diary entry reflected further good news on 5 October:[50]

'The Battle of Agp. [Army Group] Center continues along its truly classic course. Guderian is on the Orel–Bryansk highway. Enemy forces committed against his left wing have been beaten back and will eventually be encircled together with the rest. Second Army is advancing rapidly on its northern wing, meeting almost no resistance. Hoepner is driving on Vyazma, turning towards the big marshes to the west and east. His right wing, followed by the armored corps of the reserve, which has not been committed so far, has no enemy before it any longer. Fourth Army is swinging north. Enemy resistance varies according to locality and unit. It is quite evident that the enemy wants to make a stand, but cannot. Ninth Army has harder going. Armored Group 3, after being held up by lack of fuel, will not be moving again until this afternoon. The infantry is moving up with magnificent speed, so we may expect that enemy resistance, which is partly stubborn and evidently skillfully directed, will soon be broken. From the front facing the northern wing of Ninth Army, which does not participate in the attack, the enemy is drawing all available forces to the south, against the northern wing of the offensive.'

However, 6 October was a day of grave portents, as Guderian noted:[51]

'On October 6th our headquarters was moved forward to Sevsk. 4th Panzer Division was attacked by Russian tanks to the south of Mzensk and went through some bad hours. This was the first occasion on which the vast superiority of the Russian T34 to our tanks became plainly apparent. The division suffered grievous casualties. The rapid advance on Tula which we had planned had therefore to be abandoned for the moment.'

Blumentritt, in discussing the weather and strengthening Soviet resistance, also noted the problems of the T34s:[52]

'We were confronted by another and equally unpleasant surprise at this time. The first Russian T34 tanks appeared during the Battle of Vyazma. In 1941 this was a most spectacular A.F.V. [armoured fighting vehicles - Author's note], which could only be dealt with by other tanks or by the artillery: it was impervious to the infantry's anti-tank weapons, for at that time our infantry was equipped only with 37mm and 50mm anti-tank guns. These had been capable of knocking out the Russian tanks we had hitherto encountered but they had no effect on the T34. Thus a very serious state of affairs arose for the infantry divisions, which felt themselves naked and defenceless against this new tank. A gun of at least 75mm calibre was needed, and such a gun had first to be built. At Veraya the Russian tanks simply drove straight through the 7th Infantry Division to the artillery positions and literally rode over the guns. The effect on the infantryman's morale was comprehensible. This marked the beginning of what came to be called "the tank terror".'

The advent of the T34 tank was a profound shock to the Germans, as it outperformed their own tanks in every respect. It was more powerfully armed, with a 76mm gun, than any German tank at that time. It also had sloping armour, which made it almost impervious to any anti-tank guns the Germans had – apart from the 88mm flak gun when used in the anti-tank role – had wider tracks, was more manoeuvrable and could go where German tanks could not. It was a technological triumph that in an instant made all the German tanks virtually obsolete. The T34 also provided absolute physical evidence of the absurdity of the arrogant Nazi hypotheses regarding the capabilities of the Eastern *untermensch*. It was only the relatively small number of the new tanks that were then available to the Red Army, along with the skill of the German tank crews, which prevented the situation deteriorating into a rout for the panzer forces.

Guderian noted other portents in *Panzer Leader*:[53]

'During the night of October 6th–7th the first snow of the winter fell. It did not lie for long and, as usual, the roads rapidly became nothing but canals of bottomless mud, along which our vehicles could only advance at snail's pace and with great wear to the engines. We asked for winter clothing – we had already done this once before – but were informed that we would receive it in due course and were instructed not to make further unnecessary requests of this type. Nevertheless I repeated my demands on several occasions, but the clothing did not reach the front during the course of that year.'

On 7 October, Halder commented on the development of the encirclement at Vyazma:[54]

'Hoepner linked up with Hoth at Vyazma this morning. A brilliant success after a five-day battle. Next thing to be done is to push the infantry of Fourth Army sharply on Vyazma to free Hoepner at the earliest for the drive against the south-eastern front of Moscow.'

Guderian continued:[55]

'On October 8th I flew along the line of our "road" from Sevsk over Dmitrovsk to Orel, where I found my command vehicles which I had previously sent on ahead. The state of the traffic along the "road" as far as Kromy was appalling; from there on we had a metalled road as far as Orel, though already this consisted of one bomb crater after the next. General Freiherr von Geyr informed me that the enemy opposite the 4th Panzer Division had been reinforced; a tank brigade and an infantry division had been recently identified. The 3rd Panzer Division was marching northwards, with orders to capture Bolchov. The 4th Panzer's task for the 9th of October was to take Mzensk. Descriptions of the quality and, above all, the new tactical handling of the Russian tanks were very worrying. Our defensive weapons available at that period were only successful against the T34 when the conditions were unusually favourable.'

Halder recorded in his diary entry for 9 October:[56]

'AGp. Center: Guderian is feeling the increasing pressure on his western flank. He will have to drop his objections for the time being and use his tanks against this threat, even though it may delay the next move beyond Orel, against Tula. The eastern flank is free of enemy pressure! The encircling battle at Vyazma is proceeding in positively classic fashion. Outside that battle area the right wing of Fourth Army is pushing on to Kaluga, and the northern wing of Ninth Army is regrouping for the attack on Rzhev.'

On the same day, Bock's diary entry illustrates clearly the problems involved in dealing with an out-of-touch headquarters and an interfering commander:[57]

'In the morning came an order from the Fuhrer that elements of Panzer Group 3, thus north of the highway, were to be relieved by elements of Panzer Group 4 from the south of the highway for an advance to the north. That would take very much longer than a relief by infantry, involve unnecessary lateral movements over frightful roads, and open one hole in order to plug another.

'During the night of 10 October, at 03:00, there arrived an order direct from the Fuhrer according to which the 19th Panzer Division and the Infantry Regiment Grossdeutschland were to be sent to the Guderian group at once by way of Bryansk, in order to prevent the enemy south of Bryansk from breaking out to the east! I reported back that the 19th Panzer Division was at present southwest of Yukhnov and that an about face would be impossible without threatening the supply of the 4th Army and the Luftwaffe, which was on the 19th Panzer Division's road. Moreover, according to information from the 2nd Army, the road to Bryansk will not be usable until the 10th at the earliest due to numerous demolitions: on the undamaged sections of the road are the fuel transport columns of the 2nd Panzer Army. Delivery of fuel by way of the previous route, a detour far to the south, had proved impossible in the long run because of the awful road conditions. I requested orders as to which should have priority, the fuel or the Infantry Regiment Grossdeutschland. I received the reply that they would do without the 19th Panzer Division; the fuel had priority, but the Infantry Regiment Grossdeutschland was to be transferred to the 2nd Army by way of Bryansk as soon as practicable.'

This entry from Bock offers the clearest possible example that moving forces around a map at Rastenburg, 1,000km from the front, was much easier than doing so in real time in the midst of a battle while manoeuvring to accomplish the defeat of the enemy. It illustrates perfectly the great weakness in Hitler's method of command, which was almost entirely dependent on his interpretation from maps of a given situation.

During the period from 10 October to 3 November, the tone of Halder's entries changed significantly:[58]

'In AGp. Center, Second Army (reinforced by armor and motorized units) is closing up toward Kursk with the object of continuing advance on Voronezh. That is pure theory. **The grim reality is that the troops are**

stuck in the mud and will be lucky indeed if they can get enough prime movers through to get their food [Author's emphasis]. Guderian's Panzer Army has slowly and painfully worked its way loose to Tula (through Orel).

'Fourth Army in conjunction with Armored Group Hoepner has breached the Moscow defense position all the way from the Oka River, near Kaluga, to Mozhask. But to the north, the planned thrust of Armored Corps Reinhardt had to be abandoned as a result of adverse ground conditions.

'Ninth Army, after some days of critical fighting, has straightened out the situation around Kalinin and built up a sufficiently strong front facing north.

'**The problem of supply [Author's emphasis]** dominates the situation. The supply position is positively bad in Sixth Army, but this is a sector where it is not quite so serious from the operational point of view if the advance is slowed down or even falls behind that of the other groups. The position is fair in Fourth Army and Armored Group Hoepner despite the unbelievable difficulties on the supply routes through Yukhnov and Vyazma. On the other hand, it is extremely difficult north of the Moscow motor highway, so that it appears doubtful that we could carry on the planned thrust south of the Volga reservoir on the axis Klin–Rybinsk.'

Guderian commented on the difficulties encountered after 10 October:[59]

'The next few weeks were dominated by the mud. Wheeled vehicles could only advance with help of tracked vehicles. These latter, having to perform tasks for which they were not intended, rapidly wore out. Since chains and couplings for the towing of vehicles were lacking, bundles of rope were dropped from aeroplanes to the immobilised vehicles. The supplying of hundreds of such vehicles and their crews had now to be done by the air force, and that for weeks on end. Preparations made for the winter were utterly inadequate. For weeks we had been requesting anti-freeze for the water coolers of our engines; we saw as little of this as we did of winter clothing for the troops. This lack of warm clothes was, in the difficult months ahead, to provide the greatest problem and cause the greatest suffering to our soldiers – and it would have been the easiest to avoid of all our difficulties.'

He also related the worsening weather conditions:[60]

'The snow continued on October 12th. We were still sitting tight in our little town of Dmitrovsk, with the appalling mud swamps outside the door, awaiting instructions from OKH concerning reorganisation. The large encirclement south of Bryansk and the smaller one north of the town had both been completed, but our troops were stuck in the mud and immobilised, including the XLVIII Panzer Corps which at the beginning of the operation would so willingly have driven along hard roads through Sumy and which was now struggling forward through the mire towards Fatesh. In the Mzensk area the battles against the freshly arrived enemy went on.'

Bock's diary for 15 October contained a note of anxiety not previously apparent:[61]

'Guderian informed me that because of stubborn enemy resistance the advance by his army to the northwest will not be possible until the Bryansk pocket is eliminated and his forces have regrouped. This will take some days. As well there are the indescribable road conditions, which make almost any movement by motorised vehicles impossible.

'The change in the weather with its periods of snow, frost and rain, is wearing on the troops and is affecting morale. The question "what will become of us in the winter" is on everyone's mind.'

His entry for 19 October described the difficulties the armies were having with supply and movement:[62]

'Furthermore the army group is stuck fast in muck and mire. No fuel is reaching Panzer Group 3 either. Supply via Bryansk and on the highway is unbelievably difficult. The Bryansk road is in terrible shape; on the highway alone there are 33 demolitions, including 11 bridges, to be repaired.

'The elements of the 1st Panzer Division sent forward from Kalinin to Torzhok had to retire some way at the cost of men and material, since in the interim strong enemy forces had broken in between them and Torzhok.'

On the same day, Bock issued the following Order of the Day to Army Group Centre:[63]

'The battle at Vyazma and Bryansk has resulted in the collapse of the Russian Front, which was fortified in depth. Eight Russian armies with

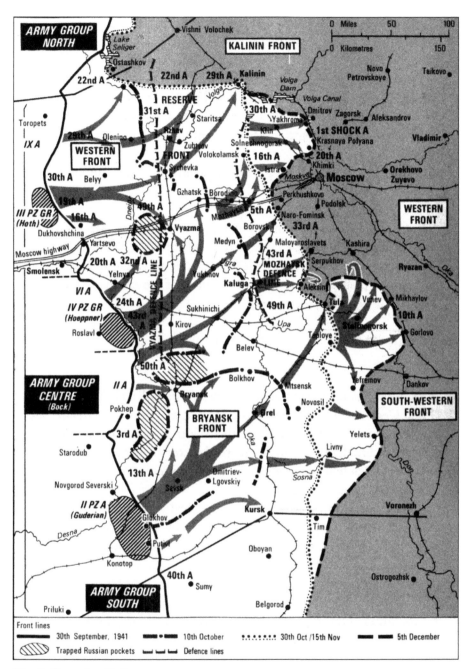

Map 3: Operation *Typhoon*.
This was the last effort to reach Moscow. This map shows the encirclement battles achieved by Army Group Centre and how close the Germans came to Moscow even though the offensive was delayed for too long and occurred during the winter.

73 rifle and cavalry divisions, 13 tank divisions and brigades and strong army artillery were destroyed in the difficult struggle with a numerically far superior foe.

'The total booty: 673,098 prisoners, 1,227 tanks, 4,378 artillery pieces 1,009 anti-tank and anti-aircraft guns and huge amounts of war material.

'This difficult battle, too, you have come through with honor and in doing so completed the greatest feat of arms of the campaign!'

Bock's diary entry of 25 October gave a characteristically clear summary of the overall situation:[64];

'The splitting apart of the army group together with the frightful weather has caused us [to be] bogged down. As a result the Russians are gaining time to bring their shattered divisions back up to strength and bolster their defense, especially since they have most of the rail lines and roads around Moscow. That is very bad!'

On the same day, Guderian considered the battles around Bryansk and Vyazma as at an end:[65]

'With the victorious end of the twin battles of Bryansk and Vyazma Army Group Centre had undoubtedly won a great tactical success. **Whether it still possessed sufficient strength to launch a further attack and thus operationally to exploit its tactical victory was the most serious question which had so far confronted the Supreme Command in this war [Author's emphasis].**

'On October 29th our leading tanks reached a point some two miles from Tula. An attempt to capture the town by a coup de main failed owing to the enemy's strong anti-tank and anti-aircraft defences; we lost many tanks and officers.

'General Heinrici, always a practical and sensible man, who commanded XLIII Army Corps, now came to see me and described the bad condition of his troops' supplies: among other things, there had been no issue of bread since October 20th.'

He went on to describe the situation of his panzer army and the attempted exploitation following the victories at Vyazma and Bryansk:[66]

'In view of the impossibility of launching a frontal attack on Tula General Freiherr von Geyr suggested that in order to continue our advance we bypass the town to the east. I agreed with this and ordered that the attack go on toward Dedilovo and the crossing-places over the Shat. General Freiherr von Geyr was also of the view that there was now no possibility of using motorised troops before the frost set in. In this he was undoubtedly correct. It was only possible to gain ground very slowly and at the cost of great wear and tear to the motorised equipment. As a result the reopening of the Mensk–Tula railroad assumed very great importance. Despite consistent exhortations to hurry, the repair work was making only slow progress. The lack of locomotives made me look around for alternative transport and I suggested the use of railway lorries, but none were sent to me.

'During the night of November 3rd–4th there had been a frost and this made it easier for the troops to move; on the other hand we were now confronted with the constant problem of the cold, from which our soldiers were already beginning to suffer.'

On 11 November, Bock's diary again deals with the problems the army group was having with supplies and the effects of the weather:[67]

'The number of trains supplying the army group has been reduced to 23 per day. That is just enough for our daily needs. I have raised objections. When Greiffenberg reported to me that this protest had been rejected and that Halder had stated on this occasion that the Army Command did not think the army group yet had the supplies necessary to attack now, I called Halder and said to him:
    "In my opinion, the objectives you marked on the recently-delivered map as worthwhile surely cannot be reached before winter, because we no longer have the required forces and because it is impossible to supply these forces after reaching those objectives on account of the inadequate potential for supply by rail [Author's emphasis]. Furthermore, I no longer consider the objectives designated 'worthwhile' by me in the army group order for the encirclement of Moscow, specifically the line Ryazan–Vladimir–Kalyazin to be attainable. All that remains, therefore, is to strive for a screening front in the general line Kolomna–Orekhovo–Zagorsk–Dmitrov, which is absolutely vital to the encirclement of Moscow. I will be happy if our forces are sufficient to obtain this line. The attack can be supplied to this point if the previous number of trains running to the army group is authorized."'

He continued:[68]

'The attack cannot become a great strategic masterpiece, because troop movements have so far largely been impossible and later will become impossible on account of the snow. The only thing that can matter, therefore, is to conduct the thrust in concentration at the tactically most favorable points. I cannot suggest waiting longer than is necessary to attack, because I fear that the weather conditions will then thwart our plans. If we get deep snow, all movement is finished.'

For Bock, one of the most successful and aggressive commanders in the German Army, to make this evaluation surely meant that the chances for the Germans to fulfil the provisions of Hitler Directive No. 21 were by now very slim. The Germans were obviously in major trouble, and these entries by Bock came over three weeks before the Soviet counterattack and the worst effects of the winter were felt.

His 14 November diary entry made clear the current difficulties:[69]

'The armies are all complaining about serious supply difficulties in all areas – rations, munitions, fuel and winter clothing. With the limited number of trains in use it is impossible to do anything about it. Naturally this has significantly complicated the attack preparations.'

Engel's diary entry for 16 November also struck a very anxious note:[70]

'Unpleasant situation conference. Supply and railways reported on. **Wild tirade by F. against Wagner (laughable theorist) [Author's emphasis]**: Gercke [Lieutenant General Rudolf Gercke, Chief of Field Transport Affairs at the General Staff, reporting to Halder – Author's note] comes off well.'

Hitler regarded Wagner, the OKH Quartermaster, as one of the impediments to his strategic aspirations. The truth is, however, that Wagner and the German supply system worked miracles within the constraints of what was possible on the Eastern Front, hampered by the almost complete destruction of the railway system by the Soviets as they retreated. Hitler's changes to the plan for *Barbarossa* made their task even more difficult than it already was.

Guderian noted that a further worrying situation had arisen on 17 November:[71]

'[W]e learned that Siberian troops [Author's emphasis] had appeared in the Uslovaia sector and that more were arriving by rail in the area

Riasan–Kolomna. The 112th Infantry Division made contact with these new Siberian troops. Since enemy tanks were simultaneously attacking the division from the Dedilova area, the weakened troops could not manage this fresh enemy. Before judging their performance it should be borne in mind that each regiment had already lost some 500 men from frostbite, that as a result of the cold the machine guns were no longer able to fire and that our 37mm anti-tank gun had proved ineffective against the T34. The result of all this was a panic, which reached all the way back to Bogorodisk. **This was the first time that such a thing had occurred in the Russian campaign, and it was a warning that the combat ability of our infantry was at an end and that they should no longer be expected to perform difficult task [Author's emphasis].**'

The Siberian troops to whom Guderian refers had been transported from the Soviet Far Eastern Front, a reinforcement that, as we have seen, consisted of eighteen infantry divisions and 1,700 tanks.[72] They were all well trained, had winter clothing and were battle-experienced, having been in two border wars in which they had soundly beaten their Japanese opponents. This reserve could only be committed because Hitler had not seen fit to involve the Japanese in the planning for *Barbarossa* or any other military preparations, or to work together to develop a role for them in threatening or taking Siberia and other eastern Soviet territories. Had he done so, it is almost certain that this crucial reinforcement would not have been available, meaning the outcome of *Barbarossa* could have been significantly different.

Bock's diary entry of 21 November provides further evidence of the tremendous strain on the front-line German troops:[73]

'Drove to Gzhatsk to VII Corps. The Commanding General has been visibly affected by the heavy fighting and described the pitiful state of his divisions, whose strength is spent.

'Losses amongst the officers, in particular, are making themselves felt. Many second lieutenants are leading battalions, one first lieutenant leads a regiment, regimental combat strengths [are] of 250 men, also [there are the effects of] the cold and inadequate shelter, in short: in his opinion the corps can do no more.'

Engel's diary note for 22 November was full of worrying omens concerning the Army High Command which would eventually come to fruition:[74]

'Schmundt referred again to the imminent change of Army Commander-in-Chief. I am in despair. He cannot be talked out of his idea to have F. take over as C-in-C Army himself. He sees in it a great opportunity for the restoration of trust. He does not understand my objections, that it would be merely symbolic and leave the Army leaderless [Author's emphasis]. Also incomprehensible is his recurrent positive opinion of Keitel: this fluctuates according to whether or not latter has upset him. At least he has turned away from the idea he had several years ago of advocating Himmler (for C-in-C): he now probably knows about this one. But the situation is depressing, and our open discussions are often violent.

'After the late situation conference I asked F. for some signatures and in conversation mentioned the C-in-C. F. spoke very calmly about Br. [Brauchitsch]. Considers him a very ill man at the end of his strength. I posed the question if he was proposing to replace him with Manstein or Kesselring. F. clammed up and left.'

Schmundt, a devoted follower of Hitler, was very influential in many personnel appointments. He was killed in the bomb blast at Hitler's headquarters on 20 July 1944 during the attempt on the Fuhrer's life known as Operation *Valkyrie*. On 22 November, a desperate tone entered Halder's diary for the first time:[75]

'Field Marshal von Bock himself has taken charge of the battle of Moscow from an advanced command post. With enormous energy he drives forward everything that can be brought to bear. Nevertheless it seems that nothing more can be gotten out of the southern wing and centre of Fourth Army for an attack. The troops here are finished (e.g., in my old 7th Division, one regiment is commanded by a first lieutenant; the battalions are commanded by second lieutenants). But northern wing of Fourth Army and Armored Group 3 still have a chance of success, and they are being driven relentlessly to achieve it. Von Bock compares the situation with the battle of the Marne, where the last battalion that could be thrown in turned the balance. Here, too, the enemy has brought in new forces. Von Bock is moving up everything he can get hold of in the new area, even 255th Division.'

On 23 November, Halder met with General Staff officers responsible for the administration and supply of the Army on the Eastern Front. He subsequently noted:[76]

'b. The means which are available to us for continuing the war are limited through use and the incredible strain imposed on our arms by the protected areas. **Certainly the Army, as it existed in June 1941, will not be available to us again [Author's emphasis].**

'3. Despite our extraordinary performance, we shall not be able to totally destroy the enemy this year. Given the vastness of this country and the inexhaustibleness of the people, **we shall not be able to totally destroy the enemy this year. Given the vastness of this country and the inexaustibleness of the people, we cannot be totally certain of success. We knew that from the beginning [Author's emphasis].** In this year we shall continue the attack until we reach the best lines for next year.'

There are two aspects of this entry of particular interest. The first is Halder's statement that the German Army would never be the same as it had been in June 1941. This was because many of the officers and enlisted men who were casualties represented the experienced core who had participated in the campaigns in Poland and France. They were the cream of the crop, and to lose a high number of them severely reduced the capabilities of the Army in every respect because they literally could not be replaced; they were the difference between the German Army and every other army in the world. The second noteworthy aspect of this entry is the statement that 'we' knew from the beginning that German forces could not be certain of destroying the enemy in one year. Once again, this harks back to the advice given to Hitler before the campaign started, and which he dismissed. This being the case, it shows clearly the reasons that motivated Halder and Brauchitsch to be so insistent that the campaign concentrate on taking Moscow as the means of inflicting a decisive strategic defeat on the USSR in the shortest possible time. They saw achieving this decisive victory as the quickest way of defeating the USSR, and this was why they strongly opposed any operation which might jeopardize the opportunity to do so by diverting units from the main effort, which had to be the drive on Moscow. It was because of Hitler's diversion of units to other objectives that the chance was lost to inflict this decisive defeat on the Soviets.

Halder's diary entry of 24 November relates to a meeting with the head of the Reserve Army, who gave a very sobering assessment of the situation:[77]

'General Fromm: Gives an overall picture of our arms production. Declining output! He thinks of the necessity to make peace!'

From was another of the generals executed for being involved in the 20 July 1944 plot to assassinate Hitler, Operation *Valkyrie*. His view at this time no doubt reflected the terrific strain that the German Army was under, the tremendous losses in men and materiel suffered so far during *Barbarossa* and the fact that it was impossible to continue in this way indefinitely. It also mirrored the orders which Hitler had given for the reduction of arms production for German ground forces after Operation *Sealion* – the proposed invasion of Britain – was cancelled in order to concentrate on equipment for the Navy and Luftwaffe, as referred to in Chapter 11 of this work.

Engel's diary entry of 24 November gave a very clear picture of the situation that reigned at Supreme Headquarters:[78]

'Another unsatisfactory, confusing situation conference. Also F. gave no orders, just delivered a long dialogue ending up with the C-in-C and Chief of the General Staff going home with the impression that they could do what they saw fit – meanwhile F. changed his thinking, everything which was is now not true and – the OKH is responsible. It is not the case, but the Field Marshal [Brauchitsch] is not the man who can ward it off.'

Halder's diary entry of 30 November made clear how heavily the German Army had suffered since the beginning of *Barbarossa*, even prior to the full force of winter setting in and before the counterattack being launched by Zhukov at the gates of Moscow:[79]

'a. The eastern army has a shortage of 340,000 men, i.e., 50 per cent of the combat strength of its infantry. Company strength is 50 to 60 men.
'b. Current losses and returning convalescents approximately offset each other at this time. **Gaps can be filled only by disbanding some divisions [Author's emphasis].**
  'In Germany we have only 33,000 men available. The bulk of the replacements are not yet broken in to the front-line routine and so have limited combat value.
'c. Trucks: Serviceability, at most 60 per cent.'

Remembering that this was the situation before the worst losses were incurred during the winter weather and the Red Army's counteroffensive launched on 5 December, this shows German forces were in a critical situation. Having to disband divisions to supply replacements elsewhere is a desperate measure for any army to consider.

Guderian related how the last advances of the Germans occurred:[80]

'On December 2nd the 3rd and 4th Panzer Divisions and Infantry Regiment Gross-Deutschland succeeded in breaking through the Russians by surprise. It was continued on December 3rd in a blizzard. The roads became icy and movement was more difficult than ever. 4th Panzer Division crossed the Moscow–Tula railroad and captured six guns: the division finally reached the Tula–Serpuchov road. By then the strength of the troops was exhausted, as was their supply of fuel. The enemy withdrew to the north and the situation remained critical.'

The situation did not improve, and Guderian continued:[81]

'On account of the threats to our flanks and rear and the immobility of our troops due to the abnormal cold, I made the decision during the night of the 5th–6th December to break off this unsupported attack, and to withdraw my foremost units into defensive positions along the general line Upper Don–Shat–Upa. This was the first time during the war that I had to take a decision of this sort, and none was more difficult. The fact that my chief of staff, Liebenstein, and my senior corps commander, General Freiherr von Geyr, were in complete agreement did not make it any easier.

'It was not only my Second Panzer Army which was in so grave a situation. **In this same night of December 5th–6th, Hoeppner's Fourth Panzer Army and Reinhardt's Third, which had reached a point only 20 miles north of the Kremlin, were forced to abandon their attacks because they lacked the necessary strength to seize the great prize that now lay so near [Author's emphasis].** In Ninth Army's sector the Russians even went over to the offensive on either side of Kalinin.

'**Our attack on Moscow had broken down. All the sacrifices and endurance of our brave troops had been in vain. We had suffered a grievous defeat which was to be seriously aggravated during the next few weeks thanks to the rigidity of our Supreme Command [Author's emphasis]:** despite all our reports those men, far away in East Prussia, could form no true concept of the real conditions of the winter war in which their soldiers were now engaged. This ignorance led to repeatedly exorbitant demands being made on the fighting troops.'

In his book *A Soldier's Record*, Field Marshal Albert Kesselring – at the time commanding Luftflotte 2 in Army Group Centre – blamed earlier delays in the campaign for the inability of the German Army to accomplish the task set for it in Russia by the Fuhrer:[82]

'The fighting on two fronts, in itself a mistake and certainly not generally wanted, need not, in the opinion of many people, necessarily have been fatal to the outcome of the war. We must therefore ask ourselves if the campaign in Russia with limited forces could have led to the capture of Moscow and the annihilation of Russian military power that is to say the armies, military centres and armament works in European Russia by the end of 1941. The starting-point of my argument must be the strategic plan adopted by Hitler. I know this central sector very well and I am certain that our worst enemies were the sporadic spells of bad weather and the bogginess of the roads, above all in 1941, but for which the capture of Moscow would have presented no problem. Nevertheless, if the inclement weather periods and their consequences are discounted as inevitable phenomena of the Russian theatre, **the objective could still have been reached if Hitler had not wasted precious weeks in overlong deliberation and secondary operations [Author's emphasis].** If on the conclusion of the encirclement battle of Smolensk at the beginning of September the offensive had been continued against Moscow after a reasonable breather, it is my opinion that Moscow would have fallen into our hands before the winter and before the arrival of the Siberian divisions. It would then in all probability have been possible to push forward a kind of umbrella bridgehead farther east which would have made it difficult for the Russians to turn our flanks and to bring-up supplies to their fronts. The capture of Moscow would have been decisive in that the whole of Russia in Europe would have been cut off from its Asiatic potential and the seizure of the vital economic centres of Leningrad, the Donets Basin and the Maikop oil fields in 1942 would have been no insoluble task.'

It must be acknowledged that this conclusion is a logical one when all the evidence of contemporary records and subsequent writings of the participants is taken into account. The precondition Kesselring sets is that the offensive against Moscow should have been continued after the encirclement battle at Smolensk, which is entirely in line with the OKH plan of operations. At the time, Kesselring was intimately involved with operational deliberations for Army Group Centre with Bock. He was subsequently a very successful commander of land forces in Italy, so his view is very persuasive.

On the night of 4/5 December, the Red Army counteroffensive began. Under Zhukov, the Soviet Northwestern Front went over to the offensive, with no less than seventeen armies involved. Soviet armies were roughly equivalent in strength to a German corps, which means that the Russian equivalent of between forty and forty-five German divisions were involved in the attack. The Germans could not endure this additional pressure and a crisis soon loomed. Any chance of *Barbarossa's* aims being achieved as set out in the Fuhrer's Directive No. 21 was now gone.

Engel's diary entry for 6 December offers clear evidence of the problem which existed between those at the pinnacle of the armed forces:[83]

> 'Trust between F. and C-in-C can no longer be patched up. Every situation conference is unpleasant. C-in-C can no longer cope with F.'s attacks and general approach to him. Told me this evening at Mauerwald he cannot handle it, also for health reasons. Is now going finally to request leave of absence. If F. decides he wants a replacement, then his suggestions [are] v. Kluge or v. Manstein definitely not Kesselring, since [he] is merely an organ of the Reichsmarschall. Reported everything to Schmundt during the night, he will speak to F. tomorrow.'

Meanwhile, the position of the German forces did not improve, as shown by Halder's diary entry for 8 December:[84]

> '**Phone talk with Field Marshal von Bock:** He outlines the situation. Result: "Army Group is not anywhere in a position to check a concentrated attack." Grave concern about von Kluge's right wing and Guderian's left wing. XXXIII Corps has only little defensive strength. Decision to withdraw involves loss of enormous quantities of material. **If the enemy were to make a concentrated attack, the consequences would be incalculable. Unless we can form a reserve, we face the danger of a serious defeat [Author's emphasis].'**

General Zhukov had wanted to launch just such a concentrated attack against Army Group Centre and inflict on it a crushing defeat. However, Stalin rejected this plan and ordered that the Red Army go over to a general offensive along the whole of the Eastern Front. Had Zhukov's strategy been implemented, it could well have resulted in the serious defeat Bock feared.

Throughout this chapter, I have included lengthy quotations because they help to illuminate a number of important conclusions. Firstly, that at the commencement of *Typhoon*, the German panzer armies were still a very potent fighting force, despite the problems referred to by Bock on 13 July, namely the reduction in their power because of wear and tear etc. Undoubtedly, they would have been in better condition and more powerful still had they not been diverted to the Kiev operation, where they suffered further casualties and inevitable attrition. Secondly, that the strategy advocated and implemented

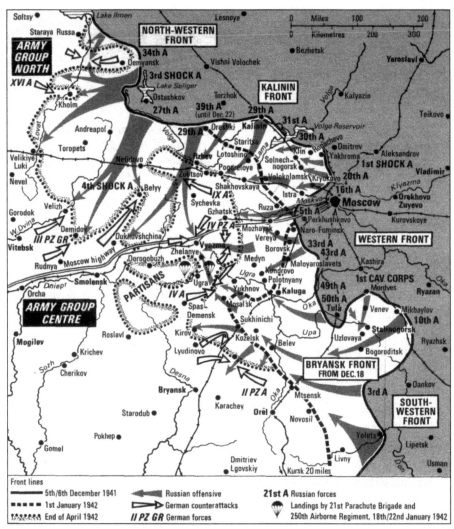

Map 4: The Red Army Counteroffensive December 1941.
Stalin's counteroffensive did not concentrate the effort of the armies against Army Group Centre as Zhukov had advised. If his strategy had been followed, it is possible that the disaster Field Marshal von Bock feared could have come to pass and the German disaster in 1941 would have been complete.

by Halder and the OKH for *Typhoon*, a classic major operational manoeuvre to encircle and destroy the Red Army, was still the most effective way for the Germans to prosecute their campaign, as opposed to Hitler's concept of small-scale tactical encirclement operations. Thirdly, that the weather conditions related by Halder and Guderian restricted Operation *Typhoon* even before the winter set in, but had far more effect once it did. Almost from the outset, this restriction significantly affected the ability of the Germans both to deploy their formations and – equally importantly – to supply them with essential materiel. Fourthly, the advent of the Soviet T34 tank was a great surprise to the Germans, who had been used to the technical superiority of their equipment, and posed a considerable operational problem for them. Had the T34 been available in larger numbers, *Typhoon* would most likely have been stopped dead. All these factors lead to the conclusion that had *Typhoon* been commenced at the time that the panzers were diverted from Army Group Centre to the Kiev operation, these problems would not have had such a significant impact on the offensive to seize Moscow, which would consequently have been much more likely to succeed. The inability of the Germans to take Moscow can thus be directly linked to the unnecessary operation around Kiev which Hitler ordered; this was a major strategic error, ultimately costing the Germans the opportunity to take Moscow, with all the advantages that would have ensued. Because the objectives of the Kiev operation were further south than Moscow, it could probably have been commenced after *Typhoon* and still had reasonable weather in which to operate, so Hitler could have had his cake and eaten it as well.

The final conclusion that can be drawn from the diary entries of the various participants is that the relationship between Hitler and the High Command of the German Army was such that it jeopardized the success of the operations being undertaken. There was no unanimity between Hitler and his most senior military advisors; in fact quite the opposite. His attitude towards them can only be described as one of ill-concealed contempt. It would have been impossible to work effectively in such an atmosphere for any length of time.

Yet regardless of the problems encountered, *Typhoon* resulted in two massive encirclements of Red Army forces around Vyazma and Bryansk. These tactical victories set the stage for the further advance on Moscow. However, because of the delay in starting *Typhoon*, the problems caused by the autumnal mud and the severe winter became worse, significantly affecting the German forces, as is apparent from the quotes above from Bock, Halder and Guderian.

Ultimately, the German Army could not maintain the offensive towards Moscow because of the weather, the lack of supplies, the losses they had already suffered and the counteroffensive unleashed by the Soviets in early December. Hitler's gamble had not succeeded.

In his memoirs, Field Marshal Keitel summarized his reasons for the failure of *Barbarossa* in 1941 and related how Hitler used these to get rid of the Commander-in-Chief of the Army, Field Marshal von Brauchitsch:[85]

'Only the real reasons for the reverse were suppressed, evident though they were: he had underestimated the enemy's ability to resist and the risk of winter closing in early that year and expected too much of the troops' fighting capacity in the endless battles from October onwards; and finally they lacked sufficient supplies. I am convinced that Brauchitsch realised that some way would have to be found around the inflexibility both of the front and of the Fuhrer; it could not be concealed from him that the guilty party would soon be looked for, and his name would not be Hitler.'

Even with all the problems mentioned above, it is likely that Moscow could have been captured had the OKH plan been followed as originally intended. This is evidenced by the successes that were achieved when Operation *Typhoon* was begun on 2 October. Taking Moscow would not of itself have guaranteed that the Germans would win the war against the USSR, but had they started the operation against the capital during August instead of being diverted to Kiev, their chances for an outright victory – or even a compromise peace – would have been increased significantly. The Soviet government could still have carried on the war from its territories in the East, which had plentiful resources and many factories that had been transported beyond the reach of German bombers. However, taking Moscow would undoubtedly have given Hitler the opportunity to set the scene quite differently for the following year's campaign, or to negotiate a peace deal with Stalin in the same way as the Germans had forced Lenin to do in 1918.

The reasons for the failure of Operation *Barbarossa*

1. Underestimation of the military abilities and resources of the USSR:
   Hitler's attitude to the capabilities of the Red Army is encapsulated in his two comments made to Keitel and Rundstedt, previously referred to in the first section of this chapter, which were to the effect that a campaign against the USSR would be a simple undertaking. This attitude was completely in line with his racial theories and bore no resemblance to reality. A more realistic factor is that he based his estimated efficiency of the Soviet forces on the very poor performance of the Red Army in its war against Finland. However, the Soviets realized that their conduct in that campaign had been extremely poor and had subsequently made reforms to their armed forces which were still being implemented when the Germans invaded. The border wars with the Japanese in Manchuria had shown that the Red Army under General Zhukov was not to be trifled with, and its performance there should have alerted the Germans that the Red Army was capable of fighting well under good leadership. Hitler had been advised by the

German military attaché in Moscow, General Kostring, that the Red Army was indeed formidable and was making significant strides in correcting its weaknesses. In addition, Goering, Rundstedt, Keitel, Brauchitsch, Halder and others all advised him that Germany should be cautious with respect to going to war with the USSR, at least while it was still fighting Britain, but Hitler did not heed their counsel. Hitler thus underestimated the Soviet forces before the invasion took place, but even more so after it had begun. He simply ignored information that did not fit with his view of the Soviets as being a beaten force. He was not totally to blame with respect to the initial force estimates, because German intelligence evaluations of the existing Soviet forces were very wide of the mark. But his refusal to take the Soviet Army seriously, and then to write it off as totally defeated at an early stage of the invasion, was foolhardy in the extreme, as was failing to adapt the conduct of the campaign to ensure that the objectives set for the Army were realistic and could be achieved before the onset of winter. His refusal to believe the information provided by the German intelligence services was so extreme that it bordered on pathological. As was pointed out by Halder, Guderian, Manstein, Zeitzler and others on numerous occasions, if you did not base decisions in military operations on reality then there was no possibility of victory.

2. The resistance made by the soldiers of the Red Army:
The ordinary soldiers of the Red Army may have been poorly led and had inferior equipment to begin with, but they fought with great heroism against the invaders. That this was the case has been documented many times. They simply would not give up even if surrounded: although the Germans inflicted vast losses on the Red Army, the Soviet soldiers continued to fight, which ultimately meant that the Germans suffered unsustainable numbers of casualties. As is shown by Halder's diary entry on 30 November 1941, referred to previously, the losses inflicted on the Germans were extremely problematic even before the winter set in and prior to Zhukov's counteroffensive which eventually ended any hopes for the quick victory envisaged in the plan for *Barbarossa*. The heroism of the Soviet troops was the main reason for this situation.

3. The difficulties presented by the terrain and underdeveloped road and rail infrastructure:
In 1941, the USSR did not have many modern roads and was in no way comparable to Western Europe in regard to transport infrastructure. The only main road that corresponded with Western ideas was the partially completed highway to Moscow from the western border of the USSR. There were few surfaced subsidiary roads within the road network, the

overwhelming majority of them being just dirt tracks. Furthermore, the Soviet rail network used a different gauge to Germany and therefore German locomotives and rolling stock could not be integrated into the existing network without modification, which took some time. This lack of development meant that the German Army's problems in supplying its troops and manoeuvring its armoured forces were dramatically increased in comparison to previous campaigns. The impact of this problem cannot be overstated and was a crucial factor in determining how and where the armoured forces could be committed. In addition, the changes Hitler made to the composition of the armoured divisions before Operation *Barbarossa* meant that they consisted of a higher proportion of wheeled transport as opposed to tracked vehicles, making them more dependent on surfaced roads. Once these problems became apparent, Hitler should have taken them into account when considering operations that could be fitted within the overall time limits of the campaign to ensure the achievement of its primary aim, the destruction of the Red Army in one offensive. However, the changes he made to the objectives to be taken and the operations needed to do so had the opposite effect, ultimately making it impossible to achieve any of the objectives set for *Barbarossa*.

4. 'General Weather':
The Soviet winter was not the only characteristic of the weather that the Germans had to deal. Autumn meant that rain turned the earth into mud, which vehicles churned up and made even worse. German tanks had relatively narrow tracks and could not easily operate in the mud, and their trucks were unable to move without assistance. The Russian winter that started in early November was one of the most intense for 100 years. However, the intensity itself is only a relative matter, as all winters in the USSR are severe compared to the rest of Europe and therefore should not have been a surprise to the Germans, especially after their experience in the First World War. Extremely low temperatures meant that equipment would not work properly or at all, with engines needing special oils and lubricants to operate. Cold weather clothing had been provided, but it wasn't issued to the troops early enough and there was never enough of it. None of these factors had been properly provided for by the Germans because Hitler's timetable had meant there would be no need for them as the campaign was to be completed before winter arrived. The operations undertaken by the Germans should have economized the use of their armoured and mechanized forces as far as possible to ensure that they could achieve the objectives of the campaign before the winter could become a problem. Hitler's requirements caused the opposite to occur.

5. Hitler's continual changes to the strategic priorities and execution of the campaign:

   Hitler completely ignored the operational difficulties imposed by his changes to the OKH plan for the campaign. Changing the emphasis of the main effort from the centre to the wings of the theatre of operations involved significant difficulties and delays in deploying the units to their new positions, which were exacerbated by the difficult terrain in the USSR. These changes also inevitably complicated the supply of the forces involved, arrangements that had been premised on the basis of the OKH plan and could not easily be switched around because of the poor state of the Soviet road network and the inability of the Germans to use rail transport as they had in their campaigns in the West. Crucially, by changing the main point of effort, the momentum achieved by Army Group Centre was lost, allowing the Soviets to reinforce their positions before Moscow and bring in fresh troops from Siberia. They would not have had the time to do this had the momentum been maintained and the attack on Moscow continued during August and September, instead of diverting forces to the Kiev operation. These new troops formed a crucial part of the Army that Zhukov used for his counteroffensive and marked the end of German expectations for the quick victory *Barbarossa* was intended to achieve.

6. Lack of co-operation between the Axis 'partners':

   The Axis 'partners' never acted as such. Whereas the Allies provided each other with war supplies, raw materials, humanitarian aid and diplomatic support, and co-ordinated their efforts toward a common strategy, the Axis nations did not act in unison in any major respect. There was no shared strategy between the Axis partners to win the war, even though it was manifestly in their interest, as the weaker grouping, to work together as closely as possible. As was the case with every campaign of the war, in *Barbarossa* the Nazis did not work with Japan to co-ordinate a strategic approach which would have given them a real chance of defeating the USSR. Hitler did not trust the Japanese at all, and the lack of co-operation between the Axis partners yielded the inevitable result. As all authority in the German state rested with Hitler, the responsibility for this fundamental error was his alone.

7. Stalin was going to attack:

   Hitler told his commanders that he was convinced that Stalin was going to attack Germany, and he used this as the main justification for his decision to invade the USSR. Yet however he may have viewed the situation, the evidence points to the conclusion that this was not correct, and that Hitler was using his suspicion of Stalin's intentions to undertake the invasion and start the war that he had always wanted. Stalin refused to countenance any rapprochement with the Western powers, and likewise to believe that the German mobilization on the borders of the USSR meant that they were about to invade. It cannot be accepted that this was a ruse on Stalin's part, as to ignore such a threat would be foolhardy in the extreme and contrary to all the evidence of Stalin's cautious nature. Furthermore, there was no evidence found when the Germans invaded that a Soviet attack as envisaged by the Fuhrer was imminent. As confirmed by the words of Rundstedt and Manstein quoted above, the dispositions of the Soviet forces did not reveal any obvious imminent intention to attack, as Hitler contended was the case.

8. Stalin was intriguing with Britain:
   The other main reason Hitler used to justify his decision to attack the USSR was that Stalin was plotting with Britain to form an alliance against Germany. This is comprehensively debunked by the evidence available from the diaries of Maisky, the Soviet Ambassador to Britain at the time. Although the idea of doing so could have been logical for the Soviets, there is absolutely no credible evidence to back Hitler's assertion. That Hitler nevertheless took this as being the case probably says more about his paranoia than the intentions of the USSR. It is important to remember that there was no co-operation between the USSR and Britain until an alliance between them was signed on 12 July 1941, three weeks after the launch of the German invasion.

These conclusions illustrate beyond reasonable doubt that Hitler's interventions in the execution of Operation *Barbarossa* were responsible for its failure.

Chapter 3

Hitler's Finest Hour? Winter 1941/42

With the failure of Operation *Typhoon* and therefore of *Barbarossa* on 6 December 1941, the German Army was in crisis. The Red Army counteroffensive caught the Germans in a very precarious position. Far from having defeated the Red Army, the Germans were on the defensive everywhere except the Crimea, where the onset of winter came later and the conditions were thus milder.

As a result of their extreme exertions, Army Group Centre was close to Moscow. However, their supply position was tenuous, the troops were at the end of their strength, they were deployed for offensive operations and could not quickly be redeployed to capitalize on their defensive power, and the winter cold had become a major problem. The first and last members of the German armed forces to look on Moscow in the Second World War, except as prisoners, had by now done so.

Meanwhile, Army Group North had not achieved its main aim of capturing Leningrad. However, it had taken all the Baltic States and Leningrad was besieged, almost encircled, cut off from any resupplies except across Lake Ladoga by ship in warmer times and by ice road and rail when it froze. Nevertheless, the besieging Germans were in a very poor situation themselves, lacking supplies, under repeated attack and exposed to the full ferocity of the winter.

Neither had Army Group South captured its assigned objectives. After the great Kiev *Kesselschlacht* victory, it had taken Rostov, but had then been bundled out by a well-timed Soviet counterattack. Rundstedt had warned Hitler that his armies were overextended and could not hold Rostov. He wanted to retire to a defensive position, using the Mius River as his base. Hitler would not agree to this, and when Rundstedt stated he could not remain in command if his judgement was not trusted, Hitler sacked him and replaced him with Field Marshal Walther von Reichenau on 30 November. Ironically, the very next day, events forced Hitler to sanction the withdrawal that Rundstedt had recommended.

Halder's diary entry of 1 December gave some idea of his frustration at these events:[1]

'Situation: The picture is dominated by developments in AGp. South, where Field Marshal von Reichenau has taken over command. The withdrawal from the intermediate position to the Mius position was already in progress when Panzer Army received the order to hold the intermediate position. There was confusion, inasmuch as the shortage of operational trucks, which hampered withdrawal, now is a serious impediment for the return to the line.'

He continued:[2]

'**1530: while ObdH sees the Fuhrer, von Reichenau calls up.** Enemy motorised forces have broken through SS "Adolf Hitler" in the intermediate position. He asks permission to fall back to the Mius position tonight. Fuhrer concurs. **Now we are where we could have been last night. It was a senseless waste of strength and time, and to top it, we lost von Rundstedt also [Author's emphasis].**'

Halder's comment can only be seen as severe criticism of the decision to delay the movement recommended by Rundstedt. In trying to avoid the necessary withdrawal from Rostov to a more defensible position, Hitler, as he always did in these situations, wasted time and ended up having to make the decision he wanted to avoid anyway. It should always have been borne in mind by Hitler that the Soviets had far more men available than Germany did, so as the numerically inferior force the Germans had to take every opportunity to economize their strength and rationalize the line they were defending. Hitler's decision not only did not achieve this aim, but actually increased the losses suffered because the Germans could not capitalize on their full defensive strength while in the exposed position he had forced them to defend. The Germans had to concentrate their forces on the shortest possible front to have the best chance to resist the numerically superior Red Army. Halder's diary entry on 3 December says everything:[3]

'Fuhrer has arrived at the conclusion that the army group and the Panzer army bear no blame for recent events in AGp. South.'

Thus, not only had Hitler's gamble to defeat the Soviets in a blitzkrieg campaign, as set out in his Directive No. 21, failed, but a catastrophe for the Germans now loomed if they could not hold off the counteroffensive commenced by Zhukov which developed, as ordered by Stalin, along the whole of the Eastern Front.

Bock's diary entry of 5 December is extremely important as it reveals the condition of Army Group Centre, bearing in mind that the Soviet counteroffensive had not yet commenced:[4]

'Panzer Group 3 reported that its offensive strength is gone and that it can only hold its positions if the 23rd Division remains subordinated. I discussed with von Kluge whether, given the situation, the attack Panzer Group 4 planned should go ahead; he said that it should not. Panzer Group 3 received orders to go over to the defensive. 23rd Division remains subordinated to it. Moreover, it and the 4th Army were ordered to make preparations for a withdrawal to the general line Nara–Moskva to Karymskoye–Istra reservoir–Sseneskoje Lake–east of Klin when the order is given. Orders for the linking up of Armored Groups 3 and 4 will be issued by the army group as soon as the intentions of both armoured groups concerning the manner of the withdrawal are known.

'Late in the evening Guderian reported that he had to call off the operation because XXXIV (Motorized) Corps was being threatened from all sides in its exposed forward position; as well the unbearable cold of more than **30 degrees below freezing** was making moving and fighting by the tired, thinned out units extremely difficult. Our own tanks are breaking down, while those of the Russians are better suited to winter conditions. After several digs by Guderian, whose Chief of Staff (von Kurowski) only yesterday evening gave a very optimistic assessment of the operation's chances, I concluded the conversation by agreeing to his suggestion that we gradually pull the army back behind the Don and Schat rivers.'

On 6 December, Bock's diary once again indicated the extremely difficult position the Germans were in because of having to fight during the winter:[5]

'The withdrawal of the 2nd Panzer Army is largely proceeding as planned. But inevitably, since motors frequently fail in the icy cold – as much as 38 degrees below freezing – some vehicles and guns have to be abandoned. A quiet day for 4th Army apart from attacks on V Corps. Heavy attacks by superior forces against the Eastern Front and especially the northeastern front of Panzer Group 3; the penetrations were for the most part eliminated by committing the last of its reserves.

'Growing complaints by the units about the enemy's air superiority. The matter of winter clothing, too, is far from satisfactory. First it was too late coming, so that even today not all units have their winter things, and now it is inadequate in quantity as well as quality.'

Bock's diary notes of 5 and 6 December are of interest for a number of reasons. Primarily, they confirm the appalling conditions that the Germans were exposed. They also show there was a plan in place to retire Army Group Centre, which was being implemented and was working, albeit with the greatest difficulty, and that this move inevitably involved some loss of equipment. Furthermore, Bock again comments on the shortage of winter clothing and other equipment problems caused by the extreme weather conditions. Finally, for the first time there is mention of enemy air superiority. This situation arose because powerful units of the Luftwaffe were having to be deployed to assist in the North African campaign, and the Red Air Force – far from having been destroyed as had previously been claimed – was beginning to cause problems for the German ground forces at the moment of their maximum discomfort. The deployment of the Luftwaffe to relieve problems in other theatres shows that the Germans were beginning, even at this comparatively early stage of the war, to suffer from problems caused by being in a global conflict, with Hitler attempting to spread their forces in an attempt to be strong enough everywhere. It is important to remember that these diary entries were made prior to the impact of Zhukov's counteroffensive being felt, and that the position of the Germans deteriorated significantly over the coming weeks.

Halder's entry for 6 December included a summary of the Fuhrer conference that day:[6]

'**Afternoon report to the Fuhrer**: He cannot be bothered with strength ratios. To him the PW [prisoner of war] figures are conclusive proof of our superiority.

'Next objectives: He recognizes the need of rehabilitation for the troops, but securing the Donets bend in the south (as a jump-off base for Maikop), eliminating the Ladoga front, and linking up with the Finns in the north **remain on the calendar as objectives which must be attained during the winter [Author's emphasis]**.

'No disbanding of divisions in France to cover replacement requirements. Comb out Germany, Romania, etc.'

This reveals that at this stage of the conflict, Hitler was still thinking of offensive operations during the winter despite the appalling conditions being experienced by the troops, which he said he was fully aware. This was at the same time as Bock had made his entries as noted above, Rundstedt had been sacked – although his estimate of the situation for Army Group South had proven correct – and Guderian had called off his attacks in the Tula area because of a combination of the weather and enemy pressure. These events indicate that Hitler was completely out of touch with the true situation at the front and was either not giving sufficient credence to daily reports he was receiving from his front commanders or was simply delusional and ignoring them.

Halder's diary entry for 7 December indicated the atmosphere that existed at the summit of the German command structure:[7]

'The occurrences of the day have again been heartbreaking and humiliating. The Fuhrer, over the head of ObdH, gets in direct touch with the commanders of army groups. But, worst of all, the Supreme Command does not realize the condition our troops are in and indulges in paltry patchwork where only big decisions could help. One of the decisions that should be taken is the withdrawal of AGp. Center to the line Ruza–Ostashkov.'

As previously noted, Halder recorded a telephone conversation he had with Bock on 8 December,[8] when he stressed that 'unless we can form a reserve, we face the danger of a serious defeat', Bock having warned that the army group was in no position to withstand a concentrated Soviet attack. Bock made it clear that in order to conduct the most effective defence, the Germans had to create a reserve. The only way to do this was to rationalize the line they held as far as possible and redeploy their forces so that they would have some defensive depth, with a reserve behind the forward line. Standing and fighting for every inch of conquered territory – as ordered by Hitler – would only lead to large-scale losses, especially as German formations had limited ability to manoeuvre. Although the weather conditions restricted their movements significantly, the Germans could redeploy their forces, but needed time to do so to capitalize on their defensive power. They thus had to carefully consider the best ways to achieve redeployment, which could only be done with a strategy in mind. Hitler's refusal to do this, an example that precipitated Rundstedt's dismissal, meant that withdrawals could not be made at the most advantageous time and therefore lost much of their effect, especially when the moves were interrupted by Red Army attacks which they were intended to forestall.

Also on 8 December, Bock recorded:[9]

'I described the situation to Halder and said that nowhere was the army group capable of withstanding a strong attack by the Russians. Halder tried to mitigate this, which I could not allow. Again and again I stressed how necessary the delivery of reinforcements was if I was to hold. Halder replied that the Army Command had no say in the sending of reinforcements from the west.'

This was an incredible admission for the Chief of the General Staff to make. He had no control over the movement of reinforcements, Hitler having appropriated total control of the armed forces, meaning that the OKH, the Supreme Command of the Army, could not redeploy any formations without his permission. At this time there were forty-nine German divisions in the West occupying the conquered territories, and these formations could certainly have been drawn on by the Germans to bolster the Eastern Front armies if Hitler had agreed. However, he would not allow any reduction in the forces in the West, despite the fact that Britain was in no position to mount any significant operation against the occupying forces in Europe.

Major Engel's diary entry for 8 December revealed his thoughts concerning the Fuhrer's running of the war on the Eastern Front:[10]

'Perplexity is self-evident: scapegoats are being sought for grinding to a halt in the thrust on Moscow. [Hitler] spoke about the OKH prattle to which he had given in. Concern about the Russian winter is now obvious but he is thinking along the lines of restarting operations towards Tula. Jodl spoke out gravely, warned about partial operations and said that one had to make an overall decision about north and south of Moscow; doubted that it would be possible for the Panzer spearhead to hold on to the advanced positions they now occupied. Either one had to break through using a small pincer movement or be forced to accept an extensive pulling back of the front. **F. disagreed and embarked – as so often – on an endless monologue [Author's emphasis]**. He did not believe in fresh Russian forces, considered it all a bluff, assumed it likely that these were the last reserves from Moscow. The OKH enemy reports were exaggerated and deliberately highly coloured. It would not be the first time that Germans had lost their nerve at the fateful hour. **He did not want to hear the expression "pull back" again. On and on it went in this tone, [Author's emphasis]** but from it all one sees how unsettled and uncertain he is. Unfortunately Keitel did not second Jodl, but as usual supported the views of F.'

The fact that Engel was chosen as an adjutant to Hitler is evidence of the regard in which he was held by the Army's highest-ranking officers. That he achieved the rank of lieutenant general before the end of the war, having started it as a captain, confirms that he continued to be viewed as more than simply competent. As he was an eyewitness to the proceedings and conferences at the Fuhrer Headquarters, his comments are therefore invaluable. There seems little doubt from his observations that he did not view Hitler's decisions or *modus operandi* positively and was not overawed by the Fuhrer's personality or position. He could see the problems that arose because of Hitler's chronic tendency to vacillate as well as the shortcomings of the most senior members of the OKW staff.

Warlimont noted that on 8 December, Hitler issued Directive No. 39, which ordered all formations to abandon completely[11] 'all major offensive operations and go over to the defensive'. The reasons given were 'the severe winter weather which has come surprisingly early and the consequent difficulties in bringing up supplies'. This directive brought the German Army's orders into line with the situation that had existed at the front since the Soviet offensive had begun two days beforehand. Implicit in this directive was recognition that the Germans had been forced onto the strategic defensive. Warlimont added:[12]

'It was nevertheless of considerable importance that Hitler now left it to OKH to issue the subsequent instructions laying down the defensive positions which they considered best calculated to economise our forces.'

He then summarized the current situation of the German forces:[13]

'From the strategic point of view these new instructions represented nothing less than an admission of the bankruptcy of Hitler's war plan of July 1940 – to say nothing of the studies and projects of the summer of 1941. ...

'All too soon however it became apparent that in his "fanatical" determination to hold on to what had been won and to restrict any initiative, Hitler proposed to contravene the principles which he himself had just laid down. In any case, this instruction did little to help the front line troops for the immediate future; the cold was intense and they suddenly found themselves without their usual superiority. Too much had already been asked of them during the offensive; now they faced a period during which they must call upon their last reserves of energy to make good past and present mistakes and retrieve the situation created by the far too ambitious objectives set by their leaders.'

Warlimont believed that it was necessary for the Germans to use what flexibility they still retained to manage the withdrawals they were being forced to carry out to economize their forces and make the most of their defensive power. Hitler's interference with this process, as epitomized by his "fanatical" determination to hold on to what had been won' and the example of Rundstedt's dismissal, restricted the possibility of planned redeployment and therefore increased the difficulty that had to be managed when any subsequent withdrawal was undertaken. Hitler's 'plan' can be reduced to merely reacting to pressure from the enemy as and where it occurred without any medium or long-term strategy at all. This lack of planning increased the casualties which occurred while formations were being pressured into new positions and reduced the German Army to being merely a series of immobile targets and accentuated the advantages the Red Army's preponderance of numbers gave it.

Halder recorded on 9 December:[14]

'**Phone talk with Field Marshal von Bock:** Guderian reports that the condition of his troops is so critical that he does not know how to fend off the enemy. "Serious break of confidence" in the field commands. Reduced fighting strength of his infantry! He is scraping together in the rear whatever forces he can get hold of (in one armored division 1,600 rifles), [although] tank gunners and drivers, of course, are not used as infantry. Army group needs more men!'

Halder also noted on this date:[15]

'Very tense situation on the northern wing of Fourth Army. Although some divisions located by our radio intelligence have not yet shown up on this front, it is safe to assume that these attacks have no depth and so are merely of tactical significance. The object of these very troublesome attacks southeast of Kalinin is probably the recapture of the city.'

He went on to mention Army Group North's current situation:[16]

'Attempts have failed to widen the Tikhvin corridor. Withdrawal will be necessary. Unfortunately, OKW interferes in this purely tactical matter with direct Fuhrer orders. The command of army group is vacillating, but this is in part due to interference from top level. Although the danger is not acute at the moment, it may well happen that the few available forces are wasted on tactical patchwork, leaving no troops to deal with the Ladoga business.'

The point Halder was stressing here was the difference between planning to ensure that future problems were averted as far as possible and simply reacting on an ad hoc basis to problems as they occurred. The former is true planning while the latter is not, which was the essential difference between Halder's approach and that of Hitler.

Bock's diary entry for 13 December included the following characteristically clear summary of the dilemma faced by the Germans when the Soviet counterattack had been underway for approximately a week:[17]

'Brauchitsch arrived. I discussed the situation with him. He has an accurate picture of what is happening and shares my opinion. I told him "I have no more suggestions to make; I made them earlier." The question that has to be decided goes beyond the military. The Fuhrer has to decide whether the army group has to fight where it stands, at the risk of being wrecked in the process, or whether we should withdraw, which entails the same risk. If he decides for withdrawal, he must realise that it is doubtful whether sufficient forces will reach the rear to hold a new, unprepared and significantly shorter position. The few reinforcements promised me are so slow in coming that they can play no decisive role in this decision.'

There can be no clearer exposition of the conundrum confronting the Germans – fighting where they were entailed the risk of the armies being wrecked where they stood, but withdrawing risked them being destroyed when they reached the new line because they may not be strong enough to defend the new positions. The basic problem was that Hitler refused to adopt one policy or the other – he just reacted, without making a strategic plan to deal with the situation. This disastrous situation had occurred as a direct consequence of Hitler's changes to the OKH plan for the *Barbarossa* campaign, including the order to carry out the Kiev encirclement which delayed the launch of Operation *Typhoon* until too late in the season to be fully effective.

Bock's diary for 14 December again stressed the seriousness of the situation facing Army Group Centre:[18]

'Toward evening Brauchitsch arrived after having spoken with Kluge and Guderian. He has come to the view that the **gradual withdrawal into a rearward position, as charted on the map by the army group, is unavoidable [Author's emphasis]**. Even the centre, which means the bulk of the 4th Army, will not be able to hold its position if the forces on its left and right are forced to fall back. Schmundt, who was also there and listened in on these discussions, called Jodl to get a decision from the Fuhrer. He decided, verbally at first, that he had nothing against a straightening of the projecting salients at Klin and Kalinin, also that a withdrawal by Army Group Guderian was inevitable. Otherwise, however, nothing must be given up and no retreat made as long as the most necessary preparations had not been made in the rearward lines. In the evening an order was sent out to coordinate, and as far as possible prepare, the withdrawal of the armies.'

It is important to note that Brauchitsch was envisaging a 'gradual withdrawal into a rearward position', not a precipitate flight that could have led to a repeat of Napoleon's disastrous retreat of 1812. Despite this, Hitler's position had clearly changed by 16 December, when Bock recorded:[19]

'When I briefed Halder on the situation, he read to me an order from the Fuhrer in which he demanded that the 4th Army "withdraw not one step farther" but authorized limited withdrawals by Army Group Guderian (2nd Panzer Army), Panzer Groups 3 and 4, and the 9th Army where unavoidable. The gaps at Lichwin and Tula are to be closed by reserves. I could only report that I have no reserves left!

'... The reason why it is questionable whether the units can hold in a new, but unprepared line is clear: I will not get my motorized units back on account of the fuel shortage and the icy roads, and also my horse drawn guns, because the horses can't do it. Typical is the 267th Division which today left behind its artillery when it fell back. The danger that we will arrive in the rear without artillery if we retire further is therefore great. On the other hand the order to hold causes me to [have] concern that the units will possibly pull back without orders.'

In this situation, the survival of the German Army depended as much on the strategy employed by the Red Army as it did on its own: would the Red Army attack, as Bock feared, with a concentrated offensive against Army Group Centre, which might overwhelm it, as he had indicated was possible in his diary entry of 8 December and related to Halder as quoted above?

To understand the course of events that ensued, it is necessary to see what was happening on 'the other side of the hill' at this critical time.

As noted above, on 5 December, the Red Army commenced a counterattack to force the Germans back from Moscow. This attack was the first phase of an offensive planned by Zhukov which was authorized by Stalin on 30 November.[20] By the middle of December, Army Group Centre had been pushed back from Moscow in considerable disarray by up to 100 miles in some sectors, so the first phase of Zhukov's strategy had succeeded. However, when Zhukov recommended to Stalin that the attack be continued and asked for reinforcements in mid-December to develop the success further against Army Group Centre, he was turned down.[21] Stalin wished to pursue a much more ambitious strategy, based on his belief that the Germans were in dire straits and would not be able to resist a general offensive. Stalin therefore ordered that all available reinforcements be used in a general offensive stretching from Leningrad in the north to the Black Sea in the south. Its aims were to break the German siege of Leningrad, destroy Army Group Centre, retake Smolensk and force Army Group South from the Ukraine, thereby relieving Sebastopol and freeing the Crimea. These aims amounted to nothing less than destroying the German Army in the USSR through a general offensive which would in effect be a Soviet version of *Barbarossa*.

At the same time as the Soviet offensive began, the British Foreign Secretary, Sir Anthony Eden, was in Moscow for discussions relating to a treaty of alliance between the USSR and Britain. Stalin told Eden on 16 December:[22]

'We are at the turning point now. The German army is tired out. Its commanders had hoped to end the war before the winter and did not make the necessary preparations for the winter campaign. The German Army today is poorly dressed, poorly fed, and losing morale. They are beginning to feel the strain. Meanwhile the USSR has prepared large reinforcements and put them into action in recent weeks. **This has brought about a fundamental change on the front [Author's emphasis]** … Our counterattacks have gradually developed into counter-offensives. We intend to follow a similar policy during the whole winter… It is hard to guess how far we shall advance in the course of our drive but, in any case, such will be our line until spring… **We are advancing and will continue to advance on all fronts [Author's emphasis]**.'

Also on 16 December, Halder noted as follows:[23]

'Midnight. Ordered to the Fuhrer: ObdH, I, Chief Op. Sec.:
'a. Order: General withdrawal is out of the question. Enemy has made substantial penetration only in a few places. The idea to prepare rear positions is just driveling [sic] nonsense. The only trouble at the front is that the enemy outnumbers us in soldiers. He does not have any more artillery. His soldiers are not nearly as good as ours.
'b. Has directed added air support of four bomber long-range fighter groups, plus a long-range fighter group. This gives an increase of 120 planes, not counting the long-range fighters.
'c. Withdrawal to shortened line only when fuel has arrived and infantry is available to take up the units.'

The order goes on to detail other steps taken to reinforce the line, but the available reinforcements were minor and were slow to arrive at the front. This order has been credited by some commentators as the reason why the German Army was able to survive the Soviet offensive and the hardships of the winter of 1941–42. However, it does not create or outline any strategy at all and led to Hitler imposing an ad hoc series of reactions to individual problems as they occurred at the front. These reactions were almost invariably the result of pressure from the Red Army and were not part of any considered strategy or plan to realign the German forces to capitalize on its defensive power. They were also usually delayed until almost too late, as is demonstrated in the following pages.

On 17 December, Halder noted the state of affairs all along the Eastern Front:[24]

'a. … Otherwise [apart from the assault at Sevastopol] all quiet on the southern front.
'b. In center, the enemy appears to be regrouping for further attacks in the penetration area at Verkhovye. Our front has been fairly consolidated, but it is rather weak.
'c. In North, local fighting, which, however, does not interfere with the orderly execution of the scheduled withdrawal to the Volkhov line.'

This entry shows that it was possible to make planned readjustments of the line and that these were carried out successfully in a limited number of cases, which is all that Hitler would allow. To be successful, the changes to the dispositions of the German formations had to be made in a considered manner, which meant that they had to be planned. This was the process permitted withdrawals the commanders had urged Hitler to undertake. There is no doubt that there would have been some situations where a considered withdrawal would not have been easily possible, for the reasons mentioned by Bock, but in reviewing each of these potential opportunities there would have been many occasions where a limited retreat to capitalize on the defensive power of the units would have been possible. The circumstances of Rundstedt's dismissal prove that this was the case. Additionally, the example given by Halder of a withdrawal to a new position in Army Group North illustrates that this strategy was successful when it was implemented as part of a plan. The problem with Hitler's 'strategy' was that there was no strategy at all, and the vast majority of permitted withdrawals were carried out under pressure from the Red Army, which meant that the troops were subject to the most difficult circumstances whenever they had to move back.

Blumentritt made the following comments with respect to the attacks against Army Group Centre:[25]

'Russian intentions were obvious. They were planning a wide double encirclement of Kluge's Fourth Army, by means of attacks both north and south, with the ultimate aim of surrounding and destroying that army in its present positions west of Moscow. The German commanders could scarcely hope to hinder, let alone defeat, the great southern pincer. A gap now existed between the Fourth Army and Second Panzer Army which the Russians were steadily widening, nor did Field Marshal von Kluge possess any reserves with which to restore the increasingly dangerous situation on his southern flank.'

These offensives were successful to a degree and caused the Germans a great deal of difficulty in containing them, but the Soviet forces did not have the power to achieve the over-ambitious goals set by Stalin. The Germans frustrated his strategy and managed to hang on despite their problems of movement and supply, albeit with heavy losses and by the smallest of margins. In essence, Stalin committed the same critical error that Hitler made in the 1941 campaign – he did not sufficiently concentrate his forces at a vital point to ensure that the attacks were strong enough to achieve a strategic victory over the Germans. If Stalin had accepted Zhukov's recommendation to reinforce the offensive success against Army Group Centre, using all the available forces in a concentrated effort there, it is quite possible – judging from the results actually achieved by the offensives – that the army group would have been overwhelmed owing to its limited manoeuvrability, the supply problems it suffered as a result of the extreme weather and the lack of reinforcements, as pointed out by Bock. Had this occurred, the course of the war would have been significantly different.

Halder's diary entry of 19 December recorded a momentous development for the German Army, indeed for the whole course of the war:[26]

'1300. Summoned to the Fuhrer:

'a. The Fuhrer is going to take over the High Command of the army himself after departure of ObdH owing to ill health. I am to carry on the business functions, while Keitel will take over the administrative part. New routine: Daily conference, along with Transportation Chief, Signal Chief and Gen Qu [Quartermaster-General, General Eduard Wagner – Author's note].'

Warlimont quoted Hitler's comment at the time he took over command:[27]

> **'Anyone can do this little job of directing operations in war [Author's
> emphasis].** The task of the Commander-in-Chief is to educate the Army
> to be National-Socialist. I do not know any Army general who can do
> this as I want it done. I have therefore decided to take over command of
> the Army myself.'

Apart from the overweening arrogance of this statement, to say that the
most important part of the role of the Commander-in-Chief of the Army
was something other than the conduct of military operations in wartime is
so illogical as to test the limits of language and understanding. It also shows
Hitler's complete failure to understand what the role of the C-in-C of the
Army entailed, with the implication that it was one that could be undertaken
part-time by someone who was already Head of State and Supreme
Commander of all the Armed Forces, which is beyond understanding on any
rational basis. One aspect Hitler entirely underrated and which he did not
even try to carry out was the maintenance of contact between the C-in-C
and his field commanders. This was a part of the role that he could not fulfil
in the same manner as would have been the case by a full-time dedicated
professional soldier. Hitler rarely went to the front to see the conditions for
himself, as Brauchitsch had frequently done, something essential to anyone
attempting to carry out the duties of C-in-C properly in order to evaluate
the condition of the Army and its commanders firsthand and be competent
to judge its capabilities. Requiring the field commanders to go to Fuhrer HQ
at Rastenburg for meetings was no substitute and wasted a great deal of their
time (as they all mention in their various memoirs). The causes of the problems
in the relations between Hitler and his generals are dealt with in detail in
Chapter 8 of Volume 1 of this work, and were fundamentally important to the
performance of the German Army.

From 20 December onwards, Halder's diary recorded the progress of the
Soviet offensives, with each day bringing more trying developments. Typical is
the entry for 30 December:[28]

> **'Again a hard day! [Author's emphasis]**....
> 'Crisis in 15th Division. Dramatic phone talk between the Fuhrer and
> von Kluge. The Fuhrer vetoes the proposal to take back the front of the
> northern portion of the Fourth Army. Very serious crisis in the Ninth
> Army, where the command must have lost its nerve for a time.
> '... Also at Lake Ladoga front disagreeable attacks. Nervous tension!'

In *The Fatal Decisions*, Blumentritt noted events that occurred during the attacks on Fourth Army in the second half of December:[29]

'Something in the nature of a miracle occurred on the southern flank of Fourth Army. Inexplicably enough the Russians, despite the local supremacy which they possessed, failed to occupy the Yukhnov–Maryaroslavets road and thus cut Fourth Army's sole supply route. Night after night Below's Cavalry Corps, which was causing us great anxiety in the second half of December, pushed on deep into our rear towards Yukhnov. Indeed it actually reached the vital road, but remarkably enough failed to close it.'

It was simply good luck on the Germans' part that the Soviets did not cut the supply line to the Fourth Army and cause the situation to be even worse than it already was. This cannot be assigned to any strategy of Hitler's, just luck that a bad situation did not become worse due to a mistake by the enemy.

While the Soviet offensive continued, the confrontations between Hitler and his generals became even worse, as indicated by Halder's diary entry for 2 January 1942:[30]

'In Fourth and Ninth armies, however, the situation is taking a critical turn. The breakthrough north of Maloyaroslavets has split the front, and we cannot at the moment see any way of restoring it again. The front of the Ninth Army has been broken through from the direction of Staritsa. As far as we can see, there was a mix up in HQ in which a non-existent "Koenigsberg position" supposed to be in back of the front, appears to have played a disastrous role. The front was taken back, and now appears to be broken again.

'In view of these situations, Field Marshal von Kluge demands withdrawal also of the adjoining sectors. Very stormy discussions with the Fuhrer, who persists in his own views. So the front will remain where it is, regardless of consequences.

'**The withdrawal of the Ninth Army against the will of the Supreme Commander occasioned mad outbursts [Author's emphasis]** on his part at the morning conference. OKH is charged with having introduced parliamentary procedures in the army, and with lacking incisiveness of direction. **These ravings interspersed with utterly baseless accusations waste our time and undermine any effective cooperation [Author's emphasis]**.'

As previously mentioned, Halder's diary is almost entirely expressed in a moderate, business-like and calm manner. He emerges from it as a very intelligent and controlled person, attempting to solve all problems through a logical, intellectual process. His remarks relating to Hitler's outbursts are therefore all the more notable because he never uses hyperbole. His is the polar opposite of Hitler's approach to solving problems and making decisions, which was undoubtedly one of the most important reasons why Hitler ultimately could not work with him.

According to Halder's diary from 3 January, casualties on the Eastern Front by 31 December 1941 were 26,755 officers and 804,148 enlisted men (a total of 830,903, or 25.96 per cent of the Army in the East as it was on 22 June when *Barbarossa* commenced). Of these, 173,722 were killed, including 7,120 officers. Naturally, these losses were concentrated in the formations where there was the fighting, so the loss ratio was even higher amongst the infantry and panzer forces, exceeding 50 per cent in some infantry divisions.

On the same day, Halder added:[31]

'Another dramatic scene with the Fuhrer, who calls in question the generals' courage to make hard decisions. **The plain truth however is that with the temperature down to thirty below freezing our troops simply cannot hold out any longer [Author's emphasis].**'

Halder's diary for 8 January noted:[32]

'**Very grave day.** The westward advance of the Sukhinichi breakthrough is becoming threatening for von Kluge. He urges taking back the Fourth Army front to free forces for the protection of his supply line – von Kluge argues his point with me already in the morning! Put before the Fuhrer! **The usual tug of war. No decision, but a great deal of energy is expended in thinking up piddling makeshifts [Author's emphasis]** to protect the supply road. Finally the Fuhrer had a talk with von Kluge, which produced nothing conclusive. In the afternoon, von Kluge again urgently requests freedom of decision over the moves of the Fourth Army, so as to enable him to disengage. I talk to the Fuhrer on this matter. He wants to talk to von Kluge himself. Result: Army Group is authorised to disengage step by step in order to free forces for the protection of the supply line.'

This is yet another example of Hitler's prevarication and refusal to make urgently needed decisions in a timely way. Kluge was one of the toughest and most successful German commanders, and for him to urgently request permission to withdraw could only mean that he felt the situation was at crisis point, as it undoubtedly then was. Hitler's vacillation also meant that additional casualties were suffered because of delays in withdrawing to a better position or in allowing units to manoeuvre to defend themselves more effectively. All this was happening when the temperature was testing the limits of human endurance. The fact that the Fourth Army was not destroyed does not prove that Hitler's orders saved it or any other part of the German Army; the survival of the German Army in the East was due much more to the fighting qualities of the German soldiers and Stalin's ill-conceived plan of attack than the Fuhrer's interventions, which were largely responsible for causing the terrible position in which the troops were struggling in the first place.

On the same day, Halder noted:[33]

'[V]on Kluge reports that Hoepner, on his own initiative, gave an order to withdraw without notifying army group. The Fuhrer at once orders his "expulsion from the army," with all legal consequences!'

In Hoepner's case, this meant he was not entitled to wear the Army uniform or to receive any pension or entitlements he would otherwise have done. It is worth noting here that Hoepner was one of the best panzer generals in the German Army, having previously been awarded the Iron Cross First and Second Class and the Knight's Cross of the Iron Cross. It is unthinkable that he would have given the order to withdraw without the utmost reluctance and only in a most critical situation.

On 14 January, Halder recorded a deteriorating situation:[34]

'The situation southwest of Rzhev is becoming increasingly dangerous. Three to four enemy divisions are already operating in our rear. XXIII Corps must be taken back. Situation in the Valdai area very uncomfortable. In these circumstances it is impossible to hold the front any longer. Von Kluge reports that he must move back if he wants to extricate himself from Rzhev. **This kind of leadership can lead only to the annihilation of the Army [Author's emphasis].**'

This pattern of vacillation, procrastination and delay on Hitler's part is typical of the manner in which he exercised command throughout the war. He would not make difficult decisions until circumstances absolutely forced him to do so. When the Germans were the stronger force and attacking, the consequences of this pattern were hidden to a large degree, but when they were on the defensive, the repercussions were more evident and profound because they no longer had the initiative. These delays meant that on numerous occasions the situation at the front was almost irreparable by the time Hitler made urgently needed decisions. These delays also resulted in higher losses than would otherwise have been the case, and were the antithesis of the rational, systematic process that should have been in place at the apex of the armed forces command.

Army Group Centre commander Field Marshal von Bock was forced to take leave on 19 December 1941 owing to medical problems, his command being taken over by Field Marshal von Kluge. Bock returned to command Army Group South on 20 January 1942 as Field Marshal von Reichenau had died on 17 January. On 18 January, Bock had met with the Fuhrer, who briefed him on the situation:[35]

> 'Reported to the Fuehrer; he brought me up to date on the situation, especially as it concerns Army Group South. **He sees the strategic threat as eliminated, although there is plenty to be ironed out. The question of Army Group South he considers "taken care of"** [Author's emphasis].'

However, when Bock arrived and took command on 20 January, he found this was most definitely not the case:[36]

> 'The situation is serious. The most critical places are north of Artemovsk and west and northwest of Izyum, where the enemy has broken through with tanks. The penetration at Artemovsk is to be headed off by committing the last reserves of the 17th Army and a reserve of the 1st Panzer Army (Kleist). At present there are no forces available for Izyum. A third dangerous penetration followed against 2nd Army northeast of Schtschigry, where a cavalry corps reinforced by infantry smashed a deep breach and is feeling its way toward Kursk.'

On 22 January, he noted the seriousness of the position in the south:[37]

> 'On the map it appears a simple matter to assemble an assault group from the 1st Romanian Division coming up by way of Dnepropretrovosk, the remains of the 298th Division in the gap west of Izyum, and the reserves gathering behind the 6th Army's south wing, and with it restore the situation at the boundary between the 17th and 6th Armies. But **things look very much different with temperatures of 30 to 40 degrees below freezing, icy roads and failing railroads, with the terrible state of the**

inadequately-fed horses and that of the vehicles, which is even worse, because all movements require a tremendous amount of time which cannot be predicted [Author's emphasis].'

These entries by Bock, who came fresh to the scene in southern Russia, can scarcely be reconciled with Hitler's view that the strategic threat was 'eliminated' or that Army Group South was 'taken care of', which were at best just completely wrong, or otherwise delusional. With the problems Bock mentions, and with no reserves, Army Group South was in great peril.

Guderian had met with Hitler on 20 December to confer with him and convince him of the need for a more flexible defence strategy. He recounted that Hitler received him with a hard expression which seemed to indicate that he had turned against him.[38] The conversation started with Hitler forbidding a withdrawal, but Guderian saying it was impossible to hold the position that the troops were in and that the withdrawal had actually started. Hitler thereupon declared:[39]

'If that is the case, they must dig into the ground where they are and hold every square yard of land.

'I: Digging into the ground is no longer feasible in most places, since it is frozen to a depth of five feet and our wretched entrenching tools won't go through it.

'Hitler: In that case they must blast craters with the heavy howitzers. We had to do that in the First World War in Flanders.

'I: In the First World War our divisions in Flanders held, on the average, sectors 2 to 3 miles wide and were supported in the defence by two or three battalions of heavy howitzers per division with proportionately abundant supplies of ammunition. My divisions have to defend fronts of 25 to 35 miles and in each of my divisions there are 4 heavy howitzers with approximately 50 shells per gun. If I use those shells to make craters I shall have 50 hollows in the ground, each about the width of a wash tub with a large black circle around it. I shall not have a crater position. In Flanders there was never such cold as we are now experiencing. And apart from that I need my ammunition to fire at the Russians. We can't even drive stakes into the ground for carrying our telephone wires; to make a hole for the stake we have to use high explosives. When are we to get sufficient explosives to blast our defensive positions on the scale you have in mind.

'But Hitler insisted on his order, that we remain where we were, being carried out.

'I: Then this means taking up positional warfare in an unsuitable terrain as happened on the Western Front during the First World War. In this case we shall have the same battles of material and the same enormous casualties as then without any hope of winning a decisive victory. If such tactics are adopted we shall, during the course of this coming winter, sacrifice the lives of our officers, our non-commissioned officers and of the men suitable to replace them, and this sacrifice will have been not only useless, but also irreparable.'

Unfortunately for the Germans, this prediction by Guderian proved only too true. Hitler's comments were completely out of step with the conditions at the front, despite his oft-repeated assertions of affinity with the front-line soldier, derived from his service during the First World War.

Warlimont observed a discussion relating to the Fuhrer's 'stand and fight' order:[40]

'Leeb and Guderian were not the only generals who, instead of being regularly visited in their headquarters by von Brauchitsch, now had to make frequent flights to the distant headquarters in East Prussia and there spend whole days arguing with Hitler as to how his principle of rigid defence could be made to accord with the actual state of affairs at the front [Author's emphasis]. Their efforts however remained fruitless, all the more so because **from the end of January 1942 the front began to solidify again on its own. This appeared to prove Hitler's theory right; he unfortunately drew from it the disastrous conclusion that his principle of rigid defence must always and in all circumstances be correct and he applied it throughout the rest of the war [Author's emphasis].**

The main reasons why the front started to solidify of its own accord were that Stalin had underestimated the residual strength of the Germans, despite the winter and its impact on their defensive power, but even more critically because he dispersed the Red Army's offensive strength too widely, contrary to Zhukov's recommendation to concentrate Soviet forces against Army Group Centre and deal it an overwhelming blow. Additionally, supplies to sustain the different Soviet offensives became problematic. Another problem the Red Army suffered resulted from the heavy losses sustained during the earlier course of *Barbarossa*, which included many lower-echelon commanders and NCOs whose replacements were inexperienced. Their rawness led to unco-ordinated attacks and frontal assaults resulting in unnecessarily high casualties even by Soviet standards.

Conclusions

1. There has been a great deal of debate relating to the effect of Hitler's order of 16 December 1941, requiring the German Army to fight where it stood, and whether this was the correct strategy for the circumstances in which the Germans found themselves. Some commentators have credited this order and Hitler's subsequent actions with saving the German Army in the winter of 1941–42, while others have assigned alternative reasons for it. A precipitate withdrawal could have led to a rout similar to that suffered by Napoleon in 1812, whether this was part of a pre-emptive general withdrawal or forced on the Germans by the attacks of the Red Army. However, the evidence shows that such a withdrawal was not what any of Hitler's commanders proposed. They wished to make timely adjustments to the front to ensure that the maximum defensive power of their units was achieved, which is precisely what Rundstedt had recommended when he was sacked. He advocated withdrawing the German line to positions that could easily be defended, but Hitler would not hear of it because of his mania to defend every piece of land that had been conquered. The result then was the same as elsewhere, with the Germans forced back by the Red Army in unfavourable circumstances. What the result would have been if the German generals had been allowed to implement their recommended withdrawal approach will never be know, except in the very few largely successful instances. The main problem caused by Hitler's order was that he made it almost impossible for any realignment of the front except as the result of Red Army pressure. It is obvious from Rundstedt's dismissal, the comments of Guderian and Warlimont, Kluge's reports and the diaries of Bock and Halder that the commanding German generals were very conscious of the difficulties involved in redeploying their forces, yet that they believed greater flexibility than Hitler allowed was not only possible, but vital to achieving the most effective defence. Additionally, they were at the front and had more intimate knowledge of what the troops could achieve than did Hitler in the far-off Fuhrer HQ in Rastenburg, East Prussia, whose limited military experience extended only to the conditions on the Western Front in the First World War. The fact that the German armies did survive the winter does not mean that this was the result of Hitler's order – there were many factors involved, including the desperation of troops who knew they were fighting for their lives, and also the inexperience of the Soviet High Command, which failed to concentrate its efforts to ensure that a breakthrough occurred in at least one sector vital to the Germans, thereby causing a major strategic defeat.

2. In reviewing the position of the Germans prior to Zhukov's counterattack around Moscow, it is apparent from all the sources that the German formations had suffered heavy casualties, were exhausted and were suffering from lack of supplies and exposure to the weather. There can be no other reason why the commanders all recognized the need to withdraw and give their troops some respite from the strain they had been under, including the appalling weather they had to endure. Yet at the same time, Hitler was still contemplating offensives during the winter, as evidenced by Halder's diary entry of 6 December, such was the state of his delusion – he clearly did not understand the position at the front. There seems no doubt that Guderian's view was correct in that Hitler's understanding of the situation at the front as seen from Fuhrer HQ at Rastenburg was dramatically different from the actual conditions and capabilities of the troops.

3. It is also apparent that regardless of the strategy pursued by the Fuhrer or the German commanders, Stalin created the opportunity enabling them to avoid defeat by insisting on his strategy of multiple offensives over the whole of the Eastern Front. Stalin did this instead of concentrating the Red Army's efforts on Army Group Centre, as Zhukov advocated, or somewhere else equally vital to the Germans. The evidence indicates that if Stalin had agreed to Zhukov's recommendation to focus the Red Army on Army Group Centre, instead of dispersing its offensive power, the Soviets may have been able to break the German Front irreparably, which would have led to the defeat of the Germans in the USSR in 1941–42. Ironically, both Hitler and Stalin thus made the same mistake, which prevented either of them from achieving a strategic victory in 1941–42; neither of them appreciated the critical importance of concentrating the strongest available power at a vital point of attack. This situation emphasized the great peril their countries were exposed to because of the practically unlimited power the dictators wielded, which enabled them to meddle in military command with such dramatic consequences.

Chapter 4

Stalingrad

The Red Army's victory at Stalingrad is rightly viewed as one of the crucial turning points of the war, not only with respect to Hitler's war against the USSR but to the ultimate defeat of Nazi Germany. This has led to one of the most debated questions of the war being whether the German disaster at Stalingrad could have been avoided? And furthermore, what role did Hitler play in it?

Partial answers to both questions can be found in Trevor Roper's *Hitler's Table Talk*,[1] a verbatim record of Hitler's views on a bewildering array of subjects, taken as a result of the Fuhrer's secretary, Martin Bormann, instructing stenographers to record for posterity remarks he made while relaxing with his intimate circle. They are revelatory, but not in the sense intended by Bormann, because they illustrate Hitler's ignorance on so many topics and the arrogance, conceit and inhumanity of his views. On 28 February 1942, for instance, the Fuhrer is recorded as saying:[2]

'Now that January and February are past, our enemies can give up the hope of our suffering the fate of Napoleon. They've lost nothing by waiting. Now we're about to switch over to squaring the account. What a relief! **I've noticed, on the occasion of such events, that when everybody loses his nerves, I'm the only one who keeps calm [Author's emphasis].** It was the same thing at the time of the struggle for power, but at that time I had the luck to be only thirty, whilst my opponents were twenty or thirty years older.'

These comments reveal that Hitler had not changed his attitude or learned anything as a result of the losses sustained during the winter crisis of 1941–42 – even though *Barbarossa* had failed, he was still thinking that attack was the strategy to follow in the war with the USSR. The remarks also highlight the selective nature of his memory, because the record shows that he did not maintain his nerve or keep calm when difficult situations arose during the campaigns in Norway, France and above all during *Barbarossa*. It was others who remained focussed and were able to calm him to a degree, and eventually to drag from him long-overdue decisions regarding the most urgent of matters.

Halder's diary entry of 21 April 1942 made clear just how costly the 1941–42 winter fighting had been:[3]

'1. Effect of winter battles:
'a. Personnel: 1.11.1941–1.4.1942, including sick: 900,000 losses, 450,000 replacements. These numbers include the almost total use of the 1942 year and strong encroachment on the economy.
'b. Material: 1.10.1941–15.3.1942: loss of 74,183 vehicles and 2,340 tracked vehicles; addition of 7,441 vehicles (10 per cent) and 1,847 tracked vehicles (80 per cent).
'Weapons: shortages include 28,000 rifles, 14,000 machine guns, 7,000 AT [anti-tank] guns, 1,900 guns.
'Horses: 15.10.41–15.3.1942: losses of 179,609, additions of 20,000.
'…
'3. Vacancies 1.5.1942: In the east, short 625,000 men.'

The figure of 625,000 men represents the normal strength of approximately thirty-five German infantry divisions at the 1940 establishment. The losses and shortages listed above, particularly those regarding anti-tank guns and artillery, were extremely serious, meaning that any attempt at offensive action had to be limited. Hitler realized this and restricted the scope of the main 1942 offensive to the southern half of the Russian Front. In order to make up the numbers in the divisions that would be used for the forthcoming offensive, other divisions in areas not involved had to be left virtually without replacements. The replacement of equipment was even more problematic because the production levels of the German economy in 1942 could make up only a fraction of what was needed. The shortage of anti-tank guns was especially dangerous, given the better quality of the new Soviet tank types. Albert Speer noted[4] that in summer 1942, Germany was manufacturing only one-third of the tanks and a quarter of the artillery pieces compared to the levels achieved in 1944, which represented much lower totals than achieved by the Soviets or the Western Allies. The comparative levels of production as set out in Appendix 1 show the tremendous gap that the Germans never came near to closing in any of the main categories of weapon production.

Apart from the other losses, there was a net loss of over 66,000 vehicles and 150,000 horses in the German Army in the East. Germany was, in effect, still on a peacetime manufacturing footing while at war with the USSR, the

British Empire and (since declaring war on 11 December) the USA – such was the ramshackle war effort co-ordinated by Hitler and the Nazi regime.

The Fuhrer's decision to take the offensive in summer 1942 was against the advice of virtually all his senior commanders, who believed that repairing and re-equipping the German armies and adopting a defensive strategic posture was the best course for them to take. The aims of Hitler's offensive were to take Stalingrad and thereby sever the flow to Soviet industry of oil and other raw materials along the Volga River, and to take the oilfields of the Trans-Caucasian area. These objectives were purely economic and would not have been selected for primarily military reasons.

In a revelatory passage in *Inside Hitler's Headquarters, 1939–1945*,[5] Warlimont stated:

'No one could have forseen how Hitler was to exercise his power of supreme command; **in fact he proved more overbearing and less open to advice than ever before [Author's emphasis]** and it was this which was the decisive factor in bringing about the awful crisis of the second Russian winter 1942–43.'

Warlimont also related that when planning the offensive, Hitler:[6]

'never considered taking the obvious course – hitherto the rule before all major operations – of testing his ambitious plans and working them out in greater detail by means of war games and paper exercises. **He apparently thought it was enough to have a short discussion of his main ideas with Army Group South, which he did on 1 June – without taking the Chief of Staff of the Army with him [Author's emphasis].'**

This incredibly amateurish approach resulted in predictable problems of supply being experienced from the beginning of the offensive, which significantly affected the forces involved.

While the offensive ordered by Hitler was underway in June 1942, Guderian was on leave due to ill health. However, he commented on it in typically succinct style:[7]

'During 1942 the German Army had once again launched an offensive – from June 28th to the end of August – which had been successful in that the southern wing (Kleist) had reached the Caucasian mountains while Paulus' Sixth Army to the north had advanced as far as Stalingrad on the Volga. These operations were once again based on an eccentric plan. The

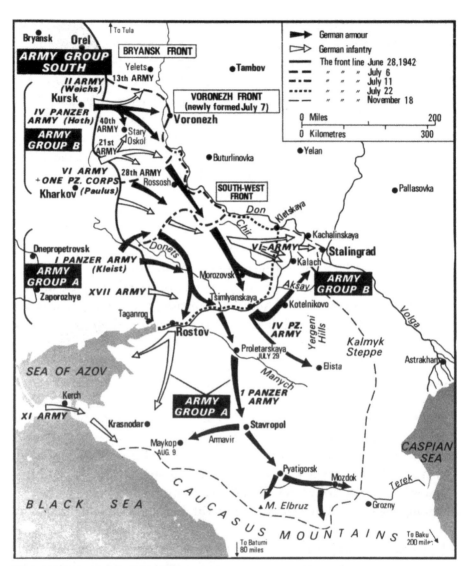

Map 5: Hitler's 1942 Stalingrad Campaign.
It is obvious from this map that Hitler's 1942 offensive led to a dramatic extension of the German Front which created insuperable supply problems. It also meant that the Allied Romanian, Italian, and Hungarian formations were deployed, on Hitler's express orders, along the flank of the advance immediately to the north of Stalingrad thus creating the opportunity for the Soviet envelopment that occurred.

objectives assigned were beyond the power of the troops, weakened as they were by the hardships of the 1941–42 winter campaign. **As in August of 1941, Hitler was driving for objectives of economic and ideological significance without first ensuring that the enemy's military strength was broken [Author's emphasis].** The capture of the Caspian oilfields, the cutting of the Volga as a maritime artery, and the neutralisation of the industrial centre at Stalingrad, **such were the motives that led him to operations which, from a military point of view were nonsensical [Author's emphasis].**'

Colonel General Kurt Zeitzler, who became Chief of the General Staff of the Army after Halder was sacked by Hitler on 24 September 1942, wrote a very clear analysis of the Stalingrad campaign in *The Fatal Decisions*, in which he identified the basic problem with Hitler's plan:[8]

'Military objectives must always correspond to the forces and other means available for their attainment. ...

'The first objective, Stalingrad, lay nearly three hundred miles beyond the front line that existed in the spring of 1942: the Caucasus was even farther away, over three hundred and fifty miles distant. Nor were these objectives close to one another. Being some three hundred and fifty miles apart, the operations must diverge.

'The question now arose whether there were sufficient forces at present available to capture two such remote and distant objectives. The answer was plainly in the negative. This question was put to Hitler by his military advisers, and the solution decided upon was, it is said, suggested to him by General Jodl. This was to demand fresh divisions from Germany's allies, thereby creating a total force upon the Eastern Front corresponding to Hitler's intentions for the coming campaign. This was the first fatal decision of the year. ...

'But Hitler was intoxicated by numbers and saw only the vast increase in divisions which now appeared on his staff maps. General Halder, who was my predecessor as Chief of the General Staff, certainly realized the dangers inherent in this plan and pointed them out to Hitler repeatedly and earnestly. However, the dictator brushed aside all his warnings.'

Zeitzler was pointing out the obvious: that the forces assigned for the 1942 campaign were not adequate to achieve the aims set by Hitler, the fulfilment of which was made even more difficult by the objectives being substantial distances apart, with the consequent splitting of the offensive power of the armies. Field Marshal Manstein stressed that another of the crucial difficulties the Germans faced in this campaign was that virtually all their supplies were based on a single Dnieper crossing, the railway bridge at Dnepropetrovsk.[9] The limited amount of supplies that could be moved across it were soon apparent and inevitably caused significant problems from an early stage of the offensive. In addition to these difficulties, a large part of the forces to be used were composed of divisions from the Romanian, Italian and Hungarian armies, which were neither equipped nor sufficiently trained for operations against the Red Army. All in all, this plan was a recipe for disaster which any moderately competent military commander would have recognized.

David Stone notes in his book *Twilight of the Gods*[10]on the 1942 campaign:

> 'Halder consistently counselled against Hitler's direction that simultaneous operations were to be conducted at the same tempo on the River Volga – including against Stalingrad – and into the Caucasus to secure the oilfields. The vast distances between them meant that these concurrent offensives really needed to be regarded almost as separate and discrete fronts for operational and command and control purposes, something that was beyond the Wehrmacht's capability. … the Chief of the General Staff's misgivings were also supported by the Quartermaster-general General Wagner, who reinforced his cautionary advice of the previous year and now stated that it was simply impracticable for the Wehrmacht to provide the required levels of logistical support for two such major offensives at the same time.'

The supply problems that occurred during the campaign crippled the forces both at Stalingrad and in the Caucasus, confirming the advice that Halder and Wagner had given.

Halder pointed out that Hitler's plan for the 1942 offensive - 'Fell Bleu' (Case Blue) – was very risky because of the use of the allied armies which were not fit to be committed to combat with the Red Army, and the supply problems which had been highlighted by General Wagner, the Army Quartermaster General. The offensive also lacked concentration being more like a thrust with open fingers, than a clenched fist. Hitler would not listen to these arguments and stated that Germany must obtain the oilfields of the Caucasus in order to continue the war. Regardless of his requirements, the most senior commanders of the Army Groups involved confirmed that the main problem in carrying out the offensive was the supply problem and that this caused its failure just when the prospects of success appeared best.[11]

Speer, Hitler's Armaments Minister, was at Supreme Headquarters very frequently, and recalled in his book *Inside the Third Reich*:[12]

> 'At the end of June 1942 I read in the newspapers, just like everyone else, that a great new offensive in the east had started. There was a mood of exuberance at headquarters. Every evening Hitler's Chief

Adjutant, Schmundt, traced the onrush of the troops on a wall map, for the edification of the civilians at headquarters. **Hitler was triumphant. Once again he had proved that he was right and the generals wrong [Author's emphasis]** – for they had advised against an offensive and called for defensive tactics, occasionally straightening out the front.'

On 28 June, the German offensive commenced by Bock's Army Group B. The attack was initially completely successful, with Red Army units facing his forces broken up within a few days. On 30 June, Army Group A under Field Marshal List began its offensive to the south of Army Group B, heading toward the Caucasus. These attacks were at first spectacularly successful too.

During the next week, Halder's diary noted the satisfactory development of the operations of both army groups. However, on 5 July he reported:[13]

'At the Fuhrer situation conferences, a warm debate developed over the conduct of the operation. The Fuhrer questions that von Bock is applying sufficient vigor in pushing toward the lower reaches of the Tikhvin-Sosna and specifically takes exception to directing 23rd Armored Division (XXXX Corps) northeastward, and 16th Motorised Division eastward instead of southeastward.'

The following day, Halder wrote:[14]

'At the Fuhrer situation conference, there is again a big scene over the conduct of the offensive by army groups; loud insistence on holding all forces together in conformity with southward objectives; prohibition to strike on Voronezh and, finally orders to stop Ninth and Eleventh Armored Divisions and speed freeing of all armored divisions and moving them behind XXXX Corps across the Tikhvin-Sosna.

'In the course of the day, phone talks with von Bock (this one highly disagreeable), with the Fuhrer, with Keitel (OKW), and with von Sodenstern, always about the same questions. **This telephoning back and forth about matters which should be thought out quietly and incorporated in clear orders is very distressing [Author's emphasis].** The hardest to endure is Keitel with his undigested spoutings.'

On 6 July, Halder also noted that Hitler was concerned that as the Soviet Front was falling apart, the Western Allies might make a landing in France to relieve the pressure on the USSR. Accordingly, the Fuhrer held back the 1st SS-Panzer Division 'Leibstandarte-SS Adolf Hitler' from being committed as part of First Panzer Army, and on 23 July also withdrew the Grossdeutschland Division and ordered that they both be sent to France. These were elite units that Halder stated could have made a significant difference to the offensive, writing prophetically:[15]'Let us hope we won't have to pay heavily for that.'

As it turned out, the forces already in France were more than adequate to deal with the Dieppe raid on 19 August, which was militarily trivial and the only operation undertaken by the Western Allies on the continent of Europe that year.

On 7 July, Halder concluded his entry with respect to the attack by Bock's Army Group B:[16]

'The enemy seems to have been caught just as he was falling back. Complete success is imminent.'

However, by 12 July, Army Group B was already experiencing problems with supply, as Halder mentioned:[17]

'[F]uel shortage unfortunately has so far held up arrival of Grossdeutschland Division and 24th Armored Division.'

This was exactly the kind of problem that could have been foreseen through the detailed staff work which Warlimont mentioned should have occurred before the plan for the campaign was adopted, and which Halder and Wagner warned Hitler would happen.

Bock recorded that during 12 July, he received a directive for his army group:[18]

'[We should] proceed in the general direction of the mouth of the Donets … with the objective of engaging the enemy north of the Don and destroying him by attacking his rear.

'Apart from being unclear, this directive scatters my weak armored units to the four winds.'

He noted that there were no less than six mouths of the Donets, and went on to describe how the carrying out of the order was 'impossible' because of road conditions. He continued:[19]

'Meanwhile the left wing of Army Group A as well as my right wing were nearing the town of Millerovo. Strong armored forces and infantry divisions will conglomerate in a small area there, in the center of the operations, while the wings are too weak! …

'Flew to 4th Panzer Army in Olkhovatka, where I discussed the continuation of the operation with Hoth and saw elements of Grossdeutschland and the 24th Panzer Division. Despite the burning heat and frightful dust the troops are in outstanding spirits. **It is regrettable that both divisions are still immobilised without fuel [Author's emphasis]**.'

On 13 July, Halder recorded:[20]

'Situation conference started with the Fuhrer's expressing [of] his utmost displeasure over the delay in the move to the front of 23rd Armored Division (pinned down by an attack from the west), 24th Armored Division, and the Grossdeutschland, as well as of the two other motorized divisions of Fourth Panzer Army. He blames this failure on the fact that 24th Panzer and Grossdeutschland, against the Fuhrer's order, were sent into Voronezh, causing a delay which could have been avoided.

'The Fuhrer accordingly rules to relieve commander of AGp.B.'

Bock wrote on the same day:[21]

'In the afternoon Feldmarschall Keitel informed me by telephone that by order of the Fuehrer the 4th Panzer Army was to join Army Group A, as had been envisaged by the supreme command. Further he took me completely by surprise by passing on to me the order that Generaloberst von Weichs was to take over command and that I was being placed at the disposal of the Fuhrer!'

Warlimont also recorded this episode:[22]

'Hitler justified his decision by quoting a previous "unfortunate proposal" by the Army Group which, however, had never been carried out: he never thereafter failed subsequently to ascribe the failure of the entire offensive to Bock's dilatoriness at Voronezh.'

Bock was regarded as one of the most able and hardest-driving field commanders in the German Army, with a spectacularly successful record in all the other campaigns in which he had been involved, for that reason Hitler had promoted him to field marshal in July 1940. It appears that the cause of any delay with committing the two divisions mentioned was primarily supply problems, not a lack of action on Bock's part. Nonetheless, he was dismissed without any explanation and not used again during the rest of the war.

Meanwhile, Halder noted ominously on 16 July:[23]

'According to reliable intelligence, we must expect that the enemy will use every available means to hold Stalingrad.'

He continued:[24]

'Conference with Gehlen and Heusinger [Lieutenant Colonel Reinhard Gehlen of the Fremde Heere Ost military intelligence service and Lieutenant General Adolf Heusinger of the Operations Planning section of the OKH – Author's note]: Preliminary planning for the forthcoming battle of Stalingrad. We shall have to prepare for, perhaps even embark upon, the battle of Stalingrad while we are still fighting the battle of Rostov north and south of the Don. Compute time and strength requirements.'

David Stone writes that on 16 July:[25]

'[Hitler ordered] Fourth Panzer Army (from Army Group B) to re-deploy to assist Army Group A, just as Army Group B was approaching Stalingrad. Then, belatedly, he realised that this city might provide a base from which Army Group A could be threatened and countermanded his earlier order, returning Fourth Panzer Army to Army Group B. This succession of "order, counter-order and disorder" meant that neither the Caucasus oilfields or Stalingrad had been accorded the higher priority.'

Halder's diary entry of 23 July was scathing:[26]

'Fuhrer situation conference: In consequence of the concentration of army ordered by the Fuhrer on 17 July over my opposition, and the diversion of 24th Armored Division to Sixth Army, directed by him on 21 July, it is becoming obvious **even to the layman** [apparently a reference to Hitler – Author's note] that the Rostov area is crammed with armor which has nothing to do, while the critical outer wing at Tsimlyanskaya is starving for it. I warned emphatically against both of these developments.

'**Now that the result is so palpable, he explodes in a fit of insane rage [Author's emphasis]** and hurls the gravest reproaches against the General Staff.

'This chronic tendency to underrate enemy capabilities is gradually assuming grotesque proportions and develops into a positive danger. The situation is getting more and more intolerable. **There is no room for any serious work. This so-called leadership is characterized by a pathological reacting to the impressions of the moment and a total lack of any understanding of the command machinery and its possibilities [Author's emphasis].**'

This entry by Halder encapsulates the problem Hitler represented as Commander-in-Chief of the Army. As his actions did not reflect reality, they either could not be carried out or were irrelevant to the actual situation of the German formations. Together with his amateurism, this meant that the Army was handicapped rather than helped by his actions.

Delays caused by lack of supplies resulted in significant problems for the Sixth Army in its march to Stalingrad at a time when the Soviet defences there were not yet properly organized. This is commented upon by Halder in his diary entry for 25 July:[27]

'Lack of fuel caused sizable elements of the armored and motorized divisions to lag behind.'

He did so again on 26 July:[28]

'Hard battles west of Stalingrad. The enemy, split into four groups, is fighting doggedly and throwing new forces, including much armor, across the Don. There must still be a strong force in Stalingrad itself. **Lack of fuel and ammunition! [Author's emphasis].**'

Halder's diary entry of 28 July revealed the difficulties that were causing delays in the advance of the Sixth Army:[29]

'Battle of Stalingrad: **Due to lack of fuel and ammunition [Author's emphasis]**, Sixth Army was unable to attack. After suffering a defeat in his violent attacks (nine new armored brigades) the enemy appears to be retreating behind the Don.'

This delay was crucial, as the Soviet defences of the city were incomplete at that time and an attack carried through to Stalingrad would probably have succeeded in taking it without much resistance.

Halder wrote on 30 July:[30]

'In AGp.B, a wild battle is raging in Sixth Army sector inside the Don bend west of Stalingrad; we do not yet have an accurate picture of its development. **Sixth Army's striking power is paralyzed by ammunition and fuel supply difficulties [Author's emphasis].**'

He also noted on the same day:[31]

'At the situation conference, Jodl is given the word: he announces pompously that the fate of the Caucasus will be decided at Stalingrad and that, in view of the importance of the battle, it would be necessary to divert forces from AGp.A to AGp.B, if possible, south of the Don. This is a dressed-up version of my own proposal, which I submitted to the Fuhrer six days ago when Fourth Panzer Army struck across the Don. At that time, though, no-one in the illustrious company of the OKW seemed to be able to grasp its significance. He goes on to explain that First Panzer Army must at once wheel south and southwest to cut off the enemy now being pushed back step by step from the Don by Seventeenth Army, before he reaches the Caucasus.

'This is rankest nonsense. The enemy is running for dear life and will be in the northern foothills of the Caucasus a good piece ahead of our armor, and then we are going to have another unhealthy congestion of forces before the enemy front.'

The situation at Stalingrad could have been cleared up earlier, but the diversion of the Fourth Panzer Army by Hitler caused a delay in it being taken, as discussed by Alan Clark:[32]

'In the result, the two Panzer armies arrived at the Don crossings together – a prodigious sledge hammer, as it had now become, to crush the tiniest of snails. For the Don crossings were virtually undefended.'

And he quotes Kleist further:

'... The 4th Panzer Army ... could have taken Stalingrad without a fight at the end of July, but was diverted to help me in crossing the Don. I did not need its aid, and it simply got in the way and congested the roads I was using.'

This is the diversion of Fourth Panzer Army on 16 July, which Stone refers to, and which Halder discussed in the entries to his diary of 23 and 30 July.

On 1 August, Halder again commented on the situation with respect to Stalingrad:[33]

'Our troops cannot attack for lack of fuel and ammunition.' The following day he noted:[34] 'In AGp.B Sixth Army is on the defensive due to failure of supply.'

These problems would have been foreseen if Hitler had carried out the detailed testing of the offensive as referred to by Warlimont. The direct consequence of these problems with supply was to restrict the impetus of the offensive, when everything depended on continuing the advance to take Stalingrad as quickly as possible to deny the Red Army the chance to consolidate its defence. This problem was the result of Hitler not taking the supply of the offensive seriously enough, which is what the General Staff's testing process was designed to do. Such a basic failure cannot be ignored and conclusively illustrates his inability to competently command the German Army.

Warlimont recorded that at the midday conference on 16 August:[35]

'Halder had produced an old map which had been captured somewhere and had pointed out the similarities between the present situation and that of the Red Army in 1920. It was commanded by Stalin at the time and had made a surprise attack across the lower Don between Stalingrad and Rostov, inflicting a severe defeat on Wrangels' "White Guard". **Hitler's interest was immediately aroused. The only result however was an order for the urgent move of one German armoured division (no. 22) to support the threatened sector which was defended by the Italian Eighth Army. A little later he ordered up two infantry divisions, one of them for the flank where the attack was in progress. A little later he ordered up two infantry divisions, one of them for the flank where the attack was in progress [Author's emphasis].'**

Another example of the problems associated with supply is provided by the situation of the III Panzer Corps:[36]

'By 16 August, the corps had reached the area east of Woroschilowsk. It was there that it ran out of fuel. It took until 22 August before the 13 Panzer Division was topped off again.'

This amounted to six days of enforced inactivity when every day was crucial to the success of the offensive. Again, this was a problem which the detailed testing work at which the General Staff excelled – but which Hitler disparaged – would have identified, as mentioned by Warlimont. That Hitler did not undertake this step before the offensive was launched meant that there was no real understanding of the potential problems that the projected operation presented, a situation that ultimately came home to roost.

There is no doubt that Halder raised with Hitler the potential difficulties associated with the extended flank held by the allied armies and urged that the situation be dealt with either through stopping the offensive and redeploying the forces being used or assigning adequate forces to ensure that it could resist an attack. On 26 August, Halder noted that 'Everything went wrong in the Italian sector on the right wing.' This was the sector which he had been highlighting to Hitler above Stalingrad where the allied formations had been deployed despite their unsuitability for combat with the Red Army. Halder was so concerned that he sent Blumentritt, who was Deputy Chief of the General Staff at the time, to review the situation at the front. Blumentritt reported that the Italian positions were weak and the supply situation problematic because the railheads were 200km away. Halder authorised the deployment of an Alpini division and part of the German 6th Division to shore up the line, but the basic problem remained. Nothing further was done to reinforce the positions although Blumentritt's report was definitely seen by Hitler:[37]

Although this report was supported by Halder and forwarded to Hitler, he did not take the steps recommended to avert the danger.

On 24 August, Halder recorded:[38]

'Fuhrer situation conference: Sharp clash over interpretation of the situation at Rzhev, where I perceive a distinct danger of attrition of our forces.'

Warlimont commented on this conference more fully:[39]

'[A]t the midday conference Halder again urged that Ninth Army, which was fighting at Rzhev, should be allowed the necessary freedom of manoeuvre and authorised to withdraw to a shorter line which could be held by its dwindling forces. **This led to a collision which, only**

nine months after the departure of its Commander-in-Chief, was to deprive the German Army of its Chief of the General Staff who had been the real brain behind its victorious campaigns [Author's emphasis]. This proposal ran counter to Hitler's cardinal principle of command and obviously annoyed him. "You always come here with the same proposal", he threw back at Halder, "that of withdrawal", and then in the same breath proceeded to make a series of highly disparaging remarks in which in this case he even included the fighting troops. He ended his tirade with the words: "I expect commanders to be as tough as the fighting troops." There was an atmosphere of extreme tension; Halder was now furious and he raised his voice as he replied: "I am tough enough, my Fuehrer. But out there brave men and young officers are falling in their thousands simply because their commanders are not allowed to make the only reasonable decision and have their hands tied behind their backs." Hitler recoiled, fixed Halder with a long malevolent stare and ground out hoarsely: "Colonel-General Halder, how dare you use language like that to me! Do you think you can teach me what the man at the front is thinking? What do you know about what goes on at the front? Where were you in the First World War? And you try to pretend to me that I don't understand what it's like at the front. I won't stand that! It's outrageous!'"

Hitler's response entirely ignored the points raised by Halder, which were about the tactics being used, not what the troops were thinking about the effect of the orders being given to them. Warlimont felt it was clear at the time that the final breach had now occurred between Hitler and Halder.

After the war, Halder was called as a witness at the trial of the major war criminals at Nuremberg. He was also interviewed by US Army psychiatrist Dr Leon Goldensohn, the record is very instructive in relation to the final breach with Hitler:[40]

'[Goldensohn:] "Were there any particular arguments with Hitler?"

'[Halder:] "There were daily quarrels all summer. The point upon which we had our final disagreement was the decision of an offensive on the Caucasus and Stalingrad – a mistake, and Hitler didn't want to see it. I told him the Russians would put in another million men in 1942 and get another million in 1943. He told me that I was an idiot – that the Russians were practically dead already. When I told Hitler about Russian armament potentials, especially for tank materials, Hitler flew into a rage and threatened me with his fists."

It was obvious that no constructive work could be carried out in such an atmosphere. Guderian and Zeitzler recorded similar episodes with Hitler when they were Chief of the General Staff. Hitler plainly did not want to be told any facts which upset his view that all Slavs were *untermensch* and could not be better at anything than the Germans.

On 26 August, Halder noted:[41]

> 'At Stalingrad, the situation is grave due to counterattacks by numerically superior enemy. Our divisions are all below strength. Severe nervous strain on the responsible commanders. Von Wietersheim wanted to withdraw his advanced outpost on the Volga, but was prevented by Paulus.'

The Germans were now paying the price for Hitler's underestimation of the Soviets and his completely amateurish approach to planning an offensive which he was warned against even undertaking by every one of his senior military advisors.

Halder's note of 29 August again related to the 'unsatisfactory' situation in the Caucasus:[42]

> 'Fuhrer situation conference: Very peevish about the conduct of operations by AGp.A. – Talk with Field Marshal List by phone to find out what could be done to get the offensive going again.'

The next day he added:[43]

> 'Today's conferences with the Fuhrer were again the occasion of abusive reproaches against the military leadership abilities of the highest commands. He charges them with intellectual conceit, mental nonadaptability, and utter failure to grasp essentials.'

On 31 August, Field Marshal List was required to attend Supreme Headquarters at Vinnitsa to report on the situation regarding Army Group A in the drive to the Caucasus. Warlimont recalled:[44]

> 'He gave a calm, balanced view of the picture which seemed to put an end to all apprehensions.'

Hitler is quoted in Trevor Roper's *Hitler's Table Talk* as making the following comments on 6 September:[45]

'The concentration of effort in the defence of Stalingrad is a grave mistake on the part of the Russians. The victor in war is he who commits the fewest number of mistakes [Author's emphasis], and who has, also, a blind faith in victory. If the Russians had not decided to make a stand at Stalingrad, they would have done so elsewhere; but it does prove that a name can give to a place a significance which bears no relation to its intrinsic value.'

Unfortunately for the German soldiers of the Sixth Army at Stalingrad, Hitler does not seem to have remembered this supremely ironic observation in his later conduct of operations which involved them.

The Fuhrer's growing dissatisfaction with the progress being made by Army Group A's offensive in the Caucasus led him to send Jodl to see List on 7 September with orders to ensure that the offensive was pursued with the utmost vigour. Warlimont stated that Hitler flew into a rage when Jodl returned and reported to him:[46]

'[T]he report he made to Hitler shook Supreme Headquarters to its foundations, the like of which was not to be seen until the last months of the war. Jodl reported that, contrary to Hitler's forebodings, Field Marshal List was adhering strictly to the instructions he had received and that he [Jodl] agreed with the views of the Army Group regarding what could be done in the future. For the first time Hitler flew into a rage with Jodl accusing him of not only being a partisan of the Army Group but of having been talked around by List when he had merely been dispatched to transmit orders. Jodl's hackles rose and he argued back.

'I was not present when this occurred. Jodl told me about it the next day.'

On 7 September, Engel made an entry relating to the same incident:[47]

'Jodl is back from Army Group A. Brought a clear appreciation of the situation confirming that it is no longer possible to force the Russians over the mountain chain and into the sea. Only flexible tactics possible in area of opportunity and in it the last attempt will be made to reach Grozny and Cas[pian] Sea with concentrated forces; not Astrakhan, no forces available for it. F. got more worked up minute by minute, sensing the failure of the offensive, had harsh words for supply service, deficiency of initiative on the part of the higher field commanders, placed all blame on OKH, Chief of the General Staff and Jodl. Final break with Jodl who is still attempting to transfer the main thrust exclusively towards the south.'

On 8 September, Halder recorded his observations on the current position:[48]

'Situation: Opposition near Novocherkassk, and advances at Stalingrad: There are no changes.

'Lack of progress in AGp.A is a bitter disappointment for the Fuhrer. Cuttingly reproaches the army group command and the generals as a whole. Jodl, on return from his visit to List, proposes not only not to advance mountain corps any further, but, on the contrary to take it back. The effect is annoyance of the highest degree.'

Regardless of the fact that Jodl's report had shown that List had complied with the orders Hitler issued, List was sacked on 9 September and not used again during the war. Hitler then took over command of Army Group A himself! Hitler was then Supreme Commander of the Armed Forces, Commander-in-Chief of the Army and C-in-C of Army Group A, not to mention being Head of State etc., an incredible situation that no-one could manage – and, not surprisingly, Hitler didn't manage to do so either.

On 9 September, Halder recorded:[49]

'16:30. Field Marshal Keitel comes to see me. List must resign. Hints of more changes in high posts, including mine.'

Halder's diary entry of 15 September set out a table of the casualties from 22 June 1941 to 10 September 1942 (it actually contains an addition error which is not material). The total number of personnel killed was 336,349, including 12,385 officers. The total wounded was 1,226,941, including 34,525 officers, with a further 75,990 missing, including 1,560 officers. The total number of casualties from all causes was 1,639,280, nearly 50 per cent of the original total forces committed to Operation *Barbarossa* (3,359,000). When one considers that the bulk of these casualties were concentrated in the infantry and armour, the scale of the German problem can be seen in its proper perspective. Furthermore, these figures were before the disastrous losses eventually suffered at Stalingrad.

Engel's diary entry of 18 September related to a meeting he and the Fuhrer's Chief Adjutant, Schmundt, had with Hitler:[50]

'After the evening conference, which was as frosty as everything else here, Schmundt and I had something else to report about. At the moment, F. seems determined to get rid of Keitel and Jodl. Schmundt asked what successor he was thinking of. He mentioned Kesselring or Paulus; the only thing that held him back was the timing. Keitel, otherwise a good worker, was apparently under the influence of Jodl, and most of his opinions were not his own. The Chief of the General Staff would have to go beforehand, there was simply nothing more there.'

Halder noted his dismissal on 24 September:[51]

'At situation conference, farewell by the Fuhrer. (My nerves are worn out; and his nerves are no longer fresh. We must part. **Necessity for educating the General Staff in fanatical faith in The Idea [Author's emphasis].** He is determined to enforce his will also into the Army.)'

Warlimont recorded what he heard Hitler say about the position of Chief of the General Staff after Halder's departure:[52]

'[I]n view of the tasks now facing the Army, **rather than relying on technical competence, it must be inspired by the fervour of belief in National-Socialism [Author's emphasis].**'

This semi-mystical utterance is impossible to understand on any rational basis. Nor could it provide any basis for improving the actual situation at the front. Halder was not given any distinction when sacked – although he had been at the centre of managing some of the most successful campaigns in military history; such was Hitler's malevolence.

Colonel General Kurt Zeitzler was appointed Chief of the General Staff after Halder's dismissal. He recalled that upon taking up his duties on 24 September:[53]

'[I] immediately became aware of the most peculiar atmosphere which prevailed at Supreme Headquarters as a result of the breakdown of the offensive in the East. To an officer coming from an operational staff in the field, this atmosphere was not only weird but positively incredible. It was compounded of mistrust and anger. **Nobody had any faith in his colleagues. Hitler distrusted everyone [Author's emphasis].**'

Commenting on Hitler, Zeitzler continued:[54]

'He would shake hands with no general. No longer did he take his meals with the members of his personal headquarters and staff, but preferred to eat alone. When attending staff conferences he would enter, bow stiffly, and listen to his adviser's brief reports, with a surly frown. Then he would once again give the assembled officers a stiff little bow and leave the room.

'… In the atmosphere which thus prevailed at Supreme Headquarters, any frank and objective discussion of the situation was impossible. This could only have one result: the conduct of our military operations was bound to suffer and the burden would be borne by the hard-fighting troops in the field.'

As soon as he could after taking up his duties, Zeitzler prepared a report for Hitler in which he stressed five major matters that needed to be addressed to rectify the situation on the Eastern Front.[55] The first was that the area occupied as a result of the summer offensive was too large for the occupying army – 'there were too few soldiers for too much ground' and a catastrophe would result if this was not addressed. Secondly, the most perilous area of the front was undoubtedly the long, exposed and thinly held flank stretching from Stalingrad to the right-hand boundary of Army Group Centre, which was held by the weakest and therefore least reliable forces on the Eastern Front – the allied Romanian, Hungarian and Italian armies. This danger had been identified by Halder and raised with Hitler but not acted upon, and now had to be eliminated. The third matter was that the flow of men, supplies and equipment to the front was entirely inadequate. Losses continually exceeded replacements, which must result in a disaster if not addressed. Fourthly, the Red Army was better led and trained than it had been in 1941, which called for greater caution on the part of the Germans than had been the case previously. Zeitzler's final point was that the railways and other supply services had to be significantly improved.

Zeitzler recorded his astonishment that Hitler listened to his report 'without flying off the handle'. When he had finished, the Fuhrer merely smiled and said:[56]

'You are too pessimistic. Here on the Eastern Front we've been through worse periods than this before you joined us and we've survived. We'll get over our present difficulties too.'

There were three alternatives Zeitzler identified to address the basic problems with the dispositions of the forces on the Eastern Front.[57] The 'large' solution was to redeploy the armies so as to entirely negate the potentially disastrous dispositions as they then stood. Hitler would have none of this. The second alternative was for the Army to prepare to evacuate the positions it presently held and retire to a stronger line if the Red Army attacked and exposed the deficiencies of the German dispositions. Hitler would not countenance this alternative either. The third suggestion was to withdraw the exposed allied forces and replace them with German troops. However, because of the strategic dispositions that Hitler had ordered for the defence of Western Europe, the Germans lacked the necessary resources for such a move; as he would not change those dispositions, this alternative was also impossible. The Germans were thus reduced to makeshift changes, which Zeitzler initiated as follows:[58]

- A small reserve was created that consisted of two armoured divisions, the German 22nd Panzer Division, which was understrength, and the Romanian Armoured Division, which was not trained or equipped to fight the Red Army. This was designated as Panzer Group H, and was deployed behind the allied front and placed in OKW reserve.
- Small German units were interspersed within the allied units to increase their fighting power. For example, OKW reserve anti-tank units were used in this role.
- German staff liaison sections were deployed with the allied headquarters units to enable them to operate more efficiently and make use of their experience.
- Radio deception activities were used to conceal the fact that there were no German units along the exposed flank and to deceive the Red Army as to the strength of the units that were there.

Reconnaissance of the obviously threatened sectors was increased, and it was soon evident that the Red Army was gradually building up its strength against the exposed flank comprising the allied units. Zeitzler recorded his concerns about the situation:[59]

'During the first half of November – by which time Hitler's Supreme Headquarters and the Army High Command had moved back from Vinnitsa to East Prussia – the picture of the future Russian offensive became increasingly clear. They were going to attack north-west of Stalingrad, probably in the sector held by the Rumanians. What we could not yet gauge was the date on which the attack would be launched.'

The makeshift changes that were carried out were plainly inadequate to address the danger posed by the extended front held by the Italians, Romanians and Hungarians, a situation that Zeitzler stressed on a number of occasions. It should be noted that these allied armies were known by all the senior German commanders – including Hitler – to be inadequately trained and equipped to fight the Red Army; this had been pointed out to Hitler by his own senior generals. Placing them in this extremely exposed position was thus not only an irresponsible move; it was reprehensible of the German Supreme Command to treat their allies in such a manner, which can only be likened to being made cannon fodder, and their subsequent performance should be seen in this light.

Manstein commented on the current German dispositions as follows:[60]

> **'Thanks to the fact that Hitler's strategic objectives were governed chiefly by the needs of his war economy [Author's emphasis],** the German offensive of 1942 had split into two different directions – the Caucasus and Stalingrad. By the time the German advance came to a halt, therefore, a front had emerged, to hold which there were not enough German forces available. To make things worse, no strategic reserve existed, the Supreme Command having squandered Eleventh Army in every conceivable direction immediately it became free in the Crimea. ...
>
> 'The attempt to hold this over-extended front for any length of time constituted the first of the mistakes which were to plunge Sixth Army into its desperate situation at the end of November, 1942.
>
> 'The second and even more fatal mistake was that Hitler compelled Army Group B to tie down its principal striking force, Fourth Panzer and Sixth Armies, in the fighting in and around Stalingrad. **The job of protecting the deep northern flank of this group along the Don was left to Third Rumanian Army, one Italian and one Hungarian army and, in the Voronezh sector, to the weak Second German Army. Hitler must have known that even behind the Don the allied armies could not stand up to a strong Soviet attack [Author's emphasis].'**

Manstein made note of another critical factor:[61]

> '[M]ention should be made of a fact which had grave repercussions on the position of the Sixth Army and the entire southern wing. The whole of Army Group A, as well as the Fourth Panzer Army, Third and Fourth Rumanian Armies and the Italian Army, were based on a single Dnieper crossing, the railway bridge at Dnepropetrovsk. ... The north-to-south link behind the German lines was equally unsatisfactory.

When it came to bringing up fresh troops or quickly switching forces behind the front, therefore, the German Supreme Command found itself at a permanent disadvantage vis-à-vis the enemy, who had much more efficient communications in every direction.'

As usual, it is impossible to find fault with Manstien's logic and deductions. This situation was at the root of the Germans' supply problems, which were raised with Hitler before the offensive by Halder and the Army Quartermaster General, Wagner.

The Red Army did finally attack on 19 November in the sector of the Romanian Army north-west of Stalingrad, as predicted by Zeitzler and feared by Manstein. The Fuhrer was at Obersalzberg and Speer, who happened to be there at the same time, recalled:[62]

'Hitler paced back and forth in the great hall of the Berghof.

'Our Generals are making their old mistakes again. They always overestimate the strength of the Russians. According to the front line reports, the enemy's human material is no longer sufficient. They are weakened: they have lost too much blood. But of course nobody wants to accept such reports. **Besides, how badly Russian officers are trained! No offensive can be organised with such officers. We know what it takes! In the short or the long run the Russians will simply come to a halt. They'll run down. Meanwhile we shall throw in a few fresh divisions; that will put things right [Author's emphasis].**'

Things looked somewhat different to Zeitzler in the cold light of day. Upon receiving the report of heavy artillery fire, which could only presage the beginning of a Red Army attack, he immediately telephoned Hitler to obtain release of the reserve which had been created to assist in such an eventuality – the two divisions of Panzer Group H, which it will be remembered consisted of one understrength German panzer division and the Romanian Armoured Division, which was not fully trained or equipped. Zeitzler noted:[63]

'I telephoned him, told him the news, and with considerable difficulty persuaded him to release Panzer Corps H from OKW reserve and give it to Army Group B. He would have preferred to postpone this decision even then, and await further reports from the front. **It required, as usual, a tremendous effort to convince him that it would then be too late [Author's emphasis]**....

'Then, under cover of a heavy snowstorm and with the thermometer showing 20 degrees of frost Centigrade, the Red Army attacked. A mass of tanks advanced on the Rumanians, with infantry riding on them or following close behind. The Russians everywhere enjoyed immense numerical superiority. Almost immediately the Rumanian front became a scene of chaos and utter confusion.'

Zeitzler related that in the succeeding days he proposed on a number of occasions that the Sixth Army be allowed to withdraw from its exposed position, but that Hitler would not countenance any such move. While he was forced to await Hitler's return to Fuhrer Headquarters at Rastenburg, he received a telephone call from Jodl, who was with Hitler in his train, proposing a solution to the evolving disaster:[64]

'General Jodl said, on the telephone, that the Army High Command should consider whether it would not be possible to bring up one armoured division from Army Group A, in the Caucasus, to act as a reserve behind the endangered front of Army Group B. Such was the solution to the crisis as envisaged aboard Hitler's command train. ...

'I was astonished and asked that I might speak to Hitler personally [Author's emphasis]. Again I asked permission to order the withdrawal of the Sixth Army. His tone was icy. He said: "We have found another expedient which Jodl will tell you about. We will talk it over tomorrow."'

Zeitzler was told that Hitler could not see him before noon the next day because he would be tired from his train trip, but the Chief of the General Staff realized that the dire situation required a more urgent decision:[65]

'I ignored these instructions, and at midnight, when his train was expected to arrive, I was waiting at his Supreme Headquarters. I insisted that he see me at once, for time was now of vital importance and even a few hours' delay could endanger the success of the operation which must be decided on immediately. To begin with both Hitler and his entourage were furious that I should have appeared there at midnight instead of waiting until noon on the following day. However, I was at last admitted to his presence. ...

'He came to me, hand outstretched, a beaming smile on his face, deliberately radiating confidence and hope. He shook me by the hand and said: "I thank you. You have done all that could be done. I myself would not have been able to do more, had I been here." Then, since I took care that my expression remained grave, he allowed a certain note of pathos to creep into his voice. He went on: "Don't let yourself be upset. We must show firmness of character in misfortune. We must remember Frederick the Great.'"

Zeitzler proceeded to conduct Hitler through an analysis of the situation, with reports from the commander of Army Group B, Field Marshal von Weichs, and other data that conclusively showed that the Sixth Army could not be relieved if it was surrounded in Stalingrad. This information clearly indicated that unless Sixth Army was permitted to withdraw it would be encircled, a situation that Zeitzler said 'must be avoided at all costs'. He later recalled:[66]

'At this point Hitler interrupted me. He lost his temper and referred to the solution which he and Jodl had worked out together. This was the transfer of the single panzer division from the Caucasus. I had expected this and could now give a detailed survey of transport conditions together with the estimated date of arrival of the division in question and the earliest possible date by which it might be expected to go into action. This would be at least a fortnight hence. ...

'Hitler lost his temper again and began to interrupt, but I went on: There is therefore only one possible solution. You must immediately order the Stalingrad army to turn about and attack westwards. This will save the Sixth Army from encirclement, will inflict great damage on the Russian armies that have broken through, and will enable us to use the Sixth Army in building a new front further to the west.

'**Hitler now lost all self-control. He crashed his fist down on the table shouting: "I won't leave the Volga! I won't go back from the Volga! [Author's emphasis]**."

The Red Army pincers closed around Stalingrad on 22 November. Speer, at Supreme Headquarters, witnessed some of the most dramatic moments in the struggle to obtain Hitler's authority for the Sixth Army to mount a breakout. He recorded:[67]

'Stalingrad was encircled. Zeitzler, his face flushed and haggard from lack of sleep, insisted that Sixth Army must break out to the west. He deluged Hitler with data on all that the army lacked, both as regards to rations and fuel, so that it had become impossible to provide warm meals for the soldiers exposed to fierce cold in the snow swept fields or the scanty shelter of ruins. ...

'Finally, after the discussion had gone on for more than half an hour, Hitler's patience snapped: "**Stalingrad simply must be held. It must be; it is a key position. By breaking the traffic on the Volga at that spot, we cause the Russians the greatest difficulties. How are they to transport their grain from Southern Russia to the north? [Author's emphasis].**"'

One need hardly point out that whether the Soviets were able to transport their grain to the north, south, east or west was hardly a military consideration relevant to the dire situation of the German forces trapped in Stalingrad.

Two days later, Speer was witness to another scene that included Hermann Goering, the Luftwaffe Commander-in-Chief:[68]

'[T]he fate of the encircled army was finally sealed. For Goering appeared in the situation room, brisk and beaming like an operetta tenor who is supposed to portray a victorious Reich Marshal. Depressed, with a beseeching tone in his voice, Hitler asked him: "what about supplying Stalingrad by air?" Goering snapped to attention and declared solemnly: "My leader! I personally guarantee the supplying of Stalingrad by air. You can rely on that." As I later heard from [Luftwaffe Field Marshal – Author's note] Milch, the Air Force General Staff had in fact calculated that supplying the pocket was impossible. Zeitzler, too, instantly voiced his doubts. But Goering retorted that it was exclusively the business of the air force to undertake the necessary calculations.

'Hitler … revived at Goering's mere words, and had recovered all his old staunchness. "Then Stalingrad can be held! It is foolish to go on talking any more about a breakout of the Sixth Army. It would lose all its heavy weapons and have no fighting strength left. The Sixth Army remains in Stalingrad."'

Zeitzler's account of this episode is materially the same as that of Speer. He added that at the end of Goering's avowal that he could supply Stalingrad by air and Hitler's decision to leave the Sixth Army where it was, he said he would like to make one further request:[69]

'Hitler said: "What is that?"

'I said: "May I submit a daily report to you giving the exact tonnage of supplies flown in to the Sixth Army during the previous twenty-four hours?"'

Although Goering objected to this procedure, Hitler agreed. Needless to say, the amounts delivered did not reach anywhere near the bare minimum specified by Zeitler that the encircled army needed on a daily basis simply to survive, and which Goering had assured Hitler the Luftwaffe could provide. Zeitzler commented that the only thing he derived from this conference was 'the enmity of the Reichsmarschall'.[70]

Panzer Group H, which had been formed at Zeitzler's instigation, was committed to battle as soon as possible to try to stem the Red Army's attack. Unsurprisingly, its strength was far short of that required to resist the forces committed to the Red Army offensive. However, this did not seem apparent to Hitler. Manstein noted that a number of counterattacks by the panzer group had been unsuccessful, and its understrength divisions were now encircled and attempting to fight their way out:[71]

'The corps commander, General Heim, had already been replaced on orders from Hitler and summoned to the latter's headquarters. There

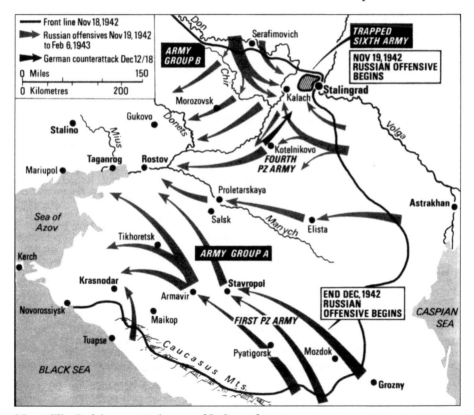

Map 6: The Red Army encirclement of Stalingrad.
This map clearly shows the effect of the Red Army counteroffensive, which encircled the Sixth Army at Stalingrad. Hitler had been warned on numerous occasions by Halder and Zeitzler that the deployment of the German forces would lead to exactly this result, but he ignored their advice. The Sixth Army was destroyed with over 200,000 casualties either dead or prisoners.

Hitler had sentenced him to death at a Court-Martial presided over by Goering, who was always available for tasks of this kind, on the ground that he, General Heim, was to blame for his corps' failure.'

Heim was later rehabilitated, but this episode shows the poisonous nature of the Hitler's mind and the atmosphere that permeated his Supreme Headquarters.

The only hope for the Stalingrad 'fortress', which Hitler had proclaimed it to be, was for it to be relieved as soon as possible by an attack commanded by Field Marshal Manstein. He was to take command of the newly formed Army Group Don, which was to consist of the Sixth Army (although Hitler stipulated that he was not allowed to order it out of Stalingrad), Fourth Panzer Army, Third Romanian Army and some other units attached for the purpose of the offensive. His task was specified as:[72]

'[T]o bring the enemy attacks to a standstill and recapture the positions previously occupied by us.'

This task was far beyond anything that could be achieved by the forces which were assigned to him. Manstein recalled:[73]

'[I] sent the Chief of the General Staff a teleprinter message pointing out that in view of the magnitude of the enemy effort, our task at Stalingrad could not be merely a matter of regaining a fortified stretch of front. What we should need to restore the situation would be forces amounting to an army in strength – none of which, if possible, should be used for counter-offensive until their assembly was complete.

'General Zeitzler agreed with me, and promised to try to let us have an armoured division and two or three infantry divisions by way of addition.'

Manstein recorded his evaluation of the situation on 24 November:[74]

'One thing was clear: even if we were able to raise the siege and re-establish contact, Sixth Army must on no account be left at Stalingrad. **The city's prestige value as far as we were concerned was non-existent [Author's emphasis].**'

This evaluation was, however, in stark contrast to Hitler's view of Stalingrad. This had been made clear in the Fuhrer's annual speech to the 'Old Fighters' of the Nazi Party in Munich on 8 November, to which he took his OKW entourage:

'But I wanted to come to the Volga, to a definite place, to a definite city. It accidentally bears the name of Stalin himself, but do not think I went after it on that account. ... A gigantic terminal was there; I wanted to take it. And you know, we're modest: that is we have it; there are only a couple of very small places left there.

'Now others say: Why aren't you fighting there? Because I don't want to make a second Verdun but would rather do it with very small shock units. Time plays no part here. **No ships come up the Volga any more - that is the decisive thing [Author's emphasis].**

'**... Whatever we once conquer, we actually hold on to so tightly that in this way at least no one else can dislodge us from wherever we gain a foothold. You may reply upon that [Author's emphasis].**'

Ignoring the obvious mistakes in the statement which must have made his senior military advisers cringe, having made this public statement, Hitler was very unlikely to ever countenance any withdrawal from Stalingrad because he believed that to do so would involve a loss of prestige for Germany with her allies as he stated on a number of occasions to Zeitzler and others. He undoubtedly also felt he would personally suffer loss of prestige, which seems to him to have been at least as important as Germany's loss. He repeatedly stated to his military advisors that he would never 'leave the Volga'. As there was no rational military reason to consign 220,000[75] of his own men to the hellish conditions they endured before either going into captivity or dying – or both – one can only assign Hitler's decision to ignore all his advisers and keep the Sixth Army at Stalingrad to a complete inability to differentiate between his duties as Supreme Commander of the Armed Forces or Commander-in-Chief of the Army and his vocation as a politician.

The units finally assigned to Manstein in Army Group Don included the Fourth Panzer Army, consisting of XVII Panzer Corps under General Kirchner, comprising the 6th and 23rd Panzer Divisions and 15th Luftwaffe Field Division, which were scheduled to arrive in the assembly area at Kotelnikovo by 3 December. A new formation, Army Detachment Hollidt, was to assemble in the sector occupied by the Third Romanian Army and consisted of the 62nd, 294th and 356th Infantry Divisions, while the XLVIII Panzer Corps under General von Knobelsdorff had the 11th and 22nd Panzer Divisions, 3rd Mountain Division and 7th and 8th Luftwaffe Field Divisions. These were expected to be available on 5 December. Manstein commented:[76]

'It was assumed from the start, of course, that the Luftwaffe divisions could at best be employed in some defensive role, such as shielding the flanks of the assault elements.

'The forces indicated – assuming they did become available in this strength and at the times stated – might conceivably suffice to make temporary contact with Sixth Army and restore its freedom of movement. In no event, however, could they administer a defeat big enough to enable us – as Hitler had put it in the jargon of static warfare – to re-occupy the positions held prior to the attack.'

Most of these forces did not become available, for a variety of reasons, including problems in transporting them from Army Group A to Army Group Don, being caught up in local crises which had to be dealt with and reinforcing the remnant of Third Romanian Army, which was under further attack. The forces that Manstein was left with for the relief effort were LVII Panzer Corps with two panzer divisions and XLVIII Panzer Corps with one panzer and one infantry division. With these forces it was impossible to carry out the planned operation to relieve the Sixth Army with any realistic hope of success.

Zeitzler provided the following comments on subsequent events:[77]

'The attack began on 12th December and we all awaited the first reports in great suspense. To begin with all went well, and Fourth Panzer Army advanced steadily. By December 18th Hoth's troops were only a little more than 40 miles from the southern perimeter of the so-called fortress. On the 19th an important river line, the Myshkova, was reached; on the 20th it was crossed. On the 21st Stalingrad was only about 30 miles away.

'And there the attack ground to a halt. Its momentum was exhausted. The troops, which were inadequate in number and desperately overtired, could only be supplied with great difficulty. Courage and determination could not alone compensate for these weaknesses.

'When it ground to a halt thirty miles from Stalingrad, the experts all knew immediately that this was the end. Not so Hitler. He told us to wait and see: the advance, he said, would certainly be resumed. It was not. On December 23rd the attack had to be finally called off.

'This was the very last moment at which the Sixth Army might still have been saved.

'Field Marshal von Manstein and I once again did all we could to persuade Hitler. Had the Sixth Army been given the order to break out, it would certainly have got through. The courage of desperation would have driven the soldiers on. Thus the final catastrophe would have been avoided. But the order to break out had to come from Hitler, and this he could not be persuaded to sign.

'Almost every night I passed several hours in his company, attempting to make him see reason. These scenes were, in their essence, repetitions of those already described.'

The result of this dismal record of appalling decisions on Hitler's part was the total destruction of the Sixth Army and the many support units attached to it.

There have been historians and other commentators who have attempted to justify Hitler's decision to leave the Sixth Army at Stalingrad as the only one available because by keeping it there it tied down Red Army forces which would otherwise have been able to attack elsewhere. Zeitzler specifically addressed this contention, as it was the very argument Hitler himself put forward:[78]

'If the Russians conduct their operations correctly – and we must assume that they will do so – they will leave the minimum number of divisions to encircle the Stalingrad army. They won't attack the fortress at all in the immediate future, but will continue to drive on westward with the mass of their forces. Our soldiers at Stalingrad will thus be compelled to accept their destiny without even fighting a battle. They will simply fall into the enemy's hand like ripe fruit.

'These predictions were proved to be correct.'

Zeitzler stated that he had this same argument with Hitler many times, both in private meetings and during the daily situation conferences. However, the answer from Hitler was always the same.

Zeitzler's view was that the best course for the Red Army to follow was to simply continue its attack westward and force the Germans further from Stalingrad with the formations that were not engaged there, which is exactly what they did. The main issue that arose from the arguments between Hitler, Zeitzler, Manstein and others as to the correct strategy to follow concerned when the withdrawal of the Stalingrad army could occur and be most effective. Zeitzler considered that the withdrawal must occur at the earliest possible moment to be most effective, and part of his proposal was that in breaking out of its encirclement the Sixth Army would attack and cause significant damage to Red Army units intending to encircle it, thereafter forming part of the forces used to reconstitute the German line to the west. Manstein's view was that 'Sixth Army must on no account be left at Stalingrad'.[79]

Clearly, these views were totally different from Hitler's opinion that the Sixth Army must stay where it was and absorb the offensive power of the Red Army forces which encircled it to save the rest of the German Front, and this is essentially how he justified his refusal to allow it to break out. The Fuhrer's 'strategy' undoubtedly condemned the German forces in Stalingrad to certain destruction from the moment it became clear where the Red Army was going to attack. The Romanian Army formations that collapsed when attacked should never have been committed to active operations in such a critical sector of the German Front. It must be remembered that the allied forces were in their exposed positions because Hitler deployed them there, knowing full well that they could not stand up to an assault by the Red Army despite being, as Manstein pointed out, behind the Don River.

In his evidence at Nuremberg, the following exchange occurred between Jodl and his defence counsel, Dr Exner:[80]

'DR. EXNER: Now, the witness Field Marshal Paulus stated before the Tribunal that the OKW was responsible for the order to hold Stalingrad; and, as a matter of fact, both Keitel and Jodl have been repeatedly accused by the foreign press of having given that disastrous order. Is that true?

'JODL: No, that is not true. The witness, for whom I feel the deepest sympathy and with whom I have worked in the most comradely fashion possible, could not have known anything at all about it. The facts are as follows: The moment danger threatened, the decision that Stalingrad must be held was made by the Fuehrer during a private conversation with Generaloberst Zeitzler and contrary to the latter's advice. Zeitzler told me so himself on his return from this interview.'

Jodl therefore indicated that Hitler's decision to keep the Sixth Army at Stalingrad was made once and for all when Zeitzler first raised the question with him, and that Hitler did not change his view subsequently regardless of any contrary views or options put to him. This corresponds with Zeitzler's recollections as previously noted.

According to Field Marshal Keitel, the correct strategy should have been as follows:[81]

'When the [Russian] counter-offensive began in November, perfectly positioned from the strategic viewpoint, first bowling over the [Third] Roumanian Army and thereby opening up deep into the flank of the Sixth Army, and when it was then on the point of surrounding Paulus's Army in Stalingrad, only one decision could possibly have staved off disaster: giving up Stalingrad and using the entire Sixth Army to fight its way out to the west.

'I have no doubt whatever that that would have worked out, that the Sixth Army would have been saved and the Russians probably defeated

– admittedly at the cost of giving up Stalingrad and our position on the bank of the Volga.'

This view, of course, corresponds with that of Zeitzler, but I can find no reference to Keitel having expressed it at the time of the events at Stalingrad.

Zeitzler recorded what Jodl and Keitel said when asked by Hitler for their opinions of what should be done at Stalingrad shortly after it was surrounded:[82]

'Keitel, standing to attention and with his eyes flashing said "My Fuhrer! Do not leave the Volga."

'Jodl spoke quietly and objectively. He weighed his words, which were as follows:

'"My Fuhrer! It is indeed a very grave decision that you now must make. If we retreat from the Volga it will mean the abandonment of a great part of the gains which we have reaped, at such heavy cost, from our summer offensive. On the other hand, if we do not withdraw the Sixth Army, its situation may become very serious. The proposed operations for its relief may succeed, or they may fail. Until we have seen the result of these operations, my opinion is that we should continue to hold out along the Volga."'

Thus fortified in his decision, Hitler continued to deny Zeitler's and Manstein's urgent and repeated entreaties to withdraw the Sixth Army. The situation that was faced once the relief operation had failed was significantly worse than it had previously been because of the deterioration in the condition of the Sixth Army resulting from the failure of the airlift to supply it. This failure inevitably resulted in the Army being less capable of fighting at anything like full efficiency because of lack of ammunition, petrol for its tanks and food for its men, all of which could have been foreseen and should have been taken into account when Hitler was making the vital decisions regarding its relief. These very problems were foreseen by Zeitzler and Manstein, but the evidence shows that Hitler would not listen to their continued requests for the withdrawal of the Army.

While the appalling events were playing out at Stalingrad, the fate of the whole of Army Group A in the Caucasus also teetered on the edge of catastrophe. If Hitler did not sanction its withdrawal in time, it would be cut off at Rostov, which the Red Army was approaching, deep in the rear of the

German forces, and in all likelihood surrounded. Just in time, Zeitzler was able to prevail upon Hitler to sanction the withdrawal:[83]

> 'One needed only to glance at the map in order to see that if the Russians continued to advance they would soon reach the Rostov area, and that if they captured Rostov the whole of Army Group A would be in imminent danger of encirclement.'

Zeitzler related that once the relief of Stalingrad had failed, he attempted on many occasions to obtain Hitler's assent for the withdrawal of Army Group A, but to no avail. Then Hitler suddenly changed his mind towards the end of December, but as Zeitzler recorded, even then it was not a straightforward matter:[84]

> 'I was alone with him. I had described the situation in the south, and I ended with the words:
> '"Unless you order a withdrawal from the Caucasus now, we shall soon have a second Stalingrad on our hands."
> 'This seemed to impress Hitler, and I thought he was about to waiver. I knew that I must exploit the moment to the full. I did so, and wrung a grudging approval from him. "Very well," he said at last, "go ahead and issue the orders." I left Hitler's room at once, but I did not go far. I telephoned from Hitler's own anteroom, where I gave the order for the withdrawal with an additional stipulation that it be passed on to the troops immediately and that the retirement was to be begun [*sic*] at once. My reason for doing so was a perfectly conscious one, and it was soon justified. I drove back to my own headquarters, which took rather less than half an hour, to find one of my staff officers waiting for me. An urgent telephone message had come in: I was to ring Hitler at once. Fully aware of what lay ahead, I picked up my telephone and asked for the connection. Hitler said: "Don't do anything just yet about the withdrawal from the Caucasus. We'll discuss it again tomorrow." This would, of course, have meant the first of an endless chain of postponements until once again it would have been too late. As it was, I was able to say: "My Fuhrer, it is too late. I despatched the order from your headquarters. It has already reached the front line troops and the withdrawal has begun. If the order is cancelled now, the confusion will be terrible. I must ask you to avoid that." He hesitated before saying: "Very well then, we'll leave it at that."'

1. General Dwight D. Eisenhower.
This picture of General Eisenhower was taken on 5 June 1944 when he was with the 101st Airborne Division. He had been told that there would be very high casualties among the airborne troops and wanted to be with them prior to their departure. He stayed until the last one was loaded onto the transport planes taking them to their vital missions in Normandy.

2. Field Marshal Ernst Busch.
Busch was unlucky enough to be in command of Army Group Centre when it was destroyed in Operation Bagration. Hitler ignored his requests for a timely withdrawal to maximise the defensive power of his Army which suffered virtual annihilation as the result.

3. Field Marshal Bernard Montgomery.

Montgomery's strategy for Normandy was to attract the German panzer forces onto the front of the British and Canadian army group and create the opportunity for the US 3rd Army to breakout from the US sector of the allied lodgement. His strategy was successful, and the German defenders of Normandy were all but destroyed in the resulting battle. Later during the 1944 Ardennes offensive, he made comments to a reporter which caused great offense to the senior commanders of the US Army which tended to imply that he had fixed problems created by the US commanders and caused hostility which remained until his death.

4. General Omar Bradley.

Bradley was a close colleague of Eisenhower and rose to 5 Star rank in the US Army. His role in the Normandy landings and battle was pivotal and involved commanding the breakout operation "Cobra" which led to the final disintegration of the German position in Normandy. He was much criticised for the disposition of the 12th Army Group before the 1944 Ardennes offensive most of which was made in retrospect, is unconvincing and out of context with the position which then existed. His response to the attack was co-ordinated with Montgomery and Eisenhower and led to its complete and irreparable defeat.

5. Field Marshal Gunter von Kluge.

For much of the war, Kluge was one of Hitler's favourite commanders and held several important commands on the Eastern Front. He was not a 'yes' man but knew how to argue with Hitler and not cause lasting offense. He was injured in October 1943 on the Eastern Front but was well enough to take command of the Normandy defense after Hitler sacked von Rundstedt in July 1944. He initially quarrelled with Rommel who Hitler had told him was not obeying orders but came to see that Rommel's view relating to the battle was correct. He committed suicide in August 1944 after the plot against Hitler as he had flirted with the conspirators and felt he would be implicated in it.

6. General Hasso von Manteuffel.

Manteuffel was the commander of the Fifth Panzer Army in the Ardennes offensive. Although it achieved the farthest penetration of the allied front, it was unable to take Bastogne which was critical to the success of the offensive. Manteuffel realised that the offensive had failed by late December 1944, but Hitler did not accept his view and ordered that it continue.

7. Field Marshal Friedrich von Paulus.

Von Paulus was a protégé of Hitler's having been promoted and made Deputy Chief of the General staff under Halder before being given command of the Sixth Army which had a critical role in Hitler's 1942 offensive aimed at taking Stalingrad and the Caucasus oil fields. The Sixth Army was surrounded in Stalingrad and destroyed thanks to Hitler's orders. He was promoted to Field Marshal by Hitler because he thought that this would motivate Paulus to commit suicide as no German Field Marshal had ever been taken prisoner. It did not.

8. Field Marshal Wilhelm List.
List was one of the most successful commanders in the German Army. He was blamed by Hitler for the failure of the 1942 offensive to take the Caucasus oil fields. Jodl defended him which led to a major conflict with Hitler who intended to sack Jodl and Keitel as a result but did not do so probably because of the complicated situation arising form the Stalingrad disaster. List was never used again in any command role after his sacking.

9. Marshal Georgy Zhukov.
Zhukov was appointed to key commands by Stalin during the war including the 1941 Moscow offensive, the offensive at Stalingrad in 1942, and the counter offensive at Kursk in 1943 following the German offensive and other major offensives in 1944 and 45 culminating in the attack on Berlin. He was probably the most successful of the Soviet Generals.

10. The Panzer V – Panther.

The Panther was a very powerful combination and was superior in single combat to almost all the allied tanks. However, it was expensive and time consuming to produce and there were never enough of them. Its interleaved drive bogeys were prone to becoming clogged with mud and this caused problems when it freezed during the winter on the eastern front.

11. The Panzer VI – Tiger 1.

The Tiger1 was a very powerful tank, but very heavy which caused problems in its commitment. It needed special flat cars for transport and had limited range on the battlefield. These were significant shortcomings, but its performance in combat was exceptional against all allied tanks. Like the Panther however, it was too expensive, took too long to make and there were never enough of them. It had the same problems with its interleaved bogeys as the Panther.

12. The Panzer VIb – Konigstiger.
The 'King Tiger'. Was the most powerful German tank produced in any numbers during the war. It was even heavier than the Tiger 1. It too took too long to make and was very expensive. It was committed in the Ardennes offensive.

13. The Soviet T34.
The T34 was a spectacularly successful design being upgraded several times during the war. To the end, it was competitive with the German tanks and was produced in such numbers that the Germans had the utmost difficulty dealing with it. It was a reliable and rugged tank which was used in Warsaw Pact and other armies for decades after WW2.

Army Group A was therefore saved, but the Sixth Army at Stalingrad was doomed. Its destruction was completed by the Red Army in a series of attacks that lasted from 10 January to 2 February, when the final Germans in the city gave up. Newly promoted Field Marshal Paulus was among those who surrendered, despite Hitler's expectation that he would commit suicide rather than be the first German officer of that rank to be taken prisoner.

Manstein made the following astute comments about Hitler's 'strategy' on the Eastern Front which led to the disaster at Stalingrad:[85]

> 'Hitler's principle, that every foot of ground had to be defended, in the hope that the Soviets would bleed themselves white in their attacks, would have had a certain justification if such a defense could have been conducted with sufficient forces. With the [divisional] frontages that existed this was not possible. ... [Hitler's direction] not only led to new crises and the danger of encirclement, but also vastly deprived the German side of the capability (by dissipating its strength) which lay in the superiority of its troops and commanders to conduct a mobile war of strategic movement.'

In the light of the facts previously reiterated, there seems no doubt that Manstein's comments are correct and his logic is unimpeachable.

Conclusions

The main conclusions that can be drawn from the evidence of the foremost military commanders involved in the 1942 summer campaign against the USSR – Halder, Manstein, Bock and Zeitzler – are as follows:

1. The plan for Hitler's 1942 offensive was far too ambitious and combines all the elements of his version of 'military command'. These errors included, firstly, that the operational plan for which he was responsible did not sufficiently concentrate the forces used for the tasks involved and had not been tested as would have been the case if the General Staff had been in command of the process.[86] General Siegfried Westphal's description of the blow being made 'not with a clenched fist, but with an open hand and the fingers extended' is perfectly apposite.[87] Secondly, the objectives were too far apart from each other and thereby lost the effect of the concentration that did exist. Thirdly, the changes Hitler made during the campaign did not contribute to the achievement of any of its objectives and complicated the serious problems that already existed relating to the supply of the

forces.[88] Fourthly, when he was told of the obvious danger that existed on the northern flank of the offensive to Stalingrad, he dismissed the concerns without due regard to the evidence that existed, and which he was told of by Halder and Zeitzler[89] of the preparations being made by the Red Army to take the offensive against the exposed flank. Fifthly, once the Red Army offensive began, he refused to take the only rational decision available which was to withdraw the Sixth Army and combine its breakout with the relief forces under Field Marshal von Manstein.[90] Sixthly, Hitler's acceptance of Goering's assurance that the Luftwaffe could supply the forces in Stalingrad was reckless in the extreme especially as he took no steps to determine whether the Luftwaffe could make good on Goering's assurance.[91]

2. The result of these decisions that Hitler was solely responsible was a strategic defeat of catastrophic proportions. There is no question that the timely withdrawal of the troops from Stalingrad would also have represented a defeat, but by adopting that course the human and material losses would have been minimised.

3. The reliance on Italian, Hungarian and Romanian allied formations – which were known to be inadequately trained and equipped to fight the Red Army – to take the place of German troops was foolhardy in the extreme. Nevertheless, these allied troops were placed by order of Hitler in the position of greatest risk in the whole Eastern Front. This decision was either based on an underestimation of the Red Army of grotesquely delusional proportions or evidenced that the Fuhrer was totally unable to understand the basic principles of military strategy; it is quite likely to have been a combination of both.

4. The supply arrangements for an offensive over such a large area were plainly inadequate. From a relatively early stage of the operation, the German forces were held up by foreseeable supply problems. Hitler was explicitly warned of this situation by Halder and Army Quartermaster General Wagner before the offensive was begun, but typically did not heed the advice given. This was also one of the results of Hitler neglecting to test the offensive plan, which had previously been the practice of the Army Supreme Command, as noted by Warlimont. This is another example of Hitler's amateurism at the most extreme and damaging level.

5. Hitler's many interventions in the disposition of the forces once the offensive was underway were the cause of numerous operational problems which could have been avoided. Halder's diary, Manstein's comments in *Lost Victories*, Zeitzler's exposition in *The Fatal Decisions*, Stone's comments in *Twilight of the Gods* and the record of the offensive in Kurowski's *Panzerkrieg* (an operational record of all the operations undertaken by the panzer forces

in the war) all provide clear evidence that this was the case. A particularly egregious example of this trait concerned the Fourth Panzer Army, when it would have been able to take Stalingrad early in the offensive, being moved to a position where it was not needed, and then being switched back when it was required, after which it had to counter stiff Soviet resistance that had developed at Stalingrad in the interim.

6. Once problems occurred as a result of the operations and dispositions he had ordered, Hitler blamed the Army commanders and sacked them without any justification. The sacking of Field Marshals von Bock and List were without any rational cause, and his assumption of the command of Army Group A when he was already Head of State, Supreme Commander of the Armed Forces and Commander-in-Chief of the Army is yet another grotesque example of his arrogance, hubris and conceit.

7. When the Red Army attack on 19 November placed the Sixth Army in peril, Hitler took undue notice of factors related to prestige – both his own and Germany's – which were entirely irrelevant to the purely military problems relating to the tactical and strategic position of the Sixth Army. He refused to adopt the only sound military solution that could have saved the Sixth Army from the predicament in which his specific orders had placed it, namely the immediate redeployment of the Army as advocated by Zeitzler and seconded by Manstein. The irrelevant considerations relating to prestige are revealed in the speech he made in Munich to the 'Old Fighters' of the Nazi Party on 8 November. The very fact that he was there shows that he did not properly understand the crucial military position of the German Army in the USSR, about which he had repeatedly been warned by Halder and Zeitzler.

8. Hitler's acceptance of Goering's assurance that the Luftwaffe could supply the forces at Stalingrad without further investigation was grossly reckless. This decision is all the more shocking when it is realized that the lives of approximately 220,000 German soldiers were in peril and the integrity of the whole of the German Eastern Front was at stake. The lack of any analytical process in this decision is key to understanding Hitler's complete unsuitability to be Commander-in-Chief of the Army and the undeniable consequences of his extreme amateurism.

9. Halder's diary entry of 23 July, which includes the phrase '*there is no room for any serious work*', encapsulates the problem of Hitler being the operational Commander-in-Chief of the Army. His life-long working patterns, inveterate impatience and lack of any process based on independent analysis – which he so abhorred – in his decision-making combined to make him completely unsuitable for a role that required precisely these

elements and the patience to watch a strategic plan evolve over the medium to long term. If any other instances of this incapacity are needed to confirm this as being the case, they can be found as noted in my first instalment of this series on the campaigns in Norway and France and in the earlier part of Operation *Barbarossa* referred to in the relevant sections of this book. The main difference in those campaigns to the Stalingrad campaign was that he did not then exercise operational command as Commander-in-Chief of the Army, which masked his influence to some degree. Furthermore, the 1940 campaigns were of relatively short duration, which gave a limited time for him to interfere. Once he arrogated the operational command of the German Army to himself, his unbridled influence was disastrous. In addition, his episodes of 'insane rage' – referred to in Halder's diary of 23 July, but also noted by others such as Guderian and Zeitzler – were not isolated instances but a normal pattern of working with Hitler. This was the polar opposite of the manner in which problems should have been resolved and trust engendered between Hitler and his senior army commanders in order that they be most effective.

The recovery of Army Group A from the perilous position in the Caucasus into which Hitler's orders had put it, and its subsequent operations under Field Marshal Manstein, showed that the German Army still outclassed the Red Army at that stage of the war when it was employed in mobile operations and properly commanded. This riposte, which stabilized the German Southern Front, was the antithesis of Hitler's policy of rigid defence, which basically just presented the Red Army with a series of stationery targets and allowed them to use the advantages which their superior numbers gave them while inhibiting those the Germans still enjoyed, namely superior tactical ability and flexibility.

In summary, any dispassionate review of the disaster that occurred to the Sixth Army can only conclude that it was the direct result of Hitler's disastrous assumption of the office of Commander-in-Chief of the Army. His complete lack of the necessary expertise to command the German Army in the field, together with his grotesque underrating of the Red Army, resulted in a plan of campaign that concentrated on non-military objectives that were beyond the power of the German Army to achieve. When this plan inevitably foundered, Hitler exacerbated its disastrous effects by refusing to countenance the retirement of the Sixth Army, leading to its entirely unnecessary destruction. It is an appropriate symbol of the utter waste and destruction caused to Germany by Hitler's rule.

Chapter 5

Operation *Citadel* – The Death Knell of the German Army in the East

The German summer offensive of 1943, Operation *Citadel*, intended to encircle and destroy the Soviet forces in the ·Kursk salient, is widely regarded as the last opportunity the Germans had to prevent total strategic defeat by the Red Army. It was also the last significant German offensive during the war and involved the largest tank battle in history, which the Germans and the Red Army fought at Prokhorovka on 12 July. The eventual German withdrawal was a strategic and tactical victory for the Soviets, and saw the initiative irrevocably move to them.

The strategic position, March 1943

The desperate defensive battles that had raged during the winter of 1942/43 after the German catastrophe at Stalingrad and withdrawal from the Caucasus caused great losses to both sides. Gradually, the Red Army's offensive was ground down, became overextended and was thwarted by counterattacks from Army Group South, masterminded by Field Marshal von Manstein. On 14 March 1943, Kharkov fell to Manstein's army group, and Belgorod was also retaken a few days later. The Red Army had suffered two defeats in quick succession, and by late March temporary stability returned to the Eastern Front. Amazingly, the front line closely resembled the position the previous summer when the Germans launched the offensive that ended at Stalingrad.

The most significant feature of the new front line was a large salient jutting west into German held territory, centred on the ancient city of Kursk and certain to exert a strong influence on the strategy of both the Red Army and the Germans. For the Soviets, it was a springboard enabling the development of future operations building on the achievements of the winter campaign, which had seen the Germans evicted from large parts of the territory they had conquered during their 1942 offensive. For the Germans, it presented an opportunity to envelop the significant Soviet forces within it and inflict a major defeat on the Red Army, enabling the negotiation of a stalemate peace which would leave them in possession of the territory they still controlled, or even the potential to recommence their quest for total victory.

Manstein observed that although the Germans had avoided a critical defeat by the Soviet forces in the winter of 1942/43, there was still much for the Supreme Command to do:[1]

> '[It] must strive with every means at its disposal to come to terms with at least one of Germany's opponents. Similarly it must realize the need to base its subsequent conduct of the war in the east on the policy of sparing its own forces – particularly by avoiding the loss of entire armies, as at Stalingrad – while seeking to wear down the offensive capacity of the enemy's. To that end, resolutely ignoring all secondary aspirations, it must switch the main effort to the Eastern theatre for so long as Germany's Western adversaries were unable to land in France.'

These comments invite the observation that by 1943, none of Germany's adversaries would have dealt with them on terms that would have been acceptable to Hitler, the only German whose opinion mattered in deciding on such matters. In December 1942 and again in June 1943, the Soviets made it known to the Germans through their Ambassador in Stockholm that they were willing to negotiate a separate peace.[2] This approach resulted from Stalin's fear that his Western Allies were watching from the sidelines while the two dictator powers fought a war of annihilation, which the West would allow to continue until both were exhausted and from which they could then profit. Stalin had come to this conclusion because he did not properly understand the difficulties associated with opening a 'Second Front' through the invasion of Europe and concluded – despite having no evidence to that end – that his allies were not committed to doing so. The Western Allies had publicly stated after the Casablanca Conference in January 1943 that they would accept no terms from Germany except unconditional surrender, so there was no hope of Hitler obtaining acceptable terms from them. His attitude to a separate peace with the Soviets is illustrated by the following statement he made to his Foreign Minister, Joachim von Ribbentrop:[3]

> 'You know Ribbentrop, if I came to an agreement with Russia today, I'd attack her again tomorrow. I just can't help myself.'

Manstein's first imperative, of reaching a negotiated compromise peace with one of Germany's adversaries, thus had no real chance of being achieved while Hitler was in power.

With respect to the changes needed to the strategy Germany followed, and the deployment of its forces, Hitler was again the immovable obstruction. There was no hope that he would ever voluntarily relinquish command of the Wehrmacht, and while he was at the apex of the command structure, the rational strategy that Manstein outlined was extremely unlikely to be implemented. The deployment of German forces in the occupied countries was largely dictated by the fact that they were held through coercion by Germany, but these deployments did not adequately reflect the urgency of the need to end or at least contain the growing crisis on the Eastern Front. In 1943, there were approximately fifty German divisions in occupied Europe, many of them in areas that were not critical to the survival of Germany, and they could have been spared for the emergency on the Eastern Front. The only time the Western Allies attacked the mainland of Europe in 1942 was at Dieppe, which was a complete failure and easily dealt with by the local German forces. The process of transferring any formations from one theatre to another could only be done with Hitler's authorization, and this would have meant changing his view of the necessary dispositions and the urgency of reinforcing the Eastern Front. So, while Manstein's proposed course of action was quite rational, it was never likely to be achieved with Hitler in power.

Manstein's two alternative strategies

The two strategic alternatives that Manstein put to Hitler in February regarding the most promising opportunities for taking the initiative from the Red Army during 1943 were as follows:[4]

> '[W]hether the overall situation allowed us to wait for the Russians to start an offensive and then to hit them hard "on the backhand" at the first good opportunity, or whether we should attack as early as possible ourselves [Author's emphasis] and – still within the framework of a strategic defensive – strike a limited blow "on the forehand".
>
> 'The Army Group preferred the former solution as one offering the best prospects operationally, and had already submitted a tentative plan to Hitler in February. It envisaged that if the Russians did as we anticipated and launched a pincer attack on the Donetz area from the north and south – an operation which could sooner or later be supplemented by an offensive around Kharkov – our arc of front along the Donetz and Mius should be given up in accordance with an agreed timetable in order to draw the enemy towards the lower Dnieper. Simultaneously all the reserves that could possibly be released – in particular the bulk of the

armour – were to assemble in the area west of Kharkov, first to smash the enemy assault forces that we expected to find there and then to drive into the flank of those driving in the direction of the lower Dnieper. In this way the enemy that be doomed to suffer the same fate on the coast of the Sea of Azov as he had in store for us on the Black Sea.

'The plan did not meet with Hitler's approval, however. ... what probably did most to prejudice him was his belief that we must fight for every foot of the ground he had won from Stalin in the winter of 1941 and which had in his view "saved the German Army from a Napoleonic retreat [Author's emphasis]". Besides this, however, he undoubtedly shrank from the risks which the proposed operation would assuredly entail. Inwardly, perhaps, he did not trust himself to cope with them, for in spite of having a certain eye for tactics, he still lacked the ability of a great captain.'

It is therefore clear that Operation *Citadel* as it actually played out did not reflect either of the strategies that Manstein had outlined to Hitler in February and occurred well outside the timeframe which he had envisaged for any attack to be made when his proposals were put forward. The reason for this was that Hitler determined the type of operation and when it would occur, and no-one else.

It is important to stress that while the German plan for *Citadel* appears in retrospect to be unrealistic and clearly beyond the power of the Wehrmacht in 1943, at the time the confidence that the Chief of the General Staff, General Zeitzler, felt to commit to an offensive was largely because no army had previously resisted the Germans in a major attack, either in the West or during Operation *Barbarossa*. Additionally, as the distances involved in the proposed offensive were not significant, the problems that had existed during the offensives in the previous two years regarding supply would not come into play.

The Red Army's strategy

The strategy of the Red Army was developed throughout April and revolved around the question of whether it would be best to strike first, as Stalin preferred, or to wait for the anticipated German attack, blunt its power from prepared defensive positions and then to attack. The Soviet Army and High Command had suffered at the hands of the Germans in 1941 and again in 1942, being initially unable to resist the German onslaught in both offensives. In addition, the offensives that Stalin had insisted upon in 1941 and 1942 following the apparent repulse of the Germans had ultimately been shown to be beyond the capabilities of the Soviet forces; they had underestimated the defensive power of the Wehrmacht and resulted in a series of costly victories and reverses. But Stalin, having learnt from the mistakes that he had made, asked the responsible commanders for their views on the best strategy for the summer 1943 period:[5]

'In fact, Stalin had always listened to and often taken the advice of his High Command. What happened from Stalingrad onwards was that he listened more, the advice got better and he got better at taking it. The Soviet generals as well as Stalin were on a steep learning curve from day one of the war and it was only through the bitter experience of defeat that they became better commanders and he became a better Supreme Commander.'

This is in marked contrast to the situation the German generals had to endure with Hitler, who rarely asked for advice and even more rarely took it, as Warlimont confirmed:[6]

'Orders were issued in a form which stifled all independent initiative; they were those of a self-satisfied know-all, shuffling battalions and divisions hither and thither and losing entire armies in the process. His pattern of personal behaviour was characterized by a complete absence of self-criticism; instead there was suspicion, nagging and raging against everybody, as a result of which the best brains in the Army gradually disappeared and proven Generals were passed on to history as cowards and traitors.'

Warlimont knew what he was talking about: he was in a unique position to observe Hitler as he was Deputy Chief of Operations at the OKW and in his presence just about every day for almost the entire war.

General Zhukov was ordered by Stalin to determine the best options and formulate a proposed strategy for the 1943 campaign. After discussing the options with senior officers of the Red Army and touring the probable Kursk battlefield himself, Zhukov proposed that they await the German attack before striking themselves. It was quite apparent to everyone that the most obvious course was for the Germans to attack at Kursk – but would they?

The Soviets were helped by some extremely valuable intelligence gained from an agent in Switzerland known as 'Lucy'. The Soviets believed that Lucy received secret information from a highly placed German source. However, the source he received his best information from was actually a British agent in Switzerland who was given highly secret 'Ultra' intercepted information to pass on to Lucy regarding the German armed forces in the USSR. This information included the German plans for *Citadel*. The British had another agent in Switzerland who also passed Ultra information to the Soviets. Ultra was the information derived from decryption at Bletchley Park in England of German transmissions using the Enigma encoding system of the German military. Ultimately, Stalin accepted the information as being genuine without knowing its provenance. Had he known that it came from the British, he probably would not have believed it, just as he had rejected British warnings – also gained from Ultra – prior to the German invasion which gave the exact composition of *Barbarossa* forces and the date of the attack.[7] The Soviets had other sources of information, which included their own agents, radio monitoring, reconnaissance and taking of prisoners through raids across the front line.

General Zhukov presented a strategic study to Stalin on 8 April, which concluded:[8]

> 'It would be better if we wore the enemy down with our defences and destroyed his tanks, and only then, after having moved up fresh reserves, went over to the offensive and destroyed his main force.'

This strategy was discussed at a meeting of Stalin, Zhukov and the Chief and Deputy Chief of Staff of the Supreme Command on 12 April:[9]

> 'Stalin accepted that the principal danger lay in the Kursk sector.... . Priority was to be given to the construction of a deeply echeloned defensive system within the Kursk salient.... . The troops were to dig in, a task to which they were ideally fitted by temperament and experience. At the same time, the Soviet defensive strategy was to be reinforced by the creation of a powerful reserve to the east of Kursk.'

This 'powerful reserve' was named the Steppe Front, and consisted of five rifle armies and a tank army, together with one tank, two mechanized and three cavalry corps, under the command of Colonel General I.S. Konev.[10] This force numbered approximately half a million men. There were also four air armies in reserve in the area, which together with the Steppe Front ground forces ensured that the German offensive had little prospect of success before it was even launched.

The Soviets constructed a series of defensive rings in the Kursk salient:[11]

'Each army in the first *front* echelon was to build three defensive lines: a main defensive zone, a second defense zone, and a rear army zone. In certain cases these zones were augmented by intermediate lines, such as along the Voronezh Front's right flank and center.

'Moreover, each *front* was to build three defensive lines: the first, second and third *front lines*, which in places were augmented by intermediate lines and reinforced along the most important axes by centers of resistance, which were built around large inhabited locales (Kursk, Staryi Oskol, Nowyi Oskol, and others).

'In this way, inside the fronts along the axes of the assumed enemy main attacks ... up to six defensive lines were to be built, which were consecutively echeloned to a depth of up to 110 kilometers along the Central Front and up to 85 kilometers along the Voronezh Front.

'... Maximum use was made in the defense construction of natural obstacles – the Severskii Donets, Psel, Svapa, Tim, Kisher and Don rivers, as well as the wooded expanses in the areas of L'gov, east of Sumy, Belgorod, Shebekino and Nechaevo.'

These defensive works were of unprecedented strength and depth, and the Soviet forces deployed to man them in the Kursk salient were as follows:[12]

The Central Front (on the northern side of the salient):

Forty-eighth Army – five rifle divisions.*

Thirteenth Army – nine rifle divisions, three tank brigades, nine artillery regiments, two anti-tank artillery regiments, six mortar regiments, two guard mortar regiments and one guards mortar battalion.

Seventieth Army – five rifle divisions, three tank regiments, seven artillery regiments, one anti-tank artillery regiment, two mortar regiments and two guards mortar regiments.

Sixty-fifth Army – nine rifle divisions, one rifle brigade, two ski brigades, three cavalry divisions, three tank brigades, one motorized rifle brigade, one artillery regiment, four anti-tank artillery regiments, five mortar regiments and two guards mortar regiments.

Sixtieth Army – three rifle divisions, four rifle brigades, two cavalry divisions, one ski brigade, one tank brigade, two artillery regiments, five anti-tank artillery regiments, four mortar regiments, two guards mortar regiments and one battalion of anti-tank rifles.

Central Front Reserve

Second Tank Army – four tank brigades and one tank regiment.

IX Tank Corps – three tank brigades and one motorized rifle brigade, 6th Guards Rifle Division, 2nd Anti-tank Artillery Division, one mortar regiment and two guards mortar regiments.

The Voronezh Front (on the southern side of the salient):

Thirty-eighth Army – four rifle divisions, one rifle brigade, two tank brigades, two artillery regiments, five anti-tank artillery regiments, two mortar regiments, one guards mortar regiment and one guards mortar battalion.

Fortieth Army – five rifle divisions, two tank brigades, one motorized rifle brigade, two tank regiments, six artillery regiments, five anti-tank artillery regiments, two mortar regiments and two guards mortar regiments.

Twenty-first Army – six rifle divisions, three artillery regiments, three guards mortar regiments, one guards mortar brigade and one battalion of anti-tank rifles.

Sixty-fourth Army – nine rifle divisions, one cavalry corps, two tank brigades, three tank regiments, two artillery regiments, four anti-tank artillery regiments and five battalions of anti-tank rifles.

Voronezh Front Reserve

Sixty-ninth Army – five rifle divisions, one tank brigade, three artillery regiments, two anti-tank artillery regiments and one mortar regiment.

First Tank Army – five tank brigades, three mechanized brigades, one motorized rifle brigade, three anti-tank artillery regiments, two mortar regiments, one guards mortar regiment and one guards mortar battalion.

(*the normal establishment of a Soviet rifle division in 1943[13] was 9,375, but a reduced establishment had been instituted which was 7,990, so they were considerably different to the normal establishment of a German infantry division.)

In addition to these forces was Konev's Steppe Front Reserve mentioned above.

The Soviet Air Force on the Central and Voronezh fronts consisted of the Sixteenth Air Army and Second Air Army, which had a combined total of 1,915 aircraft of all types. While the Soviets had a slight advantage in aircraft numbers, the Germans had technically superior types and their pilots were better trained.

The German plan for Operation *Citadel*

On 15 April, while Manstein was on medical leave, Hitler issued Operation Order No. 6, which detailed the plan as it had been developed until then:[14]

'[The attack] must seize the initiative for us in the spring and summer. Therefore, all preparations must be conducted with the greatest circumspection and enterprise. The best formations, the best weapons, the best commanders, and great stocks of ammunition must be committed to the main axes. ... The victory at Kursk must be a beacon to the entire world.'

A conference was held in Munich on 4 May, with Hitler, Manstein, Kluge, Zeitzler, Guderian, Model and Jeschonnek (the Luftwaffe Chief of Staff) in attendance. Field Marshal Walther Model, the commander of Ninth Army, had discovered through air reconnaissance that the Red Army had prepared exceptionally strong defences in precisely the areas that were to be attacked and questioned the wisdom of carrying out the operation in these circumstances. Zeitzler and Kluge were still in favour of carrying out the attack as planned, whereas Manstein indicated that the attack would have had a good chance of success if carried out in April but that he would now need further infantry to have enough power to fulfil his part of the plan. This infantry could not be provided. Guderian's view was that the operation was pointless and that the Germans should concentrate on building reserves in order to defeat any future Soviet offensives,[15] and also to have forces available if the Western Allies invaded Europe. Hitler, concerned that the attack needed more power to succeed, decided to delay the commencement date until June, when more Tiger tanks and the new Panther tanks would become available and in his opinion ensure the operation's success. This was also Zeitzler's view. Despite the hope the Fuhrer placed in them, the Panthers had not yet been committed to battle, their crews were unfamiliar with them and they were suffering from mechanical teething problems, so their value was, at this stage, questionable. There were also ninety Ferdinand heavy tank destroyers which could be deployed, but as these had no machine guns, they were vulnerable to infantry.

Manstein was sceptical of the value of delaying *Citadel*:[16]

'Hitler decided – against the advice of his two army group commanders – to postpone "Citadel" unril June, by which time, he hoped, our armoured divisions would be stronger still after being fitted out with new tanks. ... Nor would he recognise that the longer one waited, the more armour the Russians would have – particularly as their tank output undoubtedly exceeded that of Germany. As a result of delays in the delivery of our own new tanks, the Army Group was not ultimately able to move off on "Citadel" until the beginning of July, by which time the essential advantage of a "forehand" blow was lost. **The whole idea had been to attack before the enemy had replenished his forces and got over the reverses of the winter [Author's emphasis].'**

This latter point was the central matter to the whole plan of *Citadel*. Manstein's analysis of the strategic opportunity that he put to Hitler in February was based on the assumption that any operations undertaken must be implemented before the Soviets could recover from the losses they had suffered in the winter fighting and the two defeats which had been inflicted on them at Kharkov and Belgorod. The subsequent delays that were imposed by Hitler to add more firepower to the operation meant that the essential precondition for the attack – the comparative weakness of the Red Army – no longer existed.

Guderian met with Hitler again on 10 May. He noted that during their conversation, he pointed out his misgivings about the attack:[17]

"'I repeat my question: Why do we want to attack in the East at all this year?" Hitler's reply was: "You're quite right. Whenever I think of this attack my stomach turns over." I answered: "In that case your reaction to the problem is the correct one. Leave it alone." Hitler assured me that he had as yet by no means committed himself and with that the conversation was over.'

Despite these comments by Hitler, the much-delayed *Citadel* still went ahead. The forces committed to the attack included almost every formation that the Germans could spare, comprising the following:[18]

Northern Sector:

9. Armee:

XXIII Armee Korps – three infantry divisions and an additional grenadier regiment.

XXXXI Panzer Korps – one panzer division, two infantry divisions and two regiments of Ferdinand tank destroyers and Stug III assault guns.

XXXXVII Panzer Korps – one infantry division, three panzer divisions and Schwere Panzer-Abteilung 505 equipped with Tiger tanks.

XXXXVI Panzer Korps – four infantry divisions.

XX Armee Korps – four infantry divisions.

Reserves – two panzer divisions and one Panzergrenadier division.

The **Luftwaffe** drained every resource to make available the 1st Air Division, with approximately 700 aircraft of all types available.[19]

Southern Sector:

4. Panzer-Armee:

LII Armee Korps – three infantry divisions.

XXXXVIII Panzer Korps – two panzer divisions, one Panzergrenadier division with an extra regiment of Tiger tanks and an independent brigade of Panther tanks.

II SS-Panzer Korps – 1st SS-Panzer Division, including a regiment of Tiger tanks, and two SS-Panzergrenadier divisions with two regiments of Tiger tanks.

Armee Abteilung Kempf

III Panzer Korps – three panzer divisions, one infantry division and schwere Panzer-Abteilung 503 equipped with Tiger tanks.

XXXXII Armee Korps – three infantry divisions and Panzer-Abteilung 560 equipped with 88mm mobile tank destroyers.

XI Armee Korps – two infantry divisions.

Field Army Reserves – XXIV Panzer Korps with one panzer division, one Panzergrenadier division and one SS-Panzergrenadier division.

The **Luftwaffe** provided support for the southern attack through Luftflotte 4, with approximately 1,000 aircraft available.[20]

In total, there were twenty-three Army infantry divisions, twelve army panzer divisions, three army Panzergrenadier divisions, two regiments of Ferdinand tank destroyers, two divisions equipped with Tiger tanks, one brigade of Panther tanks, the 1st SS-Panzer Division and two SS-Panzergrenadier divisions. The Luftwaffe contributed approximately 1,700 aircraft of all types.

The German strategy was that the two armies would attack simultaneously from the north and south of the neck of the salient, surround the Soviet forces in it and then destroy them. This strategy had worked previously and, given the unprecedented number of armoured divisions and the new types of tanks being committed, should work again – or so Hitler thought.

The Germans attack

Operation *Citadel* was launched early on the morning of 5 July, three months later than Manstein had indicated was the best time to do so and against a thoroughly prepared opponent, which was the absolute antithesis of his original plan outlined to Hitler in February.

Model's assaulting forces became entangled in the web of Soviet defences from the start and made little headway, penetrating only 11 miles after four days and taking very heavy casualties in doing so. On 12 July, Model intended to attack with his armoured reserves to provide greater impetus, but the Red Army meanwhile assaulted Army Group Centre's front near Orel, pre-empting Model's renewed attack and requiring his armoured forces to be deployed there. Model's army's offensive part in *Citadel* was thus finished.[21]

Manstein's attack made better progress and on 6 July he asked for the release of XXIV Panzer Corps to reinforce it, but his request was refused and although he asked twice more, the authorization was never given by Hitler. On 12 July, the famous engagement involving German and Soviet armour occurred at Prokhorovka, which was the largest tank battle in history. Although the Germans held off the Soviet armour, in doing so they took casualties which they could not afford.

Manstein and Kluge received orders to attend a conference with Hitler at Rastenburg on 13 July. To say the least, this was a ridiculous time for Hitler to have both of the most senior commanders leave the battlefield. Manstein subsequently stated that Hitler should have either come forward to see the two commanders and discuss the situation with them there[22] or sent the Chief of the General Staff to do so, and it is impossible to argue with this view.

The two field marshals met with Hitler on the evening of 13 July at the Fuhrer HQ, as related by Manstein:[23]

'He opened the conference by announcing that the Western Allies had landed in Sicily that day and that the situation there had taken an extremely serious turn. ... it was necessary to form new armies in Italy and the western Balkans. These forces must be found from the Eastern Front, so Citadel would have to be discontinued.

'Thus the very thing had come to pass of which I had warned Hitler in May.

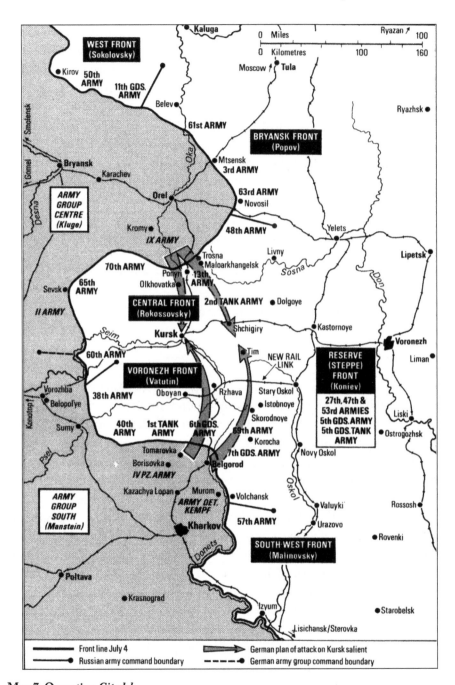

Map 7: Operation *Citadel*.

The map shows the intention of the German attack which was to cut off the forces in the Kursk salient and destroy them. The attack was unsuccessful mainly because the Red Army forces were too well entrenched in defensive positions of unprecedented strength and depth. The German forces incurred casualties in the subsequent Soviet counteroffensive, which were beyond their power to replace.

'... Speaking for my own Army Group, I pointed out that the battle was now at its culminating point, and to break it off at this moment would be tantamount to throwing victory away. On no account should we let go of the enemy until the mobile reserves he had committed were completely beaten.

'Nevertheless, Hitler ruled that "Citadel" was to be called off on account of the situation in the Mediterranean and the state of affairs in Central Army Group. The only concession he would make was that Southern Army Group should continue the attack until it had achieved the aim of smashing the enemy's armoured reserves. As a matter of fact not even this could be accomplished, for only a few days later the Army Group was ordered to hand over several armoured divisions to Central Army Group.

'... And so the last German offensive in the east ended in fiasco.'

Manstein's verdict seems to be a fitting description of affairs.

Lost opportunity?

The Kursk offensive has provoked a great deal of discussion over the ensuing years concerning whether there was ever an opportunity for the Germans to stem the Soviet tide at that time. Both sides had suffered huge losses during the two previous winter campaigns, neither having been able to achieve a strategic victory during that time. However, while the Germans' strength had been reduced by their losses, the Soviets had been able to augment their power irrespective of the casualties they had suffered. This was due to the larger manpower of the USSR but also to the deliberate moving of thousands of factories from the European territories of the USSR to sites further east, far away from the range of the Luftwaffe's bombers. The production from these facilities began to materialize during the winter of 1942/43, with Soviet arms production – particularly in tanks and artillery – significantly higher than that of Germany as is evidenced by Annexure 1. Additionally, Lend-Lease supplies from its Western Allies were starting to be a factor in Soviet capabilities. Consequently, Manstein's proposed policy of strategic defence was the only way that Germany could have hoped to defend against the Red Army.

Hitler's decision to risk everything in the attack at Kursk was an entirely characteristic gamble, as a result the Germans suffered losses from which they never recovered, accentuating the difference between their forces and the Soviet's. The opportunity that Manstein had highlighted was intended to be in the context of an overall strategic defensive stance, which Hitler ignored, and which had to be taken advantage of with great speed, which again Hitler did not do.

Manstein intended an operation that would take advantage of the higher level of operational skill which still existed in the German forces but which Hitler never fully understood. This was probably why he was so reluctant to allow his commanders to conduct a flexible defence entailing tactical manoeuvre, instead insisting upon his doctrine of inflexible defence which was so unnecessarily destructive to the Wehrmacht.

Had Manstein's proposed offensive been implemented as he intended, the result would probably not have been a strategic German victory, but may have caused substantial – although temporary – damage to the Soviets. It may therefore have led to a tactical German victory, but would not have materially altered the ensuing course of operations on the Eastern Front.

Conclusions

1. Manstein's strategy options presented to Hitler in February 1943 were based on the assumption that any German attack to 'pinch out' the Kursk salient would be made before the Red Army had time to recover from the casualties it had suffered during the winter campaign and the two recent defeats at Kharkov and Belgorod. Hitler's repeated delays in launching the attack meant that the essential basis Manstein put forward was entirely negated.

2. The preferred strategy that Manstein outlined to Hitler in February was to await the Red Army's attack and defeat it, as had been done at Kharkov. Hitler did not wish to undertake such a strategy, probably, as Manstein opined, because of his overriding demand to hold on to every square yard of land that the Germans had taken. This 'strategy' was not possible because the German Army did not have sufficient forces to do so, as was pointed out on numerous occasions by Manstein and others including Zeitzler, Halder, Brauchitsch and Rundstedt.

3. The additional forces that Hitler insisted be used in the attack were shown to be insufficient to achieve success. In particular, the use of the Panthers before the crews had completed the necessary training and their mechanical troubles had been ironed out meant that these new tanks were of little value on the Kursk battlefield. Similarly, sending the Ferdinand tank destroyers without sufficient infantry support meant that they were unable to use the advantages provided by their formidable firepower and armour, and as they had no secondary armament to deal with infantry they became sitting ducks for the Soviet troops.

4. Hitler's decision to suspend the operation in the circumstances which then existed may have been correct. However, it cannot be denied that he had created conditions under which it could not succeed because of the delays he caused in the timing and planning for the offensive. As he was the self-appointed Commander-in-Chief of the Army and in operational control of all its activities, he must bear the responsibility for the *Citadel* disaster.

The German situation on the Eastern Front was fundamentally altered by this defeat, and they were never able to regain the initiative for the remainder of the war.

Chapter 6

D-Day and the Normandy Campaign, 1944

The landings at Normandy by the Western Allies on 6 June 1944 were the largest and most complex combined services military operation ever undertaken to that time. They represented the supreme vindication of Britain's policy to pursue the war against Nazi Germany when all had seemed lost after the numerous defeats suffered in Norway, France, North Africa, Greece and Crete and the conquest of most of its Asiatic empire by Japan. The invasion of France was also the physical evidence of the material might of the Western Allies, which created an insuperable problem for the Germans, who had no hope of matching the air power or mechanized armies opposing them now that the full strength of the USA was engaged in the war effort alongside the forces of the British Empire.

That the landings and subsequent campaign were spectacularly successful is now history, but at the time there was great apprehension among senior levels of the Allies' military and governments with respect to both the anticipated level of casualties and whether the invasion would even succeed. There were known to be between fifty and sixty German divisions in France, including some of the best they had, and Germany's soldiers had shown many times how well they could fight, even in the most difficult circumstances and even, inexplicably to the Allies' mind, for the odious Nazi regime. This level of anxiety regarding the unknown aspects of the risks which were part of the invasion and the options available to Hitler are captured by General Lord Ismay who was the Deputy Secretary of the British War Cabinet and worked very closely on a daily basis with Churchill throughout the whole of the war in his memoirs where he states with respect to Hitler:[1]

'[I]n the defeat of Overlord lay his only chance of survival. Surely he would withdraw all his best troops from Italy, the Balkans, the Aegean Islands, Scandinavia, and the rest, in order to form a mass of manoeuvre to strike at our landings. Surely the almost unlimited labour at his disposal would enable him to make the Atlantic Wall impregnable. Surely he would be ready to transfer the greatest possible strength from his eastern to his western front immediately we set foot in France. Surely he would make superhuman efforts to bring his secret weapons – the V1 and V2 – into operation against our invasion forces as they concentrated for embarkation. Surely he would try to conserve his air forces for Der Tag, and accept punishment elsewhere in the meanwhile. But, as the weeks passed, he did not appear to be attaching undue importance to Overlord. He continued to refuse to give up an inch of ground anywhere.'

There had been great pressure on the Western Allies from Stalin since the German invasion of the USSR for the 'second front' – the invasion of France – to be initiated as soon as possible, causing friction and some ill-feeling between the Allies. But the date had finally been fixed for the landings during the Casablanca Conference, where Churchill and Roosevelt met in January 1943. Churchill then broke the news to Stalin that the second front would not be occurring as early as previously envisaged, but did promise it would happen in 1944, along with earlier operations aimed at knocking Italy out of the war following the successful conclusion of Operation *Torch* in North Africa. Although there were more delays before the invasion of occupied Europe occurred, the stage was finally set for the grand drama of the war in the West.

Churchill's commitment to the invasion

There has been a misinterpretation by some historians of the position of Churchill and the British Chiefs of Staff regarding Operation *Overlord*, to the effect that they were opposed to or delayed it because of fears about the level of casualties. However, this view is incorrect. Churchill was undoubtedly concerned with the difficulties that had to be overcome and the potential of a disastrous defeat. But there is equally no doubt that he did everything in his power to expedite the timing of the invasion, as shown by his decision to become personally involved in the planning and execution of *Overlord*, as noted by Ismay:[2]

'The Prime Minister, as soon as he returned from Marrakesh [in January 1944], decided that he would preside over a weekly conference on Overlord preparations. There was no limit to the range of problems which had to be settled. One day it might be a shortage of tugs; on another, it might be the bombing policy to be followed in the pre-Overlord period; on yet another the construction of the various component parts of the artificial harbours. But whatever the problem the Chairman's fiery energy and undisputed authority dominated the proceedings. Everything had to be done at once, if not sooner; the seemingly slothful or obstructive were tongue lashed; competing differences were reconciled; priorities were settled; difficulties which at first appeared insuperable were overcome; and decisions were translated into immediate action.'

It must be remembered that Ismay was Deputy Secretary of the War Cabinet and worked with Churchill on a daily basis for the entire war. If there had been any hint that Churchill was not totally committed to the invasion, he was in a unique position to see it, and to raise it with the Cabinet if there had been any evidence of such a position. There is not the slightest hint that this was the case, only that Churchill, along with everyone else in a position of senior responsibility was worried regarding the level of potential casualties and the difficulties involved in the military aspects of the invasion which, because of the unique nature of the operation, was only reasonable and quite understandable.

There were two main reasons for the delays to the invasion date. The first was that the build-up of US troops in Britain was not as rapid as expected. This was caused by shipping constraints, which were affected by the losses that had been suffered in the U-boat war, the needs of the war in the Pacific – which was fought over extremely long distances, almost entirely by shipborne forces – and the global nature of the Allied operations, involving forces in Asia, the Middle East and Europe, not to mention the Lend-Lease supplies going to the USSR. The other main reason for the delay was more prosaic – there needed to be a supply of enough landing craft because the seaborne Normandy invasion was enlarged from an original three-division landing to one involving five divisions. This factor was noted by General Dwight D. Eisenhower, the Supreme Commander of SHAEF – Supreme Headquarters Allied Expeditionary Force – in his memoirs:[3]

'Two considerations, one of them decisive in character, combined to postpone the target date from May to June. The first and important one was our insistence that the attack be on a larger scale than that originally planned ... we had to have the additional landing craft and other gear essential to the larger operation, even if this meant delaying the assault by a month. **To this the Combined Chiefs of Staff agreed [Author's emphasis]**.'

The eventual success of the operation fully justified both the enlargement of the forces involved and the delay of its launching.

The German command structure in Western Europe

When Hitler dismissed Field Marshal Brauchitsch and took the role of Commander-in-Chief of the Army himself on 19 December 1941, one of the results was that many of the functions that had previously been performed as part of Brauchitsch's role were delegated. Lieutenant General Adolf Heusinger was in charge of the Operations Planning section of the OKH for much of the war, and his career continued after the conflict when he became the first Inspector General of the West German Bundeswehr. In his book *Befel im Widerstreit* (Command in Turmoil), he commented on the effect of Hitler becoming the C-in-C of the Army:[4]

> 'Hitler is apparently interested only in two things, the actual directions of operations and the personnel department. Thus all important matters are concentrated in his hand. No one is at the moment responsible for training, organization, replacements, administration, the work of the inspectorates of each arm of the Service, or for education. Keitel is supposed to undertake the greater part of these difficult jobs, to some extent as Hitler's deputy. Soon he won't know whether he is Chief of OKW or Deputy Commander-in-Chief of the Army. Everything else will be left to the Chief of Staff of the Army. **The chaos at the head of affairs is becoming greater every moment [Author's emphasis]**.'

It is indeed ironic that in a state where unlimited power was placed in one man's hands and the whole basis of its system was the '*Fuhrerprinzip*',[5] the lines of responsibility in the command structure of the armed forces were so blurred, overlapping and redundant. Nowhere was this more apparent than the command structure of the German forces in France and Western Europe. There is no doubt that this confusion was intentional on Hitler's part to reduce the power of his senior military commanders, very few of whom he trusted, and to ensure that he was the only person able to exert control over the operations of the entire armed forces.

The various headquarters that had jurisdiction over German forces in France on 6 June 1944 were as follows:

Supreme Commander of the Armed Forces, Adolf Hitler.

Oberkommando der Wehrmacht (OKW), the Armed Forces High Command; Hitler's personal military command staff. Its chief was Field Marshal Keitel. OKW Reserves in France, which could not be committed without Hitler's agreement, comprised the 1st SS-Panzer Corps HQ –

with the 1st SS-Panzer Division, 12th SS-Panzer Division and 17th SS-Panzergrenadier Division – and the Panzer Lehr Division.

Oberkommando des Heere (OKH), the Army High Command; the Supreme Command of the Army. Hitler was its Commander-in-Chief.

Oberkommando der Luftwaffe (OKL), the Air Force High Command; the Supreme Command of the Air Force. Reichsmarschall Goering was its Commander-in-Chief.

Oberkommando der Marine (OKM), the Naval High Command; the Supreme Command of the Kriegsmarine. Grand Admiral Karl Doenitz was its Commander-in-Chief.

These Supreme Commands exercised command through a number of headquarters specific to the Western theatre of operations:

OB West (Oberbefehlshaber West), Field Marshal von Rundstedt. Commander-in-Chief of the Army in France, Belgium and the Netherlands. The formations subordinate to it were:

Army Group G, commanded by Colonel General Johannes Blaskowitz, consisting of the First and Nineteenth Armies, with reserves of the LXVI Corps, 157th Infantry Division and LVIII Panzer Corps, consisting of the 9th Panzer Division, 11th Panzer Division and 2nd SS-Panzer Division.

Army Group B, commanded by Field Marshal Erwin Rommel, consisting of the Fifteenth and Seventh Armies, Second Parachute Army and LXXXVIII Corps in the Netherlands. Army Group B had the 2nd, 116th and 21st Panzer Divisions under its command. Rommel's line of responsibility was however somewhat unclear owing to his relationship with Hitler.

Panzer Group West, General Geyr von Schweppenburg. This had no operational command responsibilities; it supervised the training of all panzer units in the West and advised Field Marshal von Rundstedt on matters pertaining to panzer forces. This headquarters was to take over command of panzer forces in France once the invasion had occurred, which would introduce yet another level of command into the already unclear structure.

Third Air Force, commanded by Field Marshal Hugo Sperrle. It had four air corps and three flak corps under its command. Its power had been reduced greatly by June 1944, and it was unable to have any effect on the total command of the airspace over Normandy and Western Europe enjoyed by the Allies.

Navy Group West, commanded by Admiral Krancke. It commanded naval units, shore installations and naval coastal batteries in the Western theatre of operations. The naval forces at its command were insignificant light forces that were unable to make any material contribution to defeating the Normandy landings. U-boats were quite ineffective in the waters around Normandy and the English Channel as they were too shallow and the currents were strong, making any attacks problematic.

Military Governors of France, North-West France and Belgium. These commanded the security troops in those areas.

It was thus possible for an army unit to be subordinate to five separate levels of headquarters.

Further 'refinements' to this structure meant that the heavy artillery in the Atlantic Wall coastal defences was subject to the jurisdiction of the Kriegsmarine, the flak units attached to the Army were subject to the jurisdiction of the Luftwaffe, the SS units were responsible to Reichsfuhrer-SS Heinrich Himmler and only under the tactical command of the Army, and OB West had jurisdiction over the Army's forces for coastal defence only. This Byzantine structure worked in one sense only, and that was to dissipate the authority of the military commanders and entrench that of Hitler.

An example of the practical problems caused by these arrangements was given in a report by Lieutenant General Max Pemsel, Chief of Staff of the Seventh Army in Normandy. He noted:[6]

'For the naval coast artillery, however, there was the restriction that any fire mission against an enemy on the sea was to be directed by the naval commanders, even though naval command posts were often a great distance from the local Heeres [army] commander. Only after the enemy had succeeded in landing was fire control to be transferred to the Heer.'

Lieutenant General Hans Speidel, who was Chief of Staff to Rommel at Army Group B, described the command structure in the West as:[7]

'The organization of major commands in the West corresponded neither to the timeless laws of warfare nor to the demands of the hour or of reason. Hitler thought he could carry through also in waging war the revolutionary principle he practiced everywhere of division of power and playing forces against each other to his own advantage. This led not only to confused chain of command, but to a command chaos.'

Speidel makes a very relevant point – it must be remembered that Hitler was a revolutionary politician, not a military man. His methods were developed during the Nazi Party's 'time of struggle' when he rose to lead Germany against his political opponents. The day-by-day tactics he used against these opponents and against resistance from within his own party were those he subsequently tried to apply to managing the military command structure. However, while 'divide and conquer' worked in the political sphere, it was totally inappropriate for creating a military chain of command where unity of purpose and clarity of hierarchy are absolutely fundamental for optimum results.

Perhaps the last word on arrangements relating to the command structure should be left to General Geyr von Schweppenburg, the Commander of Panzer Group West:[8]

'Authority to make strategic decisions passed from seasoned soldiers, well experienced in the special conditions of their respective theatres of war, to a self-complacent and pretentious dilettante, and was affected by a combination of influences. In comparison to this system, the former Vienna Court and War Council [the body directing the armies of the Habsburg Empire from the sixteenth century onwards] was a respectable and reasonable command unit.'

German strategy against an invasion

Lieutenant General Bodo Zimmerman, Chief Operations Officer to OB West, wrote a treatise on the German position in the Western theatre that was included in *The Fatal Decisions*. In it, he described their situation as follows:[9]

'The Western Army was spread in a great bow, with most of its forces disposed on or close to the coast. The bow stretched from Holland, along the Channel and Biscay coasts, to the Pyrenees, then along the Mediterranean to Toulon. ... Many German troops were locked up in the so-called "fortresses," which included exposed islands as well as fortified bases. In the Channel Isles alone, there were some 30–40,000 men consisting of one reinforced infantry division, one anti-aircraft brigade, numerous heavy naval batteries, engineers and construction workers of the Todt Organisation. This large body of troops held this isolated position, where the problems of supply were already so great that an entire year's stocks were accumulated, on Hitler's direct orders. There could be no question of Rundstedt's evacuating this or any other area of his enormous front.'

Hitler had ordered that the Channel Islands be made into the 'strongest sea fortresses in the world'.[10] Looking at a map of the Channel Islands, it is easy to see how ridiculous it was to tie up these men and resources. Any one of the Allied battleships that bombarded Normandy in June 1944 could have reduced all the German positions in the islands to rubble if it was thought important enough to do so, but the whole 'fortress' was ignored on D-Day because it was strategically irrelevant. The vast expense to make and maintain these fortifications was a total waste, yet another decision that Hitler made despite the advice he was given by his military commanders.

Zimmerman continued:[11]

'During the spring of 1943 Rundstedt attempted to report to Hitler on the actual situation as it then existed in the West. It was time wasted. The interview on the Obersalzberg, which lasted for three hours, consisted of a two-hour monologue by Hitler giving his views on the Eastern Front, followed by a tea-hour during which the discussion of official matters was forbidden. Rundstedt's mounting fury, as he shifted in his chair, can easily be imagined.'

After this interview, Rundstedt ordered that a report be prepared which he sent to Hitler in the autumn of 1943. Its effect, according to Zimmerman, was 'something of a bombshell':[12]

'The report stated that most of the German soldiers in the West were too old. Officers with artificial limbs were not infrequent. A battalion had been formed of men suffering from ear complaints. Later, a division, the 70th, was created for men with poor stomachs who needed special diets. ... As for mobility, most of the units in the West were insufficiently flexible or even completely inflexible and therefore tactically of only limited value. There was a severe lack of heavy weapons and particularly of tanks – repeated crises in the East had nullified the expectations of reinforcements contained in Fuhrer Directive 51. Only a very few parachute and panzer divisions formed an exception to this depressing picture and could be regarded as theoretically fit for operations.

'Nor was this the end. There was no strategic reserve whatever in the West, though such a reserve was supposed to intervene rapidly and effectively at the point of main effort as soon as the invasion had begun. The Air Force was so weak that it could not hope to curb the operations of the R.A.F. and the U.S.A.A.F. The Navy consisted of a few motor launches and a couple of torpedo flotillas. Submarines could not operate properly in the Channel owing to its shallowness.'

Towards the end of 1943, Hitler sent Rommel to inspect the defences in the West and report back to him on what should be done to improve them. During the winter, Hitler decided to give Rommel a command in the West, and Rundstedt suggested that he take charge of the most likely invasion area from the Netherlands to Brittany, which was covered by the forces of Army Group B.

Differences in German strategic approach

There were major differences of opinion regarding the best strategy for the Germans to defend France in the event of an invasion. The principal commanders, Field Marshals von Rundstedt and Rommel, had opposing basic views on the correct approach to adopt to defeat the landing, and each position had support from other senior officers in the military leadership hierarchy.

The basic strategic problem for the Germans in 1944 was that any successful landing in the Western theatre of operations had a shorter distance to travel to vital targets in Germany than was the case with the Eastern theatre. Consequently, they had to completely defeat any invasion in the West or suffer defeat, almost regardless of what happened on the Eastern Front. Hitler thought there was still more than enough space to trade for a gradual withdrawal in the East, where their defensive lines were still long distances from Germany and its critical industrial and other centres. Furthermore, the Germans did not have the resources – either industrial or military – to carry on a two-front war for an extended period with any realistic hope of winning. By defeating an invasion in the West, the Germans would then have the opportunity to turn again on the East with their full resources which would enable them to be victorious there – or so was Hitler's thinking. As the situation turned out however, Hitler's calculations were nullified in this regard by the timing of the Red Army's "Operation *Bagration*" which was launched on 22 June 1944, the third anniversary of the invasion of the USSR by Germany during the Normandy battles, and which added immeasurably to the strategic dilemma the Germans faced.

In an attempt to bring some clarity to the role of the Wehrmacht in the West, Hitler issued Fuhrer Directive No. 51 on 3 September 1943, which governed the defence of France against invasion. It contained the following basic approach:[13]

'Should the enemy nevertheless force a landing by concentrating his armed might, he must be hit by the full fury of our counterattack. For this mission ample and speedy reinforcements of men and material, as well as intensive training must transform available larger units into first rate, fully mobile general reserves suitable for offensive operations. The counterattack of these units will prevent the enlargement of the beachhead, and throw the enemy back into the sea.'

The necessary first step to achieving this aim was reinforcement of the units in France. As will be apparent, this did not occur on anything like the scale needed to give the strategy a chance of succeeding.

Rundstedt's view as to the best defensive strategy as summarised by Blumentritt was:[14]

'quite different from those of the Supreme Command. For example, he frequently expressed the belief that, in case of invasion across the Channel, the whole of southern France south of the Loire should be given up and all the troops employed there withdrawn as reserves into the Paris zone. An official proposal on these lines to Hitler would have been hopeless, for it was the express desire of the latter to hold the entire two thousand five hundred miles of the coastal front. Consequently, by agreement with my Commander-in-Chief, I placed this idea before Colonel-General Jodl in the form of a letter. Needless to say, no reply was received. Rundstedt's proposal was to Hitler's way of thinking so monstrous that apparently Jodl had not even dared to draw his attention to it!' Blumentritt goes on to describe the state of the Luftwaffe in the West and states that it would be carrying on a 'hopeless struggle' against the superiority of the allied air-forces.'

Colonel General Guderian, the Inspector General of Armoured Troops when the strategy was being developed, supported Rundstedt's view:[15]

'I had begun to study the problem of defending the Western Front in 1943. With the new year this problem assumed increasing importance. In February I went to France for a tour of inspection and for conversations with Field Marshal von Rundstedt and General von Geyr. We were in complete agreement that enemy sea and air superiority made our task more difficult. Allied air supremacy must in particular affect our ability to move our forces. It seemed likely that in order to achieve sufficient speed and concentration we should have to move only by night. **Our opinion was that it all depended on making ready truly adequate reserves of panzer and Panzergrenadier divisions: these must be stationed far enough inland from the so called Atlantic Wall, so that they could be switched easily to the main invasion front once it had been recognised [Author's emphasis]:** these moves must be facilitated by repairs to the French road network and by the construction of alternative river-crossings, underwater bridges or bridges of boats.

'Rommel's sad experiences in Africa had so convinced him of the overwhelming nature of allied air supremacy that he believed that there could be no question of ever moving large formations of troops again. He did not even think that it would be possible to transfer panzer or Panzergrenadier divisions by night. His views on this subject had been further strengthened by his experiences in Italy in 1943. So when General von Geyr had proposed the grouping of our motorised reserves back from the Atlantic defensive front he immediately came up against opposition on Rommel's part, since what Geyr wanted was that these reserves be employed in a mobile role and organised accordingly. ... I was therefore not surprised by Rommel's highly temperamental and strongly expressed refusal when I suggested that our armour be withdrawn from the coastal areas. He turned down my suggestion at once, pointing out that as a man from the Eastern Front I lacked his experiences of Africa and Italy; that he knew, in fact, far more about the matter in hand than I did and that he was fully convinced that his system was right. ... I therefore decided not to make any further attempts to alter his opinions and made up my mind once more to submit my contrary views to Rundstedt and Hitler.

'... Hitler had remained a man of the 1914–1918 trench-warfare epoch and had never understood the principles of mobile operations. Rommel believed such operations to be no longer possible as a result of the enemy's air supremacy. So it is little wonder that both the Commander-in-Chief West and I found that Hitler turned down our proposals for the re-distribution of our motorised formations, on the grounds that Rommel possessed more recent experiences than did either of us.'

There are two points in these remarks by Guderian that are worth examining in light of the Germans' actual experience during the invasion. Firstly, subsequent events showed that the effect of the Allied air forces had, if anything, been underestimated by Rommel, meaning switching reinforcements from as far back as Guderian suggested to anywhere in Army Group B was always going to be incredibly difficult. Kluge, when he became OB West in July 1944, soon came to realize that Rommel's assessment of the situation was correct; so as long as the Luftwaffe was unable to challenge Allied air supremacy, there was no chance of using mass formations in the way Guderian proposed. Secondly, none of the German senior military command had previously been subjected to the impact of the complete mechanization of US and British forces that had occurred since 1940. The mobility of the Allied forces was a factor that showed itself fully during the pursuit across France, which was so fast that they were almost able to move from Normandy to the Rhine in one bound. Only lack of supplies stopped them from doing so. Therefore, while Guderian's views were understandable, they did not match the reality of the situation faced by the German troops and their commanders.

General Geyr von Schweppenburg expanded on his view following the invasions of Sicily and Italy:[16]

'With the assignment of Rommel in the West, a sharp controversy arose between the concepts of Genfldm Rommel and those of Gen Panzer Geyr von Schweppenburg. Genfldm Rommel represented the school of thought that a landing should be prevented at any cost. Once the Anglo-Saxons had established a foothold on the Continent, it would be impossible to drive them back into the sea. All available forces should be kept in readiness behind the fortifications – which were in need of considerable reinforcement – in order to prevent altogether a major landing. The opinion of Gen Panzer West was that, in view of the enemy air superiority and the number, caliber and effectiveness of the naval guns of the Anglo-American battle fleets, a landing some place on 1,300 kilometers of coastline could not be prevented and would succeed in any case. **The only solution would be to utlize the only German superiority - that of speedier and more flexible leadership which employed strategic mobile reserves [Author's emphasis]**. High-quality Panzer units should be kept in reserve to crush an enemy penetration inland. Genobst Guderian, Hitler's adviser on Panzer tactics, agreed in full with the opinion of Gen Panzer Geyr von Schweppenburg, but this was of no avail.'

Whether at this stage in the war the German panzer divisions possessed the superiority as posited by Schweppenburg is at least questionable, and the events following the Normandy breakout indicate that his estimate was not correct. This was not only the case with the Americans, but also with respect to the British, with the rush by the 21st Army Group to the Dutch border being every bit as spectacular as the US Third Army's drive across France, but not as well highlighted in most military commentaries since the war. The campaign illustrated that the mobility, flexibility and command control of the Allied armoured divisions was more than equal to those of the Germans. As the panzers were the only elements of the German Army that could have provided a means of attacking the Allies, Schweppenburg's view is understandable but was not borne out by events.

General Pemsel also commented on the situation facing the German defenders:[17]

'It was of vital importance for the overall conduct of battle in Northern France to have free movement of reserves along the shortest routes between Seventh and Fifteenth Armies (across the Seine below Paris). By using French labor, as many Seine bridges as possible were to be restored to a serviceable condition.

'... In order to relieve forces for strategic reserve, OB West submitted a proposal to OKW to man the fortresses with adequate complements and simply keep watch over the intervening terrain. OB West also desired to reduce drastically the personnel and material of the Channel Islands. This proposal was rejected by OKW, since it deviated from the cordon defense theory of not yielding a foot of soil voluntarily.'

However, the tactical use of the Allied air forces made the repair of anything in France almost impossible once it was identified as being of a military or supporting nature both by direct destruction and by restricting available supplies.

Rommel's strategy

Lieutenant-General Max Pemsel was Chief-of-Staff of the Seventh Army in Normandy and had numerous conversations with Rommel. He relates that Rommel's view of the correct strategy to defeat the invasion was:

'From his extensive experience with landing operations in Africa and Italy, Rommel had formulated the opinion that an enemy, once landed and protected by covering fire from naval artillery and the air, was extremely difficult to throw back into the sea. It was therefore a proposition of making the coastal defences so strong in manpower and equipment that the enemy could never gain a foothold on the shore. Reserves which were not located close to the coast could only be used belatedly and with heavy loss because of the supporting fire from enemy naval artillery and air forces.

He concluded that as many defense troops as possible should be committed in the beach fortifications, and all reserves should be located directly on the coast and incorporated into the defense. The artillery of divisions in reserve and Panzer battalions of Panzer divisions in reserve should be moved close enough to the front that they could dominate the coast with fire from their cantonment areas. By bringing up the troops from the reserve areas, the fortress garrisons would be reinforced and more labour made available. He also expressed the view that the strength of the allies' forces made successful defence a matter of grave doubt.

… At that time, Germany no longer had the forces and material available to utilize a cordon defence in a 4,000-kilometer front. An enemy well equipped on land, on sea, and in the air, and able to attack with far superior forces at any chosen point along the front, could not be prevented from gaining a foothold on land and establishing a solid bridgehead. And if the enemy should succeed in doing this, then – according to Rommel's views – the invasion was successful and the entire Atlantic Wall built for nothing.'[18]

This strategy was consistent with the Germans' experiences in Italy at Salerno and Anzio, where although the defenders had come close to defeating the landings, once the Allies had consolidated their beachheads it proved impossible to dislodge them due to a combination of overwhelming air power and naval gunfire. The difference Rommel envisaged was that in all previous invasions, the Germans had not been able to defend using properly constructed fortifications or extensive minefields, which would make a huge difference to their chances of success. This was consistent with Field Marshal Kesselring's view of the situation:[19]

'The lessons learnt in Sicily led to the following conclusions: positions in depth were an indispensable complement to coastal fortifications, as, in view of the powerful effect of naval gunfire on visible coastal fortifications, a linear defence was useless. Despite the utter failure of the Italian coastal defence forces, concentrated fire against the enemy at his most vulnerable points, i.e. against unloading transport ships, approaching landing craft and men who had just disembarked, still appeared to be the best method of defence. **The first main reserves must be brought forward so near to the coast that they could move up into their battle areas as far as possible in the hours of darkness [Author's emphasis].'**

While Rommel and Kesselring did not see eye-to-eye on many matters, they certainly did in this respect.

According to General Speidel, Rommel's Chief of Staff, there was another reason why Rommel considered it necessary to have reserves immediately available: [20]

'His own and others' experiences had taught Genfdm Rommel that the only divisions really ready for immediate use were those subordinated and in the area. **In the case of all so-called OKW reserves, the decision to commit them usually came too late, and then frequently the units were sacrificed to Hitler's dilettantism in leadership [Author's emphasis].'**

This frank statement reflects the experience of all commanders who worked under Hitler's 'system' of command and caused them great anxiety. There are numerous examples of this problem which are referred to in this book, a particularly apposite instance being the delay in committing the OKW reserves requested by Rundstedt on D-Day.

In July 1943, after recovering from the health problems from his time in Africa, Rommel spent some weeks with Hitler at the Fuhrer Headquarters in Rastenburg, East Prussia. During that time, he discussed the position on the eastern front with Hitler and observed the developing situation with Operation Citadel during several of the daily situation conferences. He developed conclusions regarding the conduct of the war which he discussed with General Bayerlein, who had been with him in Africa. The conclusions he outlined were very much in line with those he outlined to Pemsel referred to earlier, and so can be taken to be his genuine and deeply thought through ideas of how the Germans could counter the material advantages of the allies in the east and west. At the end of this time with Hitler, he was appointed to the command of the defence of Italy necessitated by the allied landings in Sicily which were followed by landings in Italy itself. However, Hitler decided that the command in Italy would be best managed by Kesselring and so sent Rommel to evaluate the 'Atlantic Wall' and the overall defences of France. Rommel sent a report to Hitler on 31st December 1943 which was to the effect that the defences in the West were in great need of reinforcement with respect to both men and material, which motivated Hitler to choose Rommel, with the concurrence of Rundstedt, for the command of Army Group B in France, consisting of the

7th and 15th Armies. These armies were deployed at the points on the coast which had been identified by German intelligence as being the most likely for the allies to invade. Army Group 'B' was the most powerful of the German forces in France, but did not include the most powerful mobile reserves, which Hitler kept under his own control.[21]

One obvious problem with Rommel's approach was where to put the panzer and other high-quality reinforcements. If the location of the invasion was not where these troops were deployed, then they would have little or no effect on the early stages of the battle, which was the whole point of Rommel's strategy. Because the area to be covered was so large, it was impossible to concentrate enough force everywhere that an invasion could occur. The German deployments were subject to their intelligence estimates, but these were being corrupted by misinformation deliberately fed to them in accordance with the Allies' extensive deception activities. These included fabricated information being fed back to them by their own agents in Britain, who had been identified and turned by British security personnel, when a combination of accurate but unimportant and quite plausible but manufactured information was sent by them to the German intelligence network. One of the most important aspects of Operation *Overlord* – the code name for the entire invasion – was Operation *Fortitude*, which comprised the multi-faceted plan to deceive the Germans as to the place, time and strength of the invasion. It was far more successful than the planners had hoped, one result being that troops of the Fifteenth Army – vitally needed in Normandy – were kept in place around the Pas-de-Calais because Hitler believed there would be a second landing there. This was a crucial element of the misinformation that the Allies fed to the German intelligence services and which they knew to be believed because they were reading German intelligence assessments through the Ultra codebreakers at Bletchley Park.

Where would the Allies land?

The question of where the allies would land in Europe had only seriously occupied the collective mind of the German High command since March 1942, when von Rundstedt was appointed to be C-in-C West and after the failure of Barbarossa during 1941. Steps were taken to strengthen the defences from then and the construction of the 'Atlantic Wall' was commenced. Because of its proximity to England, the Pas de Calais was thought to be the most likely invasion site, as this would be the shortest route for the invasion craft, and it was conveniently under the immediate cover of allied air power. Additionally, when the Germans were planning Operation Sea Lion they had considered all the potential locations for their invasion, and this had been the site which they had chosen for sending the invasion forces to the South East of England so this would be a logical place for the allies to attack. There were also a number of ports close by which would assist the allies' in the build-up of their forces after the invasion occurred, which was an extremely important factor. The beaches in the area had also been indicated as being appropriate for landing vehicles and other infantry resources which could be expected from the allied forces by OKM, whereas Normandy was (incorrectly – Author's note) considered not to be appropriate. It was also the location of many of the V1 launch sites, and so if this area was taken, these would be neutralised.

They were almost certain that an invasion would occur in 1944 but had no conclusive evidence of the location or timing of the landing. Information from German intelligence also indicated that the build-up of allied forces in England was consistent with the invasion being in the Pas de Calais. The Germans did not realise however that the information they received from their agents in England was tainted. Because of the comparative impotence of the Luftwaffe, there had been very limited air reconnaissance over south-eastern England, and the information which it provided tended to confirm the existing thoughts regarding the location of the invasion.

In order to cloak the location of the invasion further, the tactical air interdiction and disruption campaign which the allies implemented over France indicated a false picture of the likely site of the invasion by ensuring that for every bomb dropped on the Normandy area, two bombs were dropped on the Pas de Calais. Thus, the Germans had no conclusive data as to the site of the invasion until it occurred.

The Germans therefore placed the Fifteenth Army which was the most powerful force they had in the Pas de Calais region. Because Hitler believed that there would be two landings, he would not allow these forces to be moved until it was too late to affect the outcome of the Normandy campaign.

Hitler's compromise strategy

Hitler decided on a strategy that seemed on the face of it to encompass the schools of thought of both Rundstedt and Rommel, but which in reality was a compromise and did not have any of the advantages of either. He allowed Rommel to place part of the panzer divisions close to some of the potential invasion points, as he had advocated, but also created a reserve of panzer divisions further back from the possible landing sites and placed them under OB West, with the stipulation that they could not be deployed without OKW – for which read Hitler's – agreement. If there had been sufficient forces available, this may have been a workable deployment. However, in the circumstances that applied to the German formations in the West, adopting this approach split the already inadequate available mobile forces. Consequently, those deployed in accordance with Rommel's strategy were not strong enough to repel the invasion when it came, while the other reserves were exposed to the air attack and delays which Rommel had feared when they were eventually committed to the battle. It would have been better for the Germans if Hitler had fully accepted Rommel's or Rundstedt's view and given one of them control over the deployment and commitment of the available mobile forces to ensure they intervened as soon as possible to the defence, in accordance with the terms of his own Directive No. 51. The reasons for such a course and the advantages of its adoption would have been as follows:

1. Assuming that the reserves were committed so that five or more of the panzer reserve divisions could reach the invasion beaches on the first day, in combination with the dispositions that Rommel had wanted to make but were rejected by the OKW, then there may have been a chance of inflicting a crucial defeat on the Allies at the start of the campaign when they were at their weakest. Whether this occurred or not, it was obvious that unless the Germans also used the divisions of the Fifteenth Army to reinforce the Seventh Army in Normandy, then the longer the Allies were ashore, the more likely it was that the invasion would be successful. This was because the Allies were able to build up their forces more quickly than the Germans, one of the results of the Normandy battlefield being isolated by the Allied tactical air forces on D-Day and immediately after it, and the effects of the strategic bombing campaign on the French rail transport network that had preceded the invasion. The best chance for the Germans to launch a counterattack if they had not been able to defeat the invasion on D-Day would have occurred if the Allied air forces were grounded because of bad weather, which actually did happen between 19 and 23 June when an intense storm in the Channel and along the Normandy coast significantly disrupted the Allies' build-up. Blumentritt indicates that:[22]

> In Spring of 1944 Hitler received certain information – whence, Western Command did not know – that the allies might possibly land in Normandy. In April and May reinforcements were brought to this area, including the 91st Airborne Division and strong units of the 243rd Infantry Division. There was also a Parachute Jaeger regiment from the 2nd Parachute Jaeger Division, which was in the course of formation... All these were not effective measures, but simply piecework. But the west had no more free forces at its disposal at the moment. Several complete

divisions could have been transferred from the Fifteenth Army zone, but nobody knew whether this army's important area might not likewise be attacked from the Channel.'

2. While Rundstedt, Guderian and Geyr von Schweppenburg were a formidable group of military experts and strategists, they had not faced the full might of the Allied air forces in any military operation. Rommel had been exposed to the crippling effect and ubiquitous intervention of the Allied tactical air forces in both the North African and Italian campaigns, which undoubtedly gave his opinion more weight than may otherwise have been the case. Consequently, committing to his strategy was felt to be the course most likely to maximize the defensive potential of the Germans if they actually possessed sufficient forces to defeat the invasion.

The advocates of returning the Wehrmacht to mobile operations through its mechanized forces in the West seem to have forgotten that when they achieved their greatest victories in France in 1940 and the early stages of Operation *Barbarossa*, they had done so because they had enjoyed air superiority over their enemies. They had been able to combine this air superiority with the mobility and firepower of the panzer forces, and it was this combination that was the main reason the German blitzkriegs had been so effective. The position in 1944 was drastically altered, as the Luftwaffe was not even able to defend the German ground forces against the Allies' air forces, let alone perform a critical role in any major offensive. The position on the Eastern Front was quite different in this regard, as the Red Air Force was not able to attain air superiority at the same level as occurred in the West at any time during the war until its closing stages.

3. Lastly, the Western Allied armies were much better equipped for mobile warfare than the Wehrmacht, with every British and US infantry division the equivalent in this regard of a German motorized division. Therefore, if mobile warfare was to develop in the campaign, the Allies were much more able to take advantage of it than the Germans. Indeed, this is exactly what happened after the overpowering of the German positions in Normandy until supply problems restricted the mobility of the Allied armies in September 1944 and stopped them just short of the Rhine.

On balance, there seems little doubt that Rommel's strategy was the more valid one, but Hitler – in typical fashion – prevaricated and did not fully commit to either Rundstedt's or Rommel's suggested strategy. Nor did he allow Rundstedt, Rommel or any other of the commanders in France executive authority to commit the reserves regardless of the strategy adopted, although through the terms of Directive No. 51 he had implicitly accepted that committing the counterattacking forces as early as possible was crucial to successfully repelling any invasion.

The German chances of successfully defending against the invasion were therefore almost completely compromised even before it occurred because of inadequate land, sea and air forces, a command structure that was thoroughly dysfunctional and a strategy that did not enable the commanders on the spot to use the forces the Germans possessed in the speediest way as they had to obtain Hitler's consent to do anything with them. The fact that the resistance to the invasion made the Allies' task as difficult as it did was the result of the geography of the Normandy region, especially its Bocage network of fields enclosed by thick hedges, and the bravery of the German soldiers, desperately fighting in small-scale unit and individual actions in a battle that was unwinnable from the start.

The German forces in France in June 1944

General Guderian stated that on 6 June 1944, the following German Army forces were stationed in the Western commands:[23]

> '48 infantry divisions, of which 38 were located along, and 10 behind, the coast: of these latter, 5 were between the Scheldt and the Somme, 2 between the Somme and the Seine and 3 in Brittany.

> '10 panzer and Panzergrenadier divisions, located as follows:

> '1st SS-Panzer Division Leibstandarte "Adolf Hitler" at Beverloo, Belgium;

> '2nd Panzer Division in the area Amiens–Abbeville;

> '116th Panzer Division to the east of Rouen (north of the Seine);

> '12th SS-Panzer Division Hitler Jugend in the Lisieux area (south of the Seine);

> '21st Panzer Division in the Caen area;

> 'Panzer Lehr Division in the area Le Mans–Orleans–Chartres;

> '17th SS-Panzergrenadier Division in the area Samur–Niort–Poitiers;

> '11th Panzer Division in the Bordeaux area;

> '2nd SS-Panzer Division "Das Reich" in the area Montauban–Tolouse;

> '9th Panzer Division in the area Avignon–Nines–Arles.'

Some of these divisions were the very best in the German Army and a match for any of the Allied formations. However, there was a great disparity between the divisions with respect to the standard of their equipment and training.

General Warlimont commented on the state of the formations available to defend the Atlantic Wall:[24]

'All that was available to do this, however, were "static" divisions, totally untried, mostly comprised of older classes of conscript and completely inadequately equipped. The motorized and armoured divisions were held as "mobile reserves"; they were intended, should the defence on the coasts and beach fail, to counter-attack any enemy who might have landed and defeat him; but the majority of even these divisions had no battle experience. Only ten such divisions were available in all, and on 5 June four of them were not yet operational because OKH had, as usual, been dilatory in moving such remnants of them as remained from the Eastern Front.'

The reason why the OKH had not switched the 'remnants' to the West more promptly was undoubtedly to prevent the formations from moving totally out of its jurisdiction to the Western theatre, which was an OKW area of operations, once again emphasizing the fundamentally flawed nature of the German command structure.

The divisions in the West represented a heterogeneous group, and this included the armoured and mechanized divisions. There were five different types of divisions in Army Group B:

1. Garrison divisions – these were the most numerous divisions in Army Group B, with seventeen in the Fifteenth Army and eleven in the Seventh Army. They differed from normal infantry divisions in that they had fewer troops; usually around 12,000, who were primarily German conscripts and volunteers from the occupied countries in Europe and the East. Only a few had any troops with combat experience and even less were fully trained or could be used in an attacking role. All used horse transport and were thus useless in a war of manoeuvre, and some did not even have horses. They were armed with a variety of weapons, including captured French and Soviet artillery, machine guns and in some cases self-propelled guns and armour. This complicated the supply of these formations and meant that they would have limited endurance in battle.

One such division was the 709th, which was deployed in the Cotentin peninsula between Cherbourg and Carentan. It was commanded by Lieutenant General Karl von Schlieben, who described the division and its role as follows:[25]

'The 709th Infantry Division was a division of the 15th Wave. It did not even have horses and was classified as a static division. The quality of its personnel had decreased through being drained by repeated transfers of men to the Russian front.

'... The age of the soldiers and the high percentage of men inexperienced in warfare and belonging to "Volksliste III" was striking. The latter were not Germans but had originated from countries occupied during the war. Their reliability was doubtful. In addition, two Eastern and two Georgian battalions were assigned to the division; I doubted they would fight hard in cases of emergency.'

The total strength of the 709th Division was 10,536 men, of whom 2,117 were 'Eastern elements and Foreign volunteers'. In addition to these limitations with respect to its personnel, the equipment of the division was an ad hoc mixture taken from stocks acquired from almost every country the Germans had conquered. Its field howitzers were Czech; its mortars were French; and although the majority of its small arms were German, approximately 10 per cent of the rifles, pistols and light machine guns were a mixture of French, Russian, Polish and Belgian types. Consequently, this division, which was in a crucial sector of the German defences, could hardly be described as 'first line'.

Another division in a crucial location in Normandy was the 352nd Infantry Division, which held a position between St Lo and the coast. The 352nd was formed in December 1943 and had been scheduled to be ready for service by 31 January 1944. Lieutenant Colonel Fritz Ziegelmann, the Chief of Staff of the division, commented on its readiness:[26]

'Training of the 352nd Infantry Division was carried out according to Eastern combat principles.

'... The organization itself proceeded very slowly, especially in equipment. ... The chief reasons for this were lack of materiel – beginning in the year 1944 – and the labour shortage in Germany. **(The effect of the bombing raids was becoming stronger. [Author's emphasis])** This was a strong check upon the training program of the 352nd Infantry Division.

'Thus it was possible, for example, to begin with the artillery training only at the end of February 1944, since the delivery of sighting devices and harness pieces was not possible before the middle of February. **Until the beginning of March, each soldier had only been able to throw two hand grenades and shoot during three rifle and machine gun exercises.**

The training of relief drivers had not been possible until 1 May, 1944 because of the fuel situation [Author's emphasis].'

'... Replacements consisted chiefly of young people (class of 1925/26). **Almost all these people, being physically of limited capacity as a result of the shortage of food in Germany, were fit only for limited military duties. Marches over 15 kilometers led to high casualties. ... The purchase of milk from the country, in which the French peasantry was very helpful, succeeded in correcting the dietary deficiency of these young people [Author's emphasis].'**

'The officer corps was composed of 50% inexperienced officers. 30% of the non-commissioned officer posts were vacant on 1 March 1944, because of a lack of competent non-commissioned officers. The total strength of an infantry division Type 44 amounted to around 12,000 men, which included around 1,500 Hiwis (Russian voluntary labor).'

It can therefore be seen that neither of these formations, which were deployed at locations in the German defences that turned out to be critical on D-Day, can be estimated as anything near a match for the invading Allied forces in terms of training, equipment or the standard of their personnel.

2. **Parachute divisions** – there were elements of three parachute divisions in Normandy. These were some of the best-trained units in the Wehrmacht, raised through the Luftwaffe as airborne troops but controlled tactically by the Army. The parachute divisions (Fallschirmjager) had been deployed in critical attacking roles in the early stages of the war, during the 1940 campaign in France and also in the invasion of Crete in 1941. However, they had suffered such high casualties in Crete that Hitler never used them again in their intended role. In Normandy, they were deployed as regular infantry. Their equipment did not, however, include heavy weapons, reflecting their original role. Despite these shortcomings, they were formidable units.

3. **Luftwaffe field divisions** – these formations were raised as a result of pressure for replacements and new units following the losses in the *Barbarossa* campaign. Originally, the OKW requested that the Luftwaffe and Kriegsmarine provide replacements for losses in Army units from its excess personnel, but Reichsmarschall Goering convinced Hitler to mobilize these high-quality, politically reliable troops from the Luftwaffe as units that would remain under the control of the Luftwaffe but come under the tactical control of the Army. The result was that these capable replacements, which would have been extremely valuable in reinvigorating depleted Army formations,

were committed in units that were not properly trained or equipped to fulfil an infantry role. They were also deficient in the training and experience of their officers and NCOs, who were Luftwaffe personnel with little experience in combat. The senior officers of the German Army rated these divisions very lowly, as expressed by Manstein when he related the role of the various units he was given to relieve Stalingrad:[27]

> 'It was assumed from the start, of course, that the Luftwaffe divisions could at best be employed in some defensive role, such as shielding the flanks of the assault elements.'

The creation of the Luftwaffe field divisions is yet another example of political considerations working contrary to the interests of the efficiency of the armed forces, particularly the Army, and must be rated as a complete failure.

4. Army panzer divisions – the panzer divisions were looked upon as being the elite fighting forces of the German Army. When up to establishment strength, they were equal to any formations the Allies had, except that their cross-country performance was not as good because they were not equipped to the same level with tracked as opposed to wheeled transport. However, because many of them had suffered heavy casualties on the Eastern Front, the armoured formations under the command of Army Group B were mostly not up to establishment strength, and in some cases significantly below it. The Panzer Lehr, 2nd Panzer and 116th Panzer Divisions were more or less up to strength and therefore potentially formidable adversaries. However, these formations had to compete with the SS for replacements and equipment, a further example of resources being wasted for the political ends of the Nazi regime. The state of the panzer divisions is set out in the following section with an analysis by General Geyr von Schweppenburg, commander of Panzer Group West and responsible for their training.

5. SS divisions – the Waffen-SS was a separate arm of the SS, standing apart from the guards and personnel of the concentration camps. They fought with regular German Army units, although they were under the separate jurisdiction of the Reichsfuhrer-SS, Heinrich Himmler. They were created as the Nazi equivalent of the Roman Praetorian Guard and were looked upon by Hitler as the elite formations of the armed services, receiving preferential treatment with respect to reinforcements and equipment. However, they were not easy to keep at establishment from volunteers and had to rely on being topped up with drafts from regular Army units, especially with respect to NCOs and officers.

Their establishment strengths were larger than equivalent Army formations, and therefore the fighting reputation they have is somewhat overstated. They also suffered higher casualty rates than equivalent Army formations, which has been attributed to the relatively low level of combat experience of the majority of their NCOs and junior officers.

There has been much ill-informed commentary on the combat value of the Waffen-SS divisions in comparison to equivalent Army formations, but there is no evidence that their performance was any better than the elite Army divisions. Given that their establishment levels were higher, this should have been the case. Manstein considered that the training of the Waffen-SS divisions and the lack of experience of their junior officers and NCOs led to higher-than-usual casualty rates and missed opportunities in combat, and that it was 'an inexcusable mistake to set them up as a separate military organisation'.[28]

There were two SS-Panzer divisions under Army Group B on D-Day, the 12th SS and 1st SS 'Leibstandarte SS Adolf Hitler' (LSSAH). The LSSAH was re-forming in Belgium, having suffered heavy casualties on the Eastern Front, but the 12th SS-Panzer Division was close to Caen, so within easy reach of the beaches targeted by the Allies. The 2nd, 9th and 10th SS-Panzer Divisions were also available as reserves but were not close to the landing areas. The SS divisions in the Battle of Normandy disgraced themselves and Germany by committing atrocities, killing unarmed prisoners and civilians. Their actions are inexcusable as Germany had signed the Hague and various other conventions relating to the treatment of prisoners of war and civilians which were binding with respect to the Western nations, although the USSR had not signed these agreements, so such events were more widespread on the Eastern Front. There is absolutely no reason for these divisions to be extolled in the manner that some commentators seem eager to do because of their alleged prowess on the battlefield.

Also in the OKW reserve was the 17th SS-Panzergrenadier Division, which differed from the panzer divisions in that it did not have the same number of tanks, but had an additional infantry element. In the event, the division was not fully equipped or motorized by D-Day, having to rely on commandeered French trucks for its transport.

The state of the Panzer divisions on D-Day

The panzer and Panzergrenadier divisions available in Normandy at the time of the invasion represented a mixed bag of equipment, training and combat efficiency. Panzer Group West chief General Geyr von Schweppenburg, responsible for the training of all panzer troops in the West, ranked the divisions in the following order for overall combat efficiency: [29]

A. 2nd Panzer Division
    9th SS-Panzer Division
    12th SS-Panzer Division
    Panzer Lehr Division
B. 11th Panzer Division
    2nd SS-Panzer Division
    21st Panzer Division
C. 9th Panzer Division
    17th SS-Panzergrenadier Division
    116th Panzer Division (probably)
D. 10th SS-Panzer Division
    1st SS-Panzer Division.

The 'A' level divisions were all at full strength or close to it, with good commanders and training. There were, however, some weaknesses, which were mainly traceable to high casualty levels which could not be replaced, particularly experienced NCOs.

The 'B' level divisions were still good, but uneven. For example, Geyr noted that the 2nd SS-Panzer Division was re-formed in France in 1944, so although it had a sufficient group of experienced personnel, it had not had time to attain its former level of efficiency.

Geyr noted that the 'C' level divisions had problems with either senior personnel or training. One of the issues he mentioned with respect to training was that the troops were committed to building fortifications on the Atlantic Wall or field positions and were therefore diverted from the training they needed.

With respect to the 'D' level divisions, this ranking may seem strange, especially having regard to the reputation that some of the units enjoyed subsequent to the war. However, for example Schweppenburg explained:[30]

'[The 1st SS-Panzer Division] was bled white in Russia and was unable to fill the gaps resulting from casualties and sending out cadres (the 12th SS-Panzer Division was formed by a cadre from the 1st SS-Panzer Division). Discipline was a sham; the NCOs were poor. The division did not have time for thorough training before the invasion.'

The ranking allocated to the 21st Panzer Division is of particular interest, having regard to where it was deployed and the role it was expected to carry out in the early stages of the invasion. The state of the division in 1944 is outlined by its commander, General Edgar Feuchtinger:[31]

'Even at the time of the invasion, the formation of the division had naturally not yet been completed. Particularly the Panzer Regiment had been treated rather badly, as it was only able to exchange its antiquated Hotchkiss and Somua (French) tanks for German Mark IV tanks a few weeks before the invasion. The division was not equipped with Mark V (Panthers). At the start of the invasion the 1st Battalion had eighteen tanks per company and the second only 12 tanks per company.

'The division, which had thus been formed very slowly and regrouped often, suffered considerably where its training was concerned.

'… The order calling for the formation of the division stated that all members of the former 21st Africa Armored Division now in Germany were to be transferred to the division. In this way, the division got a small but good cadre of experienced veterans (about 2,000 men). Naturally these men, many of whom only joined the division at a late date, were no full compensation.'

That this division was ranked by the general in command of Panzer Group West above five other panzer formations available in the Western theatre clearly shows that the combat efficiency of half of the German armoured divisions was low. These ratings also reflected the problems Germany experienced in replacing the casualties inflicted on the Eastern Front and the limitations of the nation's industrial capacity. Germany's limited industrial potential was, ironically, the direct result of the policies of the Nazi government. This situation was commented upon by Albert Speer, the Nazi Minister for Armaments, while he was in Spandau prison following his conviction at the Nuremberg trials:[32]

'In the middle of 1941 Hitler could easily have had an army equipped twice as powerfully as it was. For the production of those fundamental industries that determine the volume of armaments was scarcely higher in 1941 than in 1944. What would have kept us from attaining the later production figures by the spring of 1942? We could even have mobilised approximately three million men of the younger age groups before 1942 without losses in production. Nor would we have needed forced labor from the occupied territories, if women could have been brought into the labor force as they were in England and the United States. Some five million women would have been available for armaments production; and three million additional soldiers would have added up to many divisions. These, moreover, could have been excellently equipped as a result of the increased production.'

Of course, a mere increase in the production of weapons was of little consequence without the training and support services that are an integral part of the complex interaction needed before these increases are sustainable in front-line combat forces. But even if only a third of the increases postulated by Speer resulted in an equivalent addition to strength at the front, the consequences for the ability of the Allies to defeat Germany would be terrible to contemplate. Thus, the Nazi policy of not using women in the workforce – their role being seen as having as many children as possible – worked significantly to the detriment of Germany's war effort.

The Seventh Army on the eve of D-Day

The invasion front in Normandy was defended by the Seventh Army, which was part of Rommel's Army Group B. The Seventh Army was commanded by Colonel General Friedrich Dollman. According to his Chief of Staff, Lieutenant General Max Pemsel, the divisions in the Seventh Army were located as follows:[33]

'In Normandy, along the 400-kilometer front of LXXXIV Infantry Corps, there were the following:

'a. On the coastal front:
'1. 716th Infantry Division, from the Dives to the Carentan Canal;
'2. 709th Infantry Division, from the Carentan Canal to the Bay of St. Malo (inclusive);
'3. One Russian battalion guarding the 100-kilometer front from Cap de la Hague to the Bay of St Malo; and
'4. Reinforced 319th Infantry Division on the British Channel Islands.
'b. In reserve:
'1. 352nd Infantry Division around St Lo;
'2. 243rd Infantry Division, in the Cotentin peninsula (center);
'3. 30th Infantry Brigade (Mobile), north of Avranches; and
'4. 77th Infantry Division, which had been located around Caen, was – by an OKW order – to be inserted in the St Malo sector to replace the 346th Division (transferred to Fifteenth Army).

'In response to Seventh Army's pressure for additional troops, the following reinforcements were received during the Spring:

'1. 21st Panzer Division, in the area around Caen (after temporary assignment elsewhere);

'2. 91st LL [Luftlande/Air Landing] Division, in the area northwest of Carensan [*sic*]; and

'3. 6th FS [Fallschirmjager] Regiment (from the 2nd FS Division which was being reorganized in Germany), in the area around Carentan.'

Pemsel rated the combat efficiency of the units as follows:

'a. 716th and 709th Infantry Divisions: static; the two of approximately the same quality; two regiments of three battalions each; well acquainted with their sectors for years; well trained for defense; not much combat experience.

'b. 319th Infantry Division; high quality division, with three regiments of three battalions each, reinforced with one Maschinengewehr (MG) battalion, one French Panzer battalion, and naval and air force units; average age 26–27 years; well suited for attack and defense; little combat experience.

'c. 21st Panzer Division; recently reorganised with German weapons; good enlisted personnel who had completed training.

'd. 352nd Infantry Division: recently reorganized with three regiments of two battalions each, and one fusilier battalion; bulk of personnel young men with training nearly completed.

'e. 243rd Infantry Division: recently reorganized, same as 352nd Infantry Division; fusilier battalion hastily rendered mobile by equipment with bicycles; bulk of personnel young men unschooled in combined arms.

'f. 91st LL Division: newly organized with three regiments of two battalions each; weapons and equipment not yet complete; bulk of personnel young men; training completed only to platoon level; not yet suitable for assault.

'g. 30th Infantry Brigade (Mobile): name unjustified; recruit training unit with four Fahrradbewegliches (bicycle infantry) battalions and brigade staff (total strength approximately 1,200); remaining battalions located in Holland and Belgium.

'h. 6th FS Regiment: an especially good regiment in training and leadership [This was a parachute unit used as infantry].'

He also noted that four Russian battalions were with LXXXIV Corps, consisting of volunteers mainly from captured Russians. As would be expected, the trustworthiness of these battalions in combat was more than a little questionable.

Pemsel said that there were not enough troops to attempt to create a cordon defence as required by Rommel, especially because of the possibility of airborne landings cutting off the Cotentin peninsula.

The deployment of the Seventh Army's formations on 6 June had the following results:

- Its best infantry division, the 319th, was on the Channel Islands and thus not available for the defence of any of the critical sectors. This deployment was the result of a direct order from Hitler.
- The 716th Division was occupying a critical sector which was larger than it could possibly hope to effectively cover.
- The 709th Division was occupying an area just outside the landing areas of Normandy, extending to below the Cotentin peninsula, but with too few troops to adequately defend it.
- The 21st Panzer Division was located very close to where the British landings were to occur and was well placed to intervene early if given the order to do so.
- The 352nd Division was located around St Lo and was well positioned to block the landings by the US forces.
- The 243rd Infantry Division was occupying a position in the Cotentin where it was well placed to intervene against the US landings.
- The 91st LL Division was well placed to intervene against the US landings.
- The 6th FS Regiment was well positioned to intervene against the US landings.
- The 30th Infantry Brigade was just outside the critical area where the British landings were to be made.
- The 77th Infantry Division had been located at Caen, perfectly placed to intervene in the British landings, but was transferred by order of the OKW (Hitler) to St Malo, which was outside the critical landing areas of all the invading troops.
- The 116th Panzer Division was north of the Seine and was therefore not placed to intervene on D-Day.
- The 2nd Panzer Division was deployed around Caumont, north of the Somme River, too far away to intervene on the first day of the invasion.
- The OKW reserve of the 12th SS-Panzer and Panzer Lehr Divisions were west of Paris and north-east of Le Mans, and thus not well placed to intervene on the first day.

- The OKW reserve, consisting of the 1st SS-Panzer Division, was refitting near Brussels and obviously could not intervene in the fighting for some time;
- The 17th SS-Panzergrenadier Division was positioned south of Normandy in reserve at Thouars, some 200 miles from the landing sites.

The deployment was therefore far from being optimal, but some good troops were in the right places, or very close to them. Everything depended on how quickly the Germans could commit and deploy their forces in response to the landings.

The Fifteenth Army, which was also part of Army Group B, was concentrated around the Pas-de-Calais, the closest point to Britain on the Channel. The Germans had always expected that the invasion would occur at this point because of this proximity and had planned to launch their own invasion of Britain from there at least partially due to the same reason. The Atlantic Wall was at its strongest in the Pas-de-Calais. There were twenty-one divisions under the command of Fifteenth Army, which comprised four Luftwaffe field divisions and seventeen static infantry divisions, garrisoning the Atlantic Wall or stationed very close behind it. Some of these divisions were well placed to intervene in the early days of the invasion and others were able to join the battle relatively quickly, if the decision had been made to commit them when it was identified that the Normandy landings had occurred in force, which was obvious from the first day of the battle.

Mines, mines and more mines

As part of his determination to defeat any invasion on the beaches, Rommel intended to create a belt of strong field works which would be integrated with extensive mine fields. He had concluded from the experience gained in Africa where the British had used minefields extensively in their defences, that capturing defences using these minefields was very difficult. He also believed that by using them the other material inadequacies of the German army's equipment could be ameliorated. Rommel was accompanied on all his inspection tours by General-Engineer Dr. Wilhelm Meise with whom he discussed all his ideas relating to the defence of the invasion front. Rommel instructed Meise that he wanted to create a defensive belt 2 thousand yards deep which would include the beaches and the immediate adjacent land which was to be the first line of the defences and that mines would be installed at 10-yard intervals. Meise calculated it would require 20 million mines to cover the area to Rommel's specification. Additional defences inland from the coast would require another 180 million mines.[34]

These minefields did not get even close to completion. However, by 20 May more than 4 million mines had been laid, mainly in the Channel coast area. Had these minefields, and the field positions that were intended to be created with them, been completed, the complications for the invaders would have been much greater.

In addition to these extensive minefields and strongpoints, Rommel intended to emplace obstacles at and below the water level on the foreshore where the landings were likely. These included four belts of underwater obstacles which covered the entire tide levels to a depth of twelve feet below the low level and six feet above the high level which took into account the spread of the tides along the coast from the Pas de Calais to Normandy. These were to incorporate mines so that if hit by a landing craft they would explode.[35]

Although the installation of these obstacles was not complete at the time of the invasion, the Allies detected that they existed and a change was made in the timing of the landings so that the obstacles would be above the water level when the landing craft were delivering the troops to the landing beaches. It would have been much more difficult to avoid the obstacles if the installation had been completed, as they would have been at or near the water level and would have had to be individually destroyed before or at the time the troops were being landed.

Rommel knew from their use in the invasion of Sicily and intelligence reports that the allies had powerful specialised airborne troops available and expected that they would be used in the invasion of France. To mitigate their potential use, he ordered the inundation of sectors of the Normandy coast, and also behind the areas occupied by the Fifteenth Army. He was also aware that as well as being dropped by parachute, part of the airborne divisions' personnel and equipment were transported by gliders and intended to block the areas that would be suitable for landing areas with large wooden stakes driven into the ground which would be topped with artillery shells captured from the French in 1940. These obstacles were known among German troops as 'Rommel's asparagus' and would have consisted of stakes approximately 10ft high driven into the ground 100ft apart. He realized that the stakes alone would not be a lethal obstacle to troops landing in gliders, so he gave orders that they were to be fitted with captured shells at the top and for them all to be connected by wire. The shells were to be so arranged that they would be detonated by a pull on the wire. Experimentation showed that a glider landing in territory defended in this manner could not fail to suffer heavy losses, and its troops would have little hope of success. Only a few days before the invasion, Rommel succeeded in obtaining the release of a million captured shells for arming these obstacles, but it was too late – there was no time left to install them.[36]

While deploying all these obstacles would certainly have made the invasion more difficult, without an increase in the number and quality of the troops in the landing area the likelihood is that it would still have been successful. Additionally, the Panzer reserves had to be positioned close enough to the landings to be involved in the fighting when the Allied troops were coming ashore; otherwise the overwhelming Allied firepower – in the form of heavy naval guns and tactical air forces – would surely enable the invasion to succeed.

The Luftwaffe in the West at D-Day

Warlimont wrote the following regarding the strength of the Luftwaffe in Western Europe:[37]

'The air situation was even worse. The original plan was still in force laying down that the meagre reinforcements available should only be flown in when the invasion started. Accordingly, prior to 5 June, the enemy had made good use of his absolute air superiority and had seen to it that: all bridges over the lower Seine and Loire were destroyed, thus cutting all reinforcement routes to the probable battle area: no reconnaissance had penetrated for a considerable period and as a result not a single bomb had fallen on the concentration areas, ports and shipping assembly areas in and around the British Isles.

'... the enemy's air superiority was even greater than had been expected and from the first day of the invasion the Luftwaffe's inferiority was so great that it became the prime factor in making any command action or movement well nigh impossible [Author's emphasis].'

Pemsel confirmed that from the autumn of 1943, ever-increasing bombing missions had been carried out by the Allied air forces against traffic centres, bridges, aerodromes, factories and other infrastructure, and that the Luftwaffe had 'scarcely put in an appearance'. The most important consequence was that repair of the rail network fell further and further behind, leading to construction of defence works along the coast being slowed or in some cases halted. Pemsel stated that the attacks appeared to be aimed at the entire front, with no perceptible 'point of main effort'.[38] The planners of the Allied air offensive were very careful that it was not executed in a manner that indicated the intended location of the invasion by any patterns distinguishable from the bombing missions. For example, for every bomb that was dropped in the Normandy area, two were dropped in the Pas-de-Calais. Pemsel added that a 'very serious omen' was that the Luftwaffe airfields had to be moved from near the coast to the interior, out of the direct reach of enemy air activity. He also noted that during the spring of 1944, Seventh Army received only two good reconnaissance photographs of southern British ports 'which showed large concentrations of landing craft', clearly illustrating the complete dominance of the Allied air forces over the Luftwaffe by this stage of the war.

Pemsel went on to say:[39]

'How would our over-age static divisions, which were inexperienced in combat, as well as our other divisions, which were for the most part unprepared and hampered by makeshifts of every sort, fight against an enemy equipped with the most modern weapons and equipment? **The enemy's superiority over our forces was known, only the degree was uncertain. In any event, it surpassed even our most pessimistic estimates [Author's emphasis].**'

'OKW had given an orientation concerning the possibility of invasion in the Normandy sector of the Seventh Army's area. Rommel, too, figured during the last days on this possibility, but did not draw the necessary conclusion that Seventh Army must be reinforced before the invasion.

'The hope remained that in case of a large-scale attack in Normandy, OKW would do everything possible to bolster and reinforce the attacked front with all possible available forces on the ground and in the air. In all conferences, map problems, etc., the guiding principle had always been that the enemy, wherever he should first set foot on the Continent with strong forces, was to be thrown back into the sea by concentrating every possible means. To await possible enemy assaults on other fronts was considered misleading. Thus one could expect that the decisive battle would have to be fought on the attacked front within three to four days at the latest after the invasion.'

Allied forces committed to the invasion of Normandy, 6 June 1944

The disparity between the forces committed by the Allies for the invasion and the German defenders is stark. The forces available for and supporting the invasion were as follows:

British 21st Army Group: under the command of General Sir Bernard Montgomery.

The forces that landed on the three invasion beaches allotted to the Army group were:

Sword Beach (Ouistreham) – 3rd Division; 8, 9 and 185 Infantry Brigades (all British);

Juno Beach (Courselles) – 3rd Canadian Division; 7, 8 and 9 Infantry Brigades (Canadian);

Gold Beach (Asnelles) – 50th Division; 47 Royal Commando; 56, 69 and 231 Infantry Brigades (all British);

Followup forces: 7th Armoured Division, 22 Armoured Brigade Group and 153 Infantry Brigade Group; The 6th Airborne Division.

American 12th Army Group: under the command of General Omar Bradley. The forces that landed on the two beaches allotted to the army group were:

Omaha Beach (St Laurent) – 1st Division; 16th, 18th, 115th and 116th RCT (Regimental Combat Team);

Utah Beach (Varreville) – 4th Division; 8th, 12th and 22nd RCT;

Follow-up forces: 29th Division; 26th, 175th and 359th RCT; 82nd and 101st Airborne Divisions.

US Army Air Force IX/XIX Tactical Air Command: IX TAC had three fighter wings and the XIX TAC had two. There was a general understanding that the IX TAC would support the US First Army and the XIX TAC would support the US Third Army once the latter became operational in France. Eventually, on 1 August 1944, when Patton's Third Army and Bradley's 12th Army Group became operational, this arrangement was formalized.

Eighth USAAF: the strategic bombing forces under command of the 8th Air Force consisted of three bombardment divisions of fourteen bombardment wings, each of three or four bombardment groups.

RAF 2nd Tactical Air Force: consisted of three RAF groups – No. 2 Group, No. 83 Group and No. 84 Group. During the campaign, 2nd RAF's subordinate units came to directly support specific parts of the 21st Army Group, with the British Second Army assigned No. 83 Group, and First Canadian Army supported by No. 84 Group.

RAF Bomber Command: there were eighty-three squadrons in RAF Bomber Command on 6 June 1944. These squadrons had a total of over 2,000 heavy bombers which could be deployed as required.

Royal Navy: the fire support group consisted of four battleships – HMS *Warspite*, *Rodney*, *Ramillies* and *Nelson*. These mounted 15-inch and 16-inch guns, easily outclassing anything the Germans had in Normandy or the Channel Islands. Two monitors, each carrying two 15-inch guns, were also included. There were also two heavy cruisers and seventeen light cruisers. Eighty-five British and Commonwealth destroyers and escort ships were also deployed.

US Navy: the fire support group consisted of three battleships – USS *Nevada*, *Texas* and *Arkansas*. The main armament on these ships varied between 12-inch and 14-inch, also outclassing anything the Germans had in the invasion area. There were also three US heavy cruisers and forty destroyers and escort ships.

Warships from the Free French, Dutch and other Allied navies brought the total number of warships involved to 508, of which 352 were British.

With the Germans unable to match the number of Allied naval units and scale of air support, and all of the Allied divisions being equivalent to full-establishment German motorized divisions, it is clear that the scale and quality of forces arrayed against the defenders meant it was most unlikely that the invasion would be defeated.

INVASION!

Lieutenant General Warlimont, Deputy Chief of Operations at the OKW under Colonel General Jodl, was witness to the reactions of and decisions made by Hitler and the OKW Supreme Headquarters when news of the invasion was received. He recounted:[40]

> 'The first news arrived about 3am on 6 June when Commander-in-Chief West reported major air landings in Normandy. ... At about 6am General Blumentritt, Chief of Staff to the Commander-in-Chief West, gave me the first indication that in all probability this was the invasion and that Normandy was apparently the area. He urged on behalf of his Commander-in-Chief, Field Marshal von Rundstedt, that the so-called "OKW reserves", consisting of four motorized or armoured divisions, should be released so that they could move from their assembly areas to positions nearer the front.
>
> 'This was the first and most important decision which Supreme Headquarters had to take and I therefore immediately got on to Jodl by telephone. It was soon clear that Jodl was fully up to date with all

the information, but in the light of the latest reports was not yet fully convinced that here and now the real invasion had begun. He did not therefore consider that the moment had arrived to let go our last reserves and felt that Commander-in-Chief West must first try to clear up the situation with the forces of Army Group B.

'... General Jodl took this decision on his own responsibility, in other words without asking Hitler.'

It is interesting to note that Jodl had no operational command experience which could compare with that of Rundstedt or Rommel, yet he was in a position to prevent the Commander-in-Chief West from conducting the defensive battle for which he was responsible – and upon which the fate of Nazi Germany depended – in the manner he thought appropriate. Furthermore, Rundstedt was in touch with the front – Jodl was not – and was thus in the best place to determine the requirements of the battle situation. Meanwhile, as was his normal habit, Hitler was sleeping late because he always went to bed in the early hours of the morning; Jodl decided he should not be disturbed to be told of this report from the C-in-C West. It is beyond doubt that if a professional soldier had occupied the office of Commander-in-Chief of the Army, Hitler would have expected him to be available at any time during the day or night to deal with such a critical matter. This emphasizes yet again that Hitler was a part-time Commander-in-Chief; because of the way he worked and his other roles and duties, he could never be anything else.

Consequently, the only scintilla of hope that existed to defeat the invasion while the Allied ground forces were at their weakest was lost because of Hitler's failure to fully implement Rommel's defence strategy and Jodl's hesitation reflecting the Byzantine command structure which Hitler had inflicted on the Germany Army in the West.

The date the Allies chose to invade, 6 June, happened to be the day on which a Hungarian state visit to Germany was scheduled, so Hitler's regular midday situation conference was cancelled. Hitler was staying at the Berghof and had a planned meeting with the Hungarians at Klessheim Castle, near Obersalzberg. In view of events in Normandy, there was a preliminary conference before that meeting, as Warlimont recalled:[41]

'I and many of the others were keyed up as a result of the portentous events which were taking place and as we stood about in front of the maps and charts we awaited with some excitement Hitler's arrival and the decisions he would take. Any great expectations were destined to be bitterly disappointed. As often happened, Hitler decided to put on an act. As he came up to the maps he chuckled in a carefree manner and behaved as if this was the opportunity he had been awaiting so long to settle accounts with his enemy. In unusually broad Austrian he said: "so we're off". After short reports on the latest moves by ourselves and the enemy we went up to the next floor where the "show piece" was laid on for the Hungarians. ... The usual overestimates of German forces and confidence in "ultimate victory" were more than normally repellent.'

All of the shortcomings of the command system created by Hitler can be seen operating throughout these events. Everyone in the senior German military hierarchy, Hitler included, knew that there were not adequate resources to repel a serious landing on the Normandy coast, largely because it had not been regarded as the most likely location for the Allies to invade, reflecting the evaluation by the Kriegsmarine. The most likely place was still considered to be the Pas-de-Calais, for the reasons previously outlined by Rommel. The reserves requested by Rundstedt – who was regarded, even by Hitler, as one of the most capable of the German commanders – were in his estimate needed to deal with the situation, viewed with the advantage of being the commander at the front. In order to comply with the previous year's Fuhrer Directive No. 51, it was imperative that strong enough forces be available to deal with the invasion as soon as possible, so not only was Rundstedt's request quite understandable from any military viewpoint, it was also in accordance with Hitler's own instructions for defence against invasion. It goes without saying that Rundstedt, or Rommel, as the responsible theatre commanders, should have had the authority to commit the reserves when they saw the need in order to fulfil the task they had been set, which was to defeat an invasion. That would have been consistent with the tradition of the German General Staff prior to Hitler's advent and the curtailment of any initiative by his command arrangements. The method by which the German General Staff was trained to operate was to set a task for a commander, give him the forces to carry it out and then allow him broad independence in how he did so. Needless to say, events proved that Rundstedt was correct in his view and that the reserves should have been committed when he requested them because Normandy was the location of the real invasion. Whether committing the reserves when he asked for them would have made any difference to the outcome is another question, but at least they would have been directed to the correct place at the earliest possible opportunity. It is also true that Hitler did not make the decision to reject Rundstedt's request, but he, and no one else, created the utterly dysfunctional multi-level command system which required Rundstedt to get OKW permission before committing the reserves. Consequently, Hitler is responsible and accountable for the ensuing disaster. It must be stressed again that there was no militarily compelling reason for the command structure which Hitler created; it simply served his interest to dissipate the power of the Army commanders, which proved on many occasions to be at the expense of operational effectiveness.

The next important step that needed to be taken by the German Supreme Command once it became evident that there had been a landing in strength at Normandy was to move sufficient forces to the Normandy Front, quickly enough to either eliminate the bridgehead or to contain it, build up the necessary forces and then defeat it. The obvious course was to move forces from the Fifteenth Army, which was deployed along the Channel coast from Le Havre to the Scheldt area in Belgium and on into the Netherlands, with the main concentrations around the Pas-de-Calais. This involved some strategic risk for the Germans, because if there was another invasion in the Pas-de-Calais – as their intelligence seemed to indicate there would be – then there might not be sufficient forces left to deal with it. An obvious response to this conundrum was that if the invasion in Normandy was not defeated, there would be no need for a second landing by the Allies, so the immediate and urgent priority was to defeat the Normandy landing as quickly as possible. The Fifteenth Army was more powerful than the Seventh, so if this course had been taken, significant reinforcements could have been sent. There were six infantry divisions of the Fifteenth Army deployed close to Normandy which could have made it there within a day or two, plus another half-dozen deployed between Normandy and the Pas-de-Calais which would have taken approximately a week to reach the battle area by normal march. This would have been substantially faster than sending reinforcements from other parts of Europe. In addition, the troops would have been travelling through areas that had been under German military control since 1940, so supply arrangements would have been easier. While they would have been exposed to the air power of the Allies as they were being redeployed, even in this regard they would have been better off than troops coming from further afield. The composition of the Fifteenth Army on 6 June, as set out in the previous section of this chapter, suggests that if a substantial part of the infantry divisions had been committed to Normandy together with the OKW reserve, the Normandy defences would have been significantly augmented. Together with those from Brittany, between twelve and fifteen divisions would have been available within a week of the landing. Warlimont recalls that:[42]

'Rommel and the OKW Operations staff, with the significant exception of Jodl, independently reached the conclusion that every risk must be

taken [Author's emphasis] and all available forces concentrated for a rapid counter-attack against the enemy who had just landed – as indeed Directive 51 laid down; no one else reached this conclusion. **The most important step was to move from the Straits to Normandy the bulk of the Fifteenth Army [Author's emphasis]**, then to collect all forces which could be made available rapidly from the other parts of France, and so be in a position to launch a decisive counter-attack.

'This was too bold a decision for Hitler. He would allow no reduction in the strength of the Fifteenth Army. Any other possible reinforcements however could not arrive for days or even weeks [Author's emphasis]. The result was that, though the Supreme Command clung to its decision to recover the entire length of the Normandy coastline, the only forces available to do so were those already on the spot, and they had been proved to be inadequate. Just as at Anzio, it did little good to issue orders that the enemy bridgehead, which meanwhile had been extended considerably, was to be broken down and then "demolished in detail".'

Predictably, Hitler's exhortations had little, if any, effect, and the bridgehead was steadily extended and consolidated by the Allies.

Omar Bradley, in command of the US land forces committed to the invasion, understood the dangers they faced in the early days of the operation:[43]

'Hitler and his generals had one last chance to defeat us. The nineteen divisions of the Fifteenth Army in the Pas-de-Calais (120 miles away) and von Rundstedt's five panzer divisions of armoured reserve were still uncommitted. Had Hitler thrown these forces against us within the first few days or within the first week, he might well have overwhelmed us.'

So while the Allies were fully aware of the threat posed by the Fifteenth Army, Hitler was unwilling to commit it to the battle because he still expected another invasion in the Pas-de-Calais. This state of affairs was confirmed by Speer:[44]

'Hitler remained convinced that the invasion was merely a feint whose purpose was to trick him into deploying his defensive forces wrongly. ... For the time being he expected the decisive assault to take place in the vicinity of Calais – **as though he were determined that the enemy, too, would prove him to have been right [Author's emphasis]**. For there, around Calais, he had ever since 1942 been emplacing the heaviest naval guns under many feet of concrete to destroy an enemy landing fleet. This was the reason he did not commit the Fifteenth Army, stationed at Calais, to the battlefield on the coast of Normandy.'

An indication of how difficult the march to the Normandy Front was for any German reinforcements was provided by the experience of the Panzer Lehr Division, which was one of the best-equipped divisions in the German Army:[45]

'General Bayerlein [the Panzer Lehr commander] issued the order to move out at 1700 hours, and the wonderfully equipped division started its movement west. The approach was broken up into five march routes. Despite this, the Allied air forces accompanied the division on its move and attempted to bomb everything that was sighted.

'... On the evening of 7th June, the balance sheet of lost vehicles for the division read as follows: 5 tanks, 40 fuel trucks, 84 SPWs

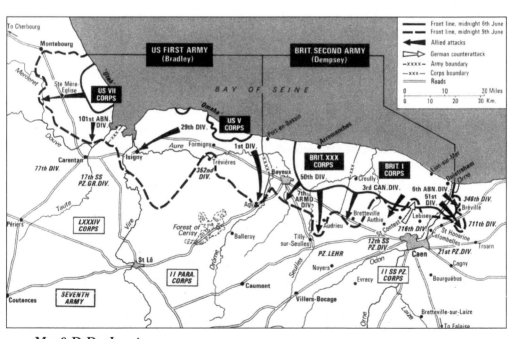

Map 8. D-Day Invasion.
This Map shows the progress made by the Allied invasions forces from 6th to 12th June, the critical phase when the Allies were at their weakest. Bradley confirms that if Hitler had authorized sending reinforcements from the Fifteenth Army which was deployed along the Pas-de-Calais, the allied position would have been made much more difficult. This is the advice that Hitler was given from all the senior operational commanders in Normandy, which he ignored.

[Schutzenpanzerwagen] and 90 cargo trucks. **Without having fired a shot, the division had already lost approximately 10% of it combat power [Author's emphasis].**'

This was the kind of interdiction by the Allied air forces Rommel had warned of, and which Hitler and other German commanders from the Eastern Front who had not experienced fighting the Western Allies continued to discount.

Field Marshals Rundstedt and Rommel meet Hitler

General Gunther Blumentritt, Chief of Staff at OB West, commented on the tardiness of the German response to the landings:[46]

'By 8 or 9 June 1944, in spite of the commitment of 12 SS-Panzer and Panzer Lehr Divisions under 1 SS-Panzer Corps, and in spite of bringing up the first, inadequate reinforcements, we did not succeed in repelling the invasion or in defeating those forces which had landed. It was evident to Genfldms von Rundstedt and Rommel that the invasion was successful. In a few days, we realised that our forces and means were not strong enough to reverse the situation. This was reported to OKW, and the envisaged reinforcements were brought up from fronts not under attack – however, only insofar as the movement was permitted or ordered by OKW, that is, by the Fuhrer himself. The Fuhrer reserved for himself the authority to move each individual division. After a few days when the Allies succeeded in joining the inner wings of the two beachheads in the vicinity of Arromanches, thus establishing one large beachhead, it was even more obvious that all counterattacks would be futile.

'... As the situation seemed threatening, Genfldm von Rundstedt requested a conference with the Fuhrer. Up to that time, all orders read: "counterattack" in order to throw back the landed enemy. However, the reinforcements necessary for this purpose arrived very slowly because of the demolished railroads and bridges, the Resistance movement, the Allied air supremacy, the limited mobility of the horsedrawn infantry divisions, and the lack of fuel and transportation. The Allies landed troops faster and in greater strength than we could reinforce our own.'

All the factors noted by Blumentritt were communicated to Hitler. They confirmed that the only way to quickly reinforce the Seventh Army was by taking the necessary units from the Fifteenth Army as soon as possible after the landings, which Hitler would not allow. In these circumstances, the defence of Normandy was bound to fail.

A further indication of the situation faced by the German forces on the ground at the time of the invasion was given by Lieutenant Colonel von Criegern, Chief of Staff of the 91st LL Division:[47]

'The command post of the 91st LL Division was attacked by air landed enemy elements in battalion strength. The tactical group of the general staff section withdrew to the command post of the supply group staff section and continued to conduct battle from there. The commander of the 91st LL Division, Gen Falley, who had gone to Rennes for a map exercise ordered by the Army, was killed during the morning of 6 June when returning to the original command post which had been captured by the enemy. Already, by 0330 hours, the division could no longer communicate with troops committed in the area of Ste Mere-Eglise.

'... The subsequently arriving reports showed that the sea landings had been in progress since 0715. It seemed that three landing sectors became apparent west of the mouth of the Orne River, east of Grandcamp, and along the coast of Cotentin, east of Ste Mere Eglise.

'By 0900, the enemy had penetrated into the artillery positions of the 716th Infantry Division west of the mouth of the Orne River, and gained a firm footing near Asnelles and St Laurent. The rapid landing of tanks, reported near Asnelles, very quickly brought about a critical situation there simultaneously with those of the 716th Infantry Division west of the Orne River and in the sector of the 352nd Division near St Laurent-sur-Mer. The lack of depth to the defense and the lack of mobile antitank weapons were especially felt.'

Once again, it is obvious there was a critical need for reinforcements at the time of the landings. Yet no such reinforcements were available anywhere along the invasion beaches. Had the tanks of the 12th SS-Panzer Division been sited where Rommel wanted them to be at the base of the Cotentin – a request rejected by the OKW – they would have made a huge difference to the strength of the defences.

Another formation in a critical area when the invasion began was the 352nd Infantry Division. As set out earlier, it was a static division with limited mobility. Lieutenant Colonel Fritz Ziegelmann, the Chief of Staff of the division, left a record of its travails:[48]

'At and after 0300 hours, the reinforced 915th Infantry Regiment (2/915th Infantry Regiment and the 352nd Rifle Battalion on bicycles, 1/915th Infantry Regiment and regimental units on French cargo trucks) were on their way to St Balaroy. As was to be expected, many of the French drivers claimed it was not possible to proceed further, due to engine trouble, and of course this held things up!'

Ziegelmann evaluated the fighting on D-Day as follows:[49]

'[The Allies'] success was to be ascribed primarily to the effect of the material and armament of his ground, naval, and air forces, which gradually brought about the breakdown of our battle installations, and these were to be designated as being only "average".

'... The infantry in the positions at field strength, without any doubt, contributed by the effect of their weapons to the casualties of the enemy in the coastal zone. At another time, on the infantry were also inflicted continuous fire of the naval artillery and that of the landing boats, and especially later on by the enemy air forces.

'... Our own personnel losses in the divisional sector amounted on 6 June to about 200 dead on the field of battle, 500 wounded and 500 missing, which meant that about one fifth of the total infantry fighting strength of 6,000 men had been rendered ineffective.'

At this rate of loss, the German formations would be rendered powerless for want of men within a few days, which is what actually occurred.

General Zimmerman of OB West noted how events developed within the German command over the first few days of the invasion:[50]

'As the success of this operation became more and more probable, Rundstedt and Rommel agreed that the time had come **for Hitler to decide personally what we must do next and how we were to go on fighting in the West; in a word what our strategy was to be [Author's emphasis]**. It was clear to the Field Marshals that limited measures could no longer hope to change the situation as it now stood. The only course open to us was to seal off Normandy along a favourable line, well to the rear of the present front. Along such a line it should be feasible once again to create a strong defensive position, which would enable us to withdraw our mobile reserves from the fighting and thus make them available for the sort of operations for which they were intended. The Field Marshals' urgent demands for an interview with Hitler were accepted.

'In circumstances of extreme secrecy, Hitler arrived at his old command post, at Margival, between Soissons and Laon. It was a particularly well-hidden installation, and there he met the two Field Marshals with their Chiefs of Staff. Their first reports on the situation certainly impressed him and he promised to lay down the necessary directives which they required for the next stage of the campaign at once. But when the conversation turned on the consequences to be drawn from the successful Allied landing, his mood changed. **Rommel expressed himself with particular force, demanding that political conclusions be drawn from the military situation in the West. Hitler became angry, took Rommel's arguments ill, and ordered him to concern himself with military, not political, matters. The gist of Hitler's remarks seem to have been that in any case no one would make peace with him [Author's emphasis].**'

It is revealing that Hitler's comments indicate that he realized none of his enemies would negotiate with him. This raises the question of when he understood that the war could no longer be won by Germany, meaning that he was using the lives of others to prolong his time in power without any real hope of a negotiated peace. Many commentators have contended that the declaration made at the Casablanca Conference, that the Allies would not make peace with Nazi Germany on any terms – in other words, that they would only accept unconditional surrender – somehow made the chances of a negotiated peace less likely. There is no doubt that as long as Hitler was in control of Germany, no peace with the Allies was possible on any terms. Hitler himself stated on numerous occasions that 'surrender' was a word that was not in his vocabulary, and he would die rather than capitulate, which of course he ultimately did. However, Lord Ismay, a member of the British War Cabinet who was at the Casablanca Conference, doubted whether the 'unconditional surrender' ultimatum made 'any material difference to the length of hostilities':[51]

'It certainly did not prevent the Italians from suing for peace at the first opportunity. Nor would it have prevented the Germans from doing likewise, if it had not been that Hitler was all-powerful, and would neither surrender himself or allow anyone else to do so.'

The situation in Germany was such that resistance to the regime of any kind was virtually impossible for any civilian group, as revealed by the fate of the 'White Rose' student movement in Munich and the 'Kreisau Circle', which included some of the foremost noble families in Germany. Virtually all the members of these resistance groups were arrested by the Gestapo and executed by guillotine after show trials for treason. The only possible effective centre of resistance was the Army, as shown by the only attempted coup that occurred against Hitler, Operation *Valkyrie*, which was smashed by the regime with comparatively little effort.

Speer recounted that he was at Obersalzberg on 17 June when Hitler returned from his meeting with Rundstedt and Rommel:[52]

'On June 17 he visited this headquarters, called W2, situated between Soissons and Laon. That same day he returned to Obersalzerg. He was sulky and cross: "Rommel has lost his nerve; he's become a pessimist. In these times only optimists can achieve anything."

'After such remarks it was only a question of time when Rommel would be relieved of his command. For Hitler still regarded his defensive positions opposite the bridgehead as unconquerable.'

Zimmerman related the outcome of the meeting:[53]

'The new instructions which resulted from this conference were simply the old ones repeated afresh. Cherbourg, together with every other square yard of Norman soil, was to be held to the last man and the last round. This was of course impossible.'

What Rundstedt and Rommel were asking Hitler for was to provide them with his strategy to defeat the invasion, not a system of makeshift moves cobbled together in an attempt to hold the line merely to buy time and postpone the inevitable.

As nothing was done by Hitler to alleviate the situation following the meeting on 17 June and the position continued to deteriorate, Rundstedt and Rommel requested another meeting which occurred on 29 June. The actions which Hitler promised at this meeting were subject to a precondition, which was that the enemy attack had to be brought to a standstill. To assist the defence, he indicated that the Luftwaffe would attack the bridgehead with the new jet aircraft and that enemy battleships would be engaged with special bombs (probably a reference to the Heinkel HS 293 which was used to sink the Italian battleship 'Roma' after its surrender – Author's note). He also indicated that the mining of the sea in the Bay of the Seine would continue, but this had already proved to be ineffective because of the superiority of the allied air forces. He also promised that 1,000 fighters would be committed, and that anti-aircraft nests would be established along the main supply routes to protect supply convoys and reinforcements.

However, none of these steps could be taken and the allied build up continued as did the inexorable progress of the bridgehead. The truth was that the Wehrmacht was virtually powerless to arrest the invasion and while the Field Marshals realised this was the case, Hitler would not see this reality:[54]

The precondition of bringing the enemy attack to a halt was of course impossible. Furthermore, none of the forces Hitler mentioned were supplied or the other actions he outlined undertaken.

Zimmerman also left an account of this meeting:[55]

'The Field-Marshals were treated with a marked lack of courtesy and were kept waiting for several hours. When at last Hitler received them, he treated them to a lengthy monologue concerning the effects to be expected from the new "miracle weapons". The Field-Marshals left in a very bad temper indeed. Back in his headquarters, Rundstedt telephoned Keitel and told him that they had better find a younger man to continue the battle: he himself was too old. When Keitel asked him what he thought they should do, Rundstedt replied loudly and clearly: "End the war, you fools!"'

Rundstedt was thus dismissed for the second time (though he was reappointed in September), placed in the Fuhrer Reserve and replaced by Field Marshal von Kluge, who arrived to take up his command on 3 July. The new Commander-in-Chief West had been at Berchtesgaden for the preceding week being 'indoctrinated' by Hitler,[56] having been convinced that Rundstedt and Rommel were too pessimistic in their assessment of a situation that he would be able to master.

By the end of June, Hitler had rejected the proposals of his two commanders in France for the conduct of the battle and sacked one of them, but had not substituted any new or alternative strategy, much less provided the forces necessary to defeat or contain the invasion. The Allies enjoyed complete mastery of the air space over the Western theatre, and because Hitler had not released formations from the Fifteenth Army quickly enough to reinforce Normandy, were also winning the race to build-up the forces at the battlefront in Normandy. In these circumstances, the success of the invasion could not be long delayed. This was the situation Kluge was confronted with when he took over command.

Rommel's analysis

Rommel sent many reports to OKW marked for Hitler's personal attention, one of the most important of which was dated 3rd July. Its substance reiterated many points he had made before and brought them together so that anyone could see the real state of the German position in Normandy and the causes from which it resulted. The most important points he made were as follows:[57]

1. As can be seen from the comparison of forces previously set out in this chapter, the German formations in Normandy were weak, in many cases over-age and suffering from the effects of injury or other physical incapacity, and were inadequately equipped to face the allies;

2. Imperative requests for reinforcement had been refused;

3. The movement of forces to positions considered critical by OB West were repeatedly changed. An example was the denial of a request to move the 12th SS-Panzer Division into the Lessay–Coutances area where it would have been on hand to immediately counterattack any enemy landing on the east or west coast of the Cotentin, as actually occurred. Another example being the command's suggestion to locate the Panzer Lehr Division where it could intervene rapidly in a coastal battle which was not accepted because of fears of an airborne landing in the vicinity of Paris. (Had this suggestion been adopted, Panzer Lehr – one of the best armoured formations the Germans had – could have made a significant contribution to defending against the invasion if committed as suggested – Author's note);

4. 7th Army requested that strong anti-aircraft forces should be located between the Orne estuary and Montebourg (which would have put them in the best place to defend against the Allied air forces over Normandy – Author's note). This request was denied and the units requested were used to protect V2 sites;

5. 7th Army requested that 7 Nebelwefer Brigade be used to strengthen the Normandy defences close to the potential landing sites. This request was also denied, and the unit was not transferred to 7th Army until after the invasion had occurred;

6. 7th Army had repeatedly requested that the Bay of the Seine to be mined but these operations were not commenced until after the invasion and therefore had very little effect;

7. It was repeatedly pointed out that because of the bombing of the French railway network, the supply position in Normandy was difficult before the invasion had occurred, but no steps were taken by the Luftwaffe to counter the problem;

8. Once the invasion had occurred Army Group B intended to eliminate the foothold on the Cotentin and then to eliminate the foothold between the Orne and the Vire. The reasons for this approach were that the Cotentin

lodgement seemed to it to be the weaker of the two and that by taking this course the danger to Cherbourg would have been eliminated. OKW however, gave orders for the main effort of the defence to be made on the eastern flank at the Orne estuary. (This fitted perfectly into the strategy which the Allied leaders had agreed to pursue for the development of the bridgehead – Author's note.);

9. The 12th SS-Panzer Division was located by order of OKW to a position 75 miles from Normandy and was not able to at their defensive position until 9.30 am on 7 June. They were attacked by enemy aircraft on the way and suffered needless casualties and delay. When they arrived, there was not time to deploy in depth and their attack could not be driven home. Similarly, because of its positioning by OKW, Panzer Lehr had 110 miles to cover to reach the battlefield and did not arrive at Caen until 1.00 pm on 7 June. They were attacked on their journey by allied aircraft and its elements became separated. Because of this their attack could not be made on that day. Contrary to their role and the intention of the command, they then became involved in defensive battles on their own front and were not able to support the 352nd Division, which was still fighting at Bayeux. The leading elements of the 2nd Panzer Division were disrupted on their approach to the battlefield and did not arrive until 13 June after which they required a further seven days before being committed to action as a division;

10. Panzer Lehr had 110 miles to cover and did not arrive at Caen until 1.00 pm on 7 June. They were hindered in their advance by Allied aircraft and the wheeled units became separated from the tracked vehicles. As a result, their attack could not be put in. They then became involved in defensive battles and were not able to support the 352nd Division, which was still fighting at Bayeux.

11. The leading elements of the 2nd Panzer Division did not arrive until 13 June and required a further seven days before they could be committed to action as a division.

12. The 3rd Parachute Division needed six days to get to the battlefield from Brittany. When it arrived, it was no longer possible to make the attack intended as the enemy had taken the forest of Cerisy.

13. The 77th Division required six days before it could intervene in the fighting in the north of the Cotentin peninsula. This division had been moved from the Cotentin to St Malo by order of Hitler.

14. Support from the Luftwaffe was not forthcoming on the scale originally foreseen. The enemy had complete command of the air over the battlefield, up to a point 60 miles behind the front.

15. German naval activity was not on the scale that had been promised. As a result, large-scale landing of further enemy forces was still taking place. The daily bombardment by naval guns 'on a scale hitherto unknown' caused serious difficulties for the troops at the front.

16. Army Group B had no authority to take part in the system pertaining to its own supply.

17. Channels of command were unsatisfactory. Only unified, close-knit command of all services, after the pattern of Montgomery and Eisenhower, would vouchsafe final victory.

This catalogue of errors and negligence in command can only be marvelled at for its breadth and comprehensive nature. It is hardly possible to envisage how the situation could have been managed worse. One can only imagine the reaction of Hitler and those in the OKW to the last item, which must have struck a particularly raw nerve.

Kluge and Rommel

When Field Marshal von Kluge took over command, he had an almost immediate falling out with Rommel. Kluge could be a difficult superior and had argued with other senior officers before, an example being when he sacked Guderian from his command during the winter campaign in 1941. Subsequently he even challenged Guderian to a duel which Hitler heard of and prevented. On this occasion he berated Rommel for his 'defeatist attitude' (note 61). Apparently, this view resulted from the two weeks he had spent previously with Hitler at Berchtesgaden, where he had stressed to Kluge that Rommel was taking too dark a view of events. However, soon after he arrived Kluge undertook a series of meetings and visited the front himself, after which he changed his view. General Zimmerman recalls:[58]

'It was not long, however, before he realized the true nature of the position. **His repeated visits to the front [Author's emphasis]** soon showed him the contrast between the poor equipment of the German troops and the lavish means at the disposal of the enemy. He saw with his own eyes the terrible effects of Allied air supremacy. After a few days he had no choice but to admit that Rommel and Rundstedt had been correct in their appreciation of the situation.'

On July 21, Kluge forwarded Rommel's last report to Hitler and also stated:[59]

'I came here with the fixed intention of making effective your order to make a stand <u>at any price</u>. But when one sees that this price must be paid by the slow but sure destruction of our troops – I am thinking here of the Hitler Youth Division, which has earned the highest praise – when one sees that the reinforcements and replacements sent to all areas are nearly always hopelessly inadequate, and that the armaments, especially artillery and anti-tank guns and the ammunition for them, are not nearly sufficient for the soldiers' needs, so that the main weapon in the defensive battle is the good spirits of our brave men, then the anxiety about the immediate future on this front is only too well justified.

... However, in spite of all endeavours, the moment is fast approaching when this overtaxed front line is bound to breakup. And when the enemy once reaches the open country a properly coordinated command will be almost impossible, because of the insufficient mobility of our troops.'

Two days later, on 17 July, Rommel was severely injured when his car was strafed by an Allied fighter-bomber as he was returning from an inspection at the front. He suffered serious fractures to the skull, which were, for a while, thought to be fatal.

During the convalescence following his injury, Rommel had several conversations with his son, Manfred. Manfred recalled his father saying that Hitler continually interfered in the dispositions he intended to make and that his role was reduced to that of a sergeant-major, which is entirely consistent with the matters mentioned in his various memoranda to Hitler, particularly as quoted above, his memorandum of 3rd July:[60]

Warlimont recalled the following incident:[61]

'Hitler might now have thought back to his statement that an allied success in the West would decide the war and have drawn the necessary conclusions from it; but instead he was to be seen in front of the assembled company at a briefing conference, using ruler and compass to work out the small number of square miles occupied by the enemy in Normandy and compare them to the great area of France still in German hands. **One's thoughts went back to those early days of the Polish war. Was this really all he was capable of as a military leader? Or did he think that this elementary method would have some propaganda effect on his audience? It was a sight I shall not readily forget [Author's emphasis].'**

On the 'other side of the hill', the Allies were implementing their strategy relentlessly. Since the beginning of the invasion, Montgomery had been applying severe pressure to the Germans in and around Caen, to obtain more room for the 21st Army Group to fully deploy and create the strongest threat of a breakout there. This meant that the Germans would have to send their most powerful formations, the panzer and mechanized divisions, against the British and Canadians. The Germans had to defend against this possibility because the shortest route to Paris and ultimately Germany was through the open country close to Caen in the British and Canadian sector of the front. By attracting the German reinforcements, it would allow the US section of the bridgehead under the command of General Bradley to gain space to deploy General George Patton's Third US Army so that it could develop its offensive which was intended to lead to a breakthrough. This successful strategy left the Germans with no other choice than to feed reinforcements into the front as they came to the battlefield against the British and Canadians; they were unable to accumulate any reserves to mount a concerted counteroffensive. Moreover, Hitler had ordered that the units should be committed as soon as they arrived at the front, so many were deployed piecemeal and suffered higher casualty rates than would have occurred if they had been committed as complete units.

Montgomery provided a summary of this strategy:[62]

'The enemy had attempted to "rope us off" in the "bocage" country some 15 to 20 miles inland from the assault area. For a time this policy was successful; but it was only successful by a continuous expenditure of reserves to plug holes in his defences and at a heavy cost in men and materials. These enemy reserves prevented any substantial gain on our part east and south of Caen, but in doing this they were not available to counter the thrusts on the western flank. In short, they were being committed. As at Alamein, we had forced the enemy to commit his reserves on a wide front; we were now ready to commit ours on a narrow front, and so win the battle.'

Despite the repeated crises that occurred on the British Front because of this strategy, the situation on the American flank of the German line eventually became so critical that on 2 July Hitler allowed the Panzer Lehr Division to be redeployed from facing the British to a position near St Lo in the American sector. On July 25 'Operation Cobra', the break-out from the American sector of the front, commenced. It was preceded by a bombardment from 1,500 US bombers which was directed against the Panzer Lehr division's position.

Although part of the bombardment fell short onto US troops, the effect of the bombing on Panzer Lehr was devastating, destroying communications and heavy equipment and stunning the surviving troops. This initial blow was then followed by the commitment of the tactical air force which completely paralysed the defence[63]

Once it had completed its move on 7 July, the Panzer Lehr was holding a 6,000-yard front, which was too long for its depleted state and meant it could not deploy to beyond 4,000 yards in depth, which its commanding General Bayerlein did not regard as an effective defensive depth.

The tactical use of the Allies' strategic air forces in Normandy emphasized further the utter hopelessness of the German situation. They could not possibly counter, defeat or even less emulate the use of these forces, which caused problems on a scale not even Rommel had previously experienced. This use of the strategic air forces in this tactical role had never been done before the Normandy campaign. It is important to note that Eisenhower had insisted on having authority over the strategic air forces as one of the conditions to achieve victory which he set out when he was appointed Supreme Commander of the Allied invasion forces.[64] Although initially resisted, he was successful in obtaining the power to use these forces as he wished, and the result was the virtual destruction of any German formation upon which they were targeted. This carpet-bombing tactic was used on German units by both allies with devastating effect, and was all the more demoralizing because there was absolutely nothing the Germans could do to counter it.

The effect of one such bombing by the RAF, which occurred on the British Front at the outset of Operation *Goodwood*, was related by Lieutenant Richard Freiherr von Rosen, who was company commander of one of the sections of heavy tank unit PzAbt 503, armed with the Tiger Mk.1, PzKpfw VI:[65]

'Finally the attack seemed to come to an end. ... I went to the panzer on our right. It had received a direct hit and looked like a giant opened sardine tin. Flames licked the wreckage. Of Unteroffizier Westerhausen and his crew there was no trace. I walked my way through a veritable primeval woodland and now came to the gigantic crater in front of Oberfeldwebel Sach's Tiger 313. The panzer itself had been flipped over by the blast and now lay on its turret, wheels in the air. We found two crewmen dead under it, and of the other three there was no trace. Where my front-line repair group had been was only a crater.'

A small group of the tanks was able to operate, but only after hours spent in digging them out and repairs being carried out on them. However, because of the power of the Tigers, they were just able to prevent a complete breakthrough by the British. Thereafter, the main German strength in Normandy continued to be committed against the British sector of the front.

In early August, Warlimont was sent to obtain a first-hand impression of the situation in the West from the Commander-in-Chief and other commanders at the front. He met with Kluge on 3 August:[66]

'An order had just arrived from Supreme Headquarters to mount a strong counter-attack from the area east of Avranches in order to re-establish positions on the coast and so once again close the ring in southern Normandy.

'As far as I was concerned I had no new instructions; I could therefore only state that before I left there had not even been a hint of such plans and in so far as they were not occupied with day-to-day developments, the staffs had been working primarily upon future strategy much farther back in the western theatre. As the Field Marshal knew from his visit to Berchtesgaden it had been recognized by the end of June that there were no further possibilities of conducting an offensive defence. There could be no doubt that Hitler had taken a snap decision without any preliminary study or other form of preparation by his staff; it looked as if this must have been taken the previous night; there was no need for me to point this out. ... Kluge said that this was so obvious an idea that he had of course considered it. If however by his order Hitler was now prepared to take responsibility for the withdrawal of considerable armour and artillery from the other flank at Caen, which was equally hard pressed, that of course produced a new situation. He was afraid that even these forces would be inadequate, but in any case – and on this we were in complete agreement – very rapid action was necessary if the ground was not to be cut from under the feet of the operation by the continuous progress of the breakthrough. While I was still in his office Commander-in-Chief West started the first telephone calls to subordinate headquarters to get more precise information on which to base his orders.

'... The counter-attack from which so much was expected, began early on 7 August in the area of Mortain.'

The orders sent by Hitler, according to General Zimmerman, read as follows:[67]

'The enemy will not be permitted to break out into the open country: every man must hold fast to the end.

'The Fuhrer orders that all available panzer forces will be withdrawn from the front, will be placed under the command of General Eberbach and will counter-attack with the objective Avranches.'

Warlimont stated that on 8 August:[68]

'When I got back to headquarters I found that people already knew that, after making some initial progress, the attack had been smothered by mass Allied air attack.

'... I found myself facing Hitler in the gloomy room in his bunker to make my report to him. Hitler said nothing as I entered and equally nothing as I described the enormous difficulties of combat and movement in Normandy, the overwhelming superiority of the enemy and the efforts made on all hands to ensure the success of the counter-attack. He did not even interrupt when in fulfilment of my special instructions – though in a sense quite different from that which he supposed – I gave a summary of what I had heard in connection with 20 July. ... I concluded by commenting that the failure of the counter-attack was certainly not due to any lack of preparation. This drew from Hitler his only comment: with a harsh edge to his voice he said: "the attack failed because Field Marshal von Kluge wanted it to fail".'

Kluge had previously been one of Hitler's favourite commanders. He was similar to Rommel in that he believed in going to the front frequently to see developments for himself. He had served Hitler devotedly, mastering many difficult situations on the Eastern Front from the beginning of *Barbarossa* until he was badly injured in a motor vehicle accident. For Hitler to make such a statement illustrates his total lack of comprehension of the conditions at the front and his paranoid distrust of all generals, which was even more pronounced after the 20 July bomb plot. Such a situation only worsened the already dysfunctional command structure, making any real understanding and co-ordinated effort between Hitler and his commanders almost impossible to achieve.

Eisenhower provided the following assessment of the German counterattack at Avranches and the measures taken to defeat it:[69]

'As the enemy saw the American First Army attack gather momentum to the southward and finally break through the Avranches bottleneck, his reaction was swift and characteristic. Chained to his general position by Hitler's orders as well as the paralyzing action of our air forces, he immediately moved westward all available armor from the Caen area to counterattack against the narrow strip through which American forces were pouring deep into his rear. His attack, if successful, would cut in behind our breakout troops and place them in a serious position. Because our corridor of advance was still constricted the German obviously felt that the risks he was assuming were justified even though, in case of his own failure, the destruction he would suffer would be vastly increased. His attacks, which were thrown in at the town of Mortain, just east of Avranches, began on August 7.

'The air co-operation against the enemy attack was extraordinarily effective. The United States Ninth Air Force and the RAF destroyed hundreds of enemy tanks and vehicles. The Royal Air Force had a large number of Typhoons equipped with rocket firing devices. These made low flying attacks against the enemy armor and kept up a sustained assault against his forces that was of great help to the defending infantry.

'Bradley and I, **aware that the German counterattack was under preparation [Author's emphasis]**, carefully surveyed the situation. We had sufficient strength in the immediate area so that if we chose merely to stand on the defensive against the German attack he could not possibly gain an inch. However, to make absolutely certain of our defenses at Mortain, we would have to diminish the number of divisions we could hurl into the enemy's rear and so sacrifice our opportunity to achieve the complete destruction for which we hoped. Moreover, by this time the weather had taken a very definite turn for the better and we had in our possession an Air Transport Service that could deliver, if called upon, up to 2,000 tons of supplies per day in fields designated by any of our forces that might be temporarily cut off.

'When I assured Bradley that even under a temporary German success he would have this kind of supply support, he unhesitatingly determined to retain only minimum forces at Mortain, and to rush the others on south and east to begin an envelopment of the German spearheads. I was in his headquarters when he called Montgomery on the telephone to explain his plan, and although the latter expressed a degree of concern about the Mortain position, he agreed that the prospective prize was great and left the entire responsibility for the matter in Bradley's hands. Montgomery quickly issued orders requiring the whole force to conform to this plan, and he, Bradley, and Lieutenant General Miles Dempsey, commanding the British Second Army, met to co-ordinate the details of the action.'

The American breakout – Operation *Cobra* – and the co-ordination of the action of the armies of Bradley and Patton with those of the British and Canadians led to the envelopment of German forces and their catastrophic defeat at Falaise, in which the bulk of the Seventh Army and most of the German armour in the West were destroyed. Any comparison of the Allied command structure with that of the Germans reveals that not only did the Allies have the forces necessary to defeat their enemy, but they also had a command organization which helped them to achieve this aim. Meanwhile, the German command structure impeded initiative, flexibility and operational efficiency at every turn and involved irrelevant political considerations in military decision-making in a way that had proven to be overwhelmingly negative.

Eisenhower's comment that he and Bradley 'were aware that the German counter-attack was under preparation' is a veiled reference to probably the Allies' most important secret weapon, which was the decoding of the German military command communications, carried out at Bletchley Park. On this occasion, the decoding was completed in time to let the Allied commanders know of Hitler's intentions and prepare an overwhelming response. It was not always possible for this to be achieved – if for no other reason than the desire not to let the Germans know their coded messages were being intercepted – but when it was, the intelligence was priceless.

Eisenhower commented on the movement towards the front of German reserves from the Fifteenth Army and elsewhere in an attempt to shore up the disintegrating position in Normandy:[70]

'[I]n late July the German had started the divisions of the Fifteenth Army across the Seine to join in the battle. They were too late. Every additional soldier who then came into the Normandy area was merely caught up in the catastrophe of defeat, without exercising any particular influence upon the battle. In the defeat were involved, also, a number of divisions that the enemy had been able to spare from the south of France, from Brittany, from Holland, and from Germany itself. When the total of these reinforcements had not proved equal to the task of stopping us, the enemy was momentarily helpless to present any continuous front against our advance.'

Warlimont recounted what happened when Hitler heard that the first attack at Mortain had achieved some initial success:[71]

'Hitler had issued a further order laying down – no less – that once the coast had been reached at Avranches a beginning should be made with rolling up the entire position in Normandy!

'This was a completely unrealistic object but the Supreme Commander clung to it, issuing a bewildering series of orders following each other with ever-increasing rapidity, and with equal rapidity being overtaken by the even faster moving course of events. An end was finally put to this method of command when the encirclement of the army in Normandy in the Falaise pocket on 19 August brought another disastrous defeat. The Operations Staff War Diary indeed records that "a good half" of the troops thus encircled fought their way out, characterizing this as "one of the great feats of arms of this campaign". But this is no excuse for the Supreme Command; by clinging rigidly to impracticable plans it had once more sent a great army to death or imprisonment without any major strategic object to justify the sacrifice.'

It goes without saying that the Germans could not afford many more such 'great feats of arms' if they were to have any chance of holding on in the West, much less of winning the war.

Model takes command

Kluge was relieved of command on 17 August, Hitler sending him a letter stating that he had worn himself out commanding the forces in Normandy and needed a rest. Kluge replied that he could not bear the failure of his command, and that he would 'no longer be' when Hitler read his letter. However, there are also good grounds for believing that he felt Hitler knew of his flirtation with the 20 July conspirators and that, although he had not participated in the bomb plot itself, his life was in jeopardy. Hitler also thought – wrongly as it happens – that Kluge was in touch with the Allies to arrange a truce on the Western Front. Hitler believed this because Kluge had been out of contact with his headquarters for most of the day on 13 August when he went to the front. He was suspicious that Kluge took only his driver and a radio vehicle with him, but any enquiry would have established that he did this often, having also done so during his time on the Eastern Front. What apparently happened was that the radio vehicle was bombed, and Kluge turned up on foot at the headquarters of the Fifth Panzer Army after having taken some hours to get there. With Kluge choosing suicide rather than the anticipated arrest and execution, he was a victim of Hitler's paranoia in the same sense as was Rommel. Warlimont offered the following comment on Kluge's actions:[72]

'As far as I know it is still uncertain whether there is any truth in the vague accusations that Field Marshal von Kluge was trying to arrange for a surrender in the West. Had he done so however he would, when all is said and done, merely have been drawing the logical conclusion from Hitler's view that if the invasion succeeded the war was lost.'

Kluge was succeeded in command of both the Western theatre and Army Group B by Field Marshal Model. Having previously been successful in stemming the course of Red Army offensives on the Eastern Front, Model was given the nickname of 'the Fuhrer's Fireman' because he had put out so many fires for Hitler. He was a very aggressive and determined commander who achieved results where others had not. He did not spare himself or others and was ruthless in his treatment of subordinates. However, there was nothing that Model could do to fundamentally alter the course of the catastrophe which the Germans suffered because of their weakness in men and materiel and the shortcomings of their Supreme Commander.

General Zimmerman provided an assessment of the situation following Model's arrival in the West:[73]

'Field Marshal Model, who had hitherto seen action only on the Eastern Front, did not immediately grasp the full gravity of the situation in France and hoped that he might yet restore it. But he was soon to realise the unimaginable effects of the enemy's air supremacy, the massive destruction in the rear areas, the impossibility of travelling along any major road in daylight without great peril, in fact the full significance of the invasion.

'He decided to withdraw all the forces that he could behind the lower Seine, and to do this regardless of all other considerations. This meant a final attempt to extricate what troops could still be saved from the Falaise pocket, which was not yet quite sealed off, even if they had to leave their heavy weapons behind. At this time the pocket contained the staffs of Seventh Army, of Panzer Group Eberbach, of four corps headquarters and the remnants of some thirteen divisions. Although the enemy artillery now covered the remaining escape routes from the pocket, a break out with armoured support succeeded during the night of August 21st–22nd. Those troops of Seventh Army which managed to escape were the first to be ferried across the lower Seine. They were then moved to rest areas in the north, where they were to be made ready for combat once again. The battle along the Seine between Paris and Rouen was now left almost entirely to Fifth Panzer Army.'

When the Allies closed the pincers at Falaise, the first stage of the campaign in the West – the Normandy campaign – can be said to have ended. The losses of the German Wehrmacht were immense in both men and materiel, neither of which could be afforded. Although this overwhelming victory had occurred within three months of the initial landings, there has been continued criticism of the Allied commanders for not closing the gap at Falaise earlier and more completely. Such criticism is easy when carried out in the abstract, but achievement in reality is much more difficult. It is sufficient to say that the result was more than enough to utterly cripple the German armies in the West and precipitate a retreat which did not stop until the Allies' supply situation imposed a pause on them close to the German border; it was not the Wehrmacht that stopped the Allies, but the very speed of their progress across France.

According to a report of 28 September 1944 by the Commander-in-Chief West and the chief surgeon of the German Army, the approximate German losses in the West from 6 June to 31 August were 30,000 killed, 80,000 wounded and 210,000 missing.[74] Approximately 70 per cent of the missing were later classified as being taken prisoner. The losses in personnel were therefore larger than those suffered at Stalingrad. Meanwhile, the losses in equipment were such that there were only some 80 to 100 operational tanks left in Fifth Panzer Army at the end of August, according to General Zimmerman. The heavy equipment of almost all the German divisions involved in the defence of Normandy had been destroyed or left behind in the retreat.

Eisenhower commented on the scale of the Allied victory at Falaise:[75]

'The battlefield of Falaise was unquestionably one of the greatest "killing grounds" of any of the war areas. Roads, highways and fields were so choked with destroyed equipment and with dead men and animals that passage through the area was extremely difficult. Forty-eight hours after the closing of the gap I was conducted through it on foot, to encounter scenes which could only be described by Dante. It was literally possible to walk for hundreds of yards at a time, stepping on nothing but dead and decaying flesh.'

Since the war, there has been a great deal of controversy relating to the strategy pursued by the Allies in Normandy and whether Montgomery had to change it during the campaign. Montgomery's original strategic intention has also been questioned. This commentary has largely ignored the actual course of events, as it has the remarks of the general best placed in the US armies to clarify the position. Omar Bradley was the commander of US Army forces in

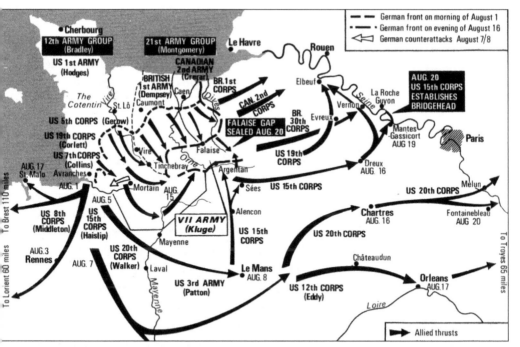

Map 9: The Allied Breakout from Normandy – 1–16 August 1944.
This map shows the speed of the Allied advance form Normandy once Operation *Cobra* had succeeded. It took only from 1 August to 16 August to completely rout the German armies and breakout from the Normandy battlefield. Paris was taken on August 25 and the allied armies continued to roll across the whole of France until the supply situation imposed a regrouping from September 18.

Normandy and made the following comment relating to the operational plan and how it unfolded during the campaign:[76]

> 'These statements foster at least two quite erroneous impressions: That in the original plan Monty had been expected to "break out" in the east and failed, and after this failure the plan was changed to have me "break out" in the west. … [The original strategy] called for Monty not to "break out" but to hold and draw the Germans to his sector, while I "broke out" in my sector and wheeled to the east. We adhered to this basic concept throughout the Normandy campaign with no major changes in strategy or tactics.'

While this issue has nothing to do with Hitler's leadership, it shows that even in victorious coalitions, national and personal jealousies can obscure brilliant results. In this regard, Eisenhower's contribution to victory by being able to reconcile the various demands of the commanders in the Allied armies cannot be overstated.

Conclusions

There are several fundamental conclusions that can be made from the evidence relating to the Normandy campaign and its sequel which illuminate Hitler's role in the conduct of German military operations. The main points are as follows:

1. The strategic compromise that Hitler decided upon, given the inadequate forces which the Germans disposed of in the Western theatre, could not have been better calculated to make the task of his commanders in Normandy impossible. There was too little power committed to implement Rommel's strategy, while not enough was left to Rundstedt to ensure that he could achieve victory, if indeed that was possible for either of them. Similarly, if Rundstedt's had been the favoured strategy, too much was taken from his control to give him a chance of victory. Hitler's compromise was such that it effectively destroyed the chances of successful defence before the invasion had even begun by trying to cover all potential scenarios and not giving either strategy the power to prevail. It is worth noting that the disparity between the forces of the Allies and Germany was such that once the Allies successfully landed, the only realistic chance of victory the Germans had was to commit all their forces at once, and to concentrate them on the focal points of the invasion. Hitler made a bad situation even worse by the deployment he chose, which fragmented the German forces and their control.

2. Hitler's refusal until it was too late to use formations from the Fifteenth Army to reinforce the Normandy position merely compounded all the mistakes he previously made in his strategy to deal with the invasion. Once the landings at Normandy had successfully taken place, it was patently obvious that they had to be eliminated, regardless of any other potential problems, because unless they were, on Hitler's own admission the war was lost. But he would not act to concentrate the forces necessary to achieve this imperative aim, once again trying to cover all possibilities and thereby achieving nothing because he was unable to identify and act against the main problem. It was also clear that if the Normandy landings succeeded, it would not be necessary for the Allies to make any others, which logically meant that every effort should be made to eliminate them as quickly as possible.

3. The command structure that Hitler created was one of the prime reasons that the Germans were unable to effectively defend against an invasion of Europe. The Byzantine arrangement that he imposed did not have any

justification from a military viewpoint, existing only to entrench his power. One of the results of the failings of this absurd structure in action was Jodl's refusal of Rundstedt's request for the release of the OKW reserves early on D-Day. Jodl should never have been able to deny a request from Rundstedt for such a purely operational matter; he had no experience compared to Rundstedt, whose request, it should be stressed again, was shown to be correct by subsequent events. The delay Jodl caused meant that the immediate deployment of the Panzer reserves was prevented, making it impossible for them to provide the early contribution to the defence which was so vital if the Germans were to have any chance of defeating the invasion. In this case, minutes were vital and slow reactions fatal. The imperative need for speed in the reaction to the invasion was recognized by Hitler's own Directive No. 51, but the command structure he created led to delays which ensured the German defeat.

In contrast to the absurd confection of the German command structure in the Western theatre was the clear and logical command organization of the Allied invasion forces, with lines of authority that were simple, clear-cut and enabled co-ordination of the efforts of all three services to achieve victory. No starker contrast could be made than the comparison of these command arrangements. This was the last item pointed out by Rommel in his memorandum to Hitler of 3 July, which must have been a very unwelcome observation for such an audience.

4. Rommel's memorandum of 3 July clearly shows the operational steps he tried to take to augment the defence of Normandy. There is no doubt that if his recommendations had been adopted, the defence of the invasion front would have been much more effective. One example is the deployment of the 12th SS-Panzer Division, which Rommel wished to locate at the base of the Cotentin. Had those troops been there on the day of the invasion, the difficulties the US 1st and 29th Divisions had on Omaha would have been worse – and possibly much worse. Not to mention the problems that could have been visited upon the comparatively lightly equipped airborne forces, in the same manner as occurred several months later at Arnhem. Another of Rommel's denied requests related to the positioning of the 2nd Panzer Division, which he wished to have near what ended up being the British landing beaches. There are more than enough important examples noted in his memorandum to show that Hitler's baleful influence did nothing to assist the defence against the invasion.

5. As had been the case in the past when his orders led to debacle, Hitler's reaction was to blame and sack the commanders on the spot, who had done nothing other than attempt to follow his orders. Once again, Rundstedt

was relieved of his position, followed by Kluge, who had been a devoted and successful commander on the Eastern Front. Then Model was appointed and Rundstedt was reappointed in September, as if to Hitler these changes were of no importance to the chances of success. This continuous changing at the apex of the command structure could not help but be injurious to the performance of the German forces and further demotivate their commanders.

6. In addition to the events mentioned above, Rommel was forced to commit suicide on evidence – which was never conclusive – that he was involved in the 20 July bomb plot. Then Kluge also committed suicide because he believed he was implicated in the same conspiracy. These appalling events further illustrate the true nature of Hitler's murderous tyranny and the casual cruelty associated with it. These deaths and the attempt on Hitler's life starkly reveal the extreme loathing of Hitler by many of the senior members of the Wehrmacht and their despair at his methods, which they believed – correctly, as it turned out – would result in utter defeat for Germany.

All of these problems stem from one overriding source, Hitler's mania for control, which meant that he could not let others, even those who were more competent than himself, command the German forces and carry out the defence of their position more effectively than he could ever have done. This was the great irony and paradox of his position and the influence he exerted on events; ultimately, he was by far his own worst enemy.

Chapter 7

Operation *Bagration* –
The Destruction of Army Group Centre

On 22 June 1944 – the third anniversary of the commencement of Hitler's Operation *Barbarossa* – the Soviets unleashed their largest offensive of the war so far. The USSR had made a remarkable comeback since the summer of 1941, despite having suffered some 20 million casualties in prisoners, dead and wounded[1] to repel the German attack, as well as losing a great deal of its most productive territory and industries.

The German Army Group Centre – which had been the vanguard of Hitler's forces in 1941 – was the target for the new Soviet onslaught. Its units had almost reached Moscow, but now the aim of the Red Army was to destroy the tormenters who had caused so much agony and loss to their country. The very name chosen for the offensive emphasized how far the conflict had metamorphosed into Stalin's 'Great Patriotic War', being named after one of the most important Czarist generals of the Napoleonic era, Peter Bagration, who commanded an army corps at the Battle of Borodino and died of wounds suffered there. The Soviet strategy of summer 1944, of which Operation *Bagration* was a major part, was intended to evict the Germans from European Russia.

This offensive was the first time in the war that the campaigns of the three allies had combined to squeeze Germany in the strategic vice which was possible now that Britain and the USA had landed in Normandy to commence the liberation of Western Europe. Two weeks before *Bagration* was launched, the 'second front' had finally been opened. Hitler was thus faced with the destruction of German armies in the West and in the East, and could no longer use his central position to shuffle reinforcements to the straining Eastern Front from anywhere in his imperilled empire.

The strategic situation in June 1944

The strategic position on the Eastern Front in June 1944 resulted from the failure of the German offensive at Kursk, Operation *Citadel*, and the subsequent Soviet counteroffensives. These began on 12 July 1943, against

Army Group Centre, and developed from there during the summer and winter into a concerted campaign, pushing the Germans back on the fronts of Army Group Centre and the various southern army groups by hundreds of miles south of the Pripet Marshes.

Army Group South, commanded by Field Marshal von Manstein, had narrowly avoided disaster in several partial encirclements by the Red Army, escaping with great difficulty and at great cost, precipitated primarily by Hitler's 'stand fast' orders. These instructions gave rise to serious arguments between Hitler and Manstein, for example during a meeting on 4 January 1944, when Manstein was trying to persuade him of the seriousness of the position and the need for changes to the command structure:[2]

'The briefing room emptied leaving only Hitler, Manstein and Zeitzler. Hitler invited the Field Marshal to speak. He cut to the quick "One thing we must be clear about, mein Fuhrer, is that the extremely critical situation we are now in cannot be put down to the enemy's superiority alone, great though it is. It is also due to the way in which we are led."

Although Manstein did not record an immediate reply, he gives us a vivid and striking impression of 'the wordless struggle of will played out between us within a few seconds':

'As I spoke these words, Hitler's expression hardened. He stared at me with a look which made me feel he wished to crush my will to continue. I cannot remember a human gaze ever conveying such willpower. In his otherwise coarse face, the eyes were probably the only attractive and certainly the most expressive feature, and now they were boring into me as if to force me to my knees.

'... As for establishing a Commander-in-Chief East, who, in Manstein's opinion should "enjoy full independence within the framework of grand strategy" this only aggravated Hitler's increasing ire. As he had stated often before, no other individual in the Reich would have his authority. After all, "Even I cannot get the Field Marshals to obey me," he shouted. "Do you imagine", he then asked Manstein, "that they would obey you more readily? If it comes to the worst, I can dismiss them. No one else would have the authority to do that."

'The vast majority of German generals would have bitten their lips at this point. But Manstein ventured a bold reply to the effect that his orders were always carried out. Hitler made no further comment, bringing the meeting to a brusque close.'

These entirely fruitless confrontations did nothing to assist the position of the German armies. Hitler was convinced of his own infallibility and completely disregarded the events his own 'generalship' caused to the great detriment of the overall German position, and especially the long-suffering front-line troops he attempted to command.

Manstein's contention was that the operational tactics which Hitler employed were completely wrong and ignored the main strengths of the German Army while allowing the Red Army to use its greater numbers to most effect:[3]

> '[I]t is generally recognized that defence is the stronger of the two forms of fighting. This is only true, however, when the defence is so efficacious that the attacker bleeds to death when assaulting the defender's positions. Such a thing was out of the question on the Eastern Front, where the number of German divisions available was never sufficient for so strong a defence to be organized. The enemy, being many times stronger than we were, was always able, by massing his forces at points of his own choice, to break through the fronts that were far too widely expended. As a result, large numbers of German forces were unable to avoid encirclement. Only in mobile operations could the superiority of the German staffs and fighting troops have been turned to account and, perhaps, the forces of the Soviet Union ultimately brought to naught.'

Manstein also commented upon Hitler's insistence for 'hanging-on' at all costs:[4]

> '[This] may be found deep down in his own personality. He was a man who saw fighting only in terms of the utmost brutality. His way of thinking conformed more to a mental picture of masses of the enemy bleeding to death before our lines than to the concept of a subtle fencer who knows how to make the occasional step backwards in order to lunge for the decisive thrust. **For the *art of war* he substituted a brute force which, as he saw it, was guaranteed maximum effectiveness by the will-power behind it [Author's emphasis].'**

The differences were fundamental, but Manstein's avoidance of defeat in the battles against the Red Army in 1943–44 should have convinced Hitler that his operational flexibility was the most effective form of defence. Manstein's conduct of the 1943–44 defensive battles with Army Group South are regarded by military historians and analysts as clear evidence that his proposal to Hitler regarding the best course for the Germans to take against the Red Army was correct.

Following the Soviet winter offensive, Army Group Centre's strength had been significantly reduced because the Fuhrer expected that the next Soviet offensives would concentrate on the German armies south of the Pripet Marshes in the area of Army Group North Ukraine, commanded by Field Marshal Model. In order to defend against this eventuality, he had taken almost all the armoured and mechanized infantry divisions from Army Group Centre and diverted them to Army Group North Ukraine.[5]

Consequently, Army Group Centre had become critically reduced in strength and exposed to a Red Army attack concentrating on its weakened defences. Typically, Hitler would not listen to the warnings given by Army Group Centre commander Field Marshal Ernst Busch and continued to believe an intelligence assessment that his forces should expect a 'quiet summer'.[6] Army Group Centre's own intelligence assessment, however, had repeatedly warned of Soviet troop concentrations on its front, indicating an offensive aimed at Brobruisk, Mogilev, Orscha and Vitebsk.[7] These warnings were not heeded.

Partisans

Since the beginning of the German occupation of Soviet territory, the policies pursued by the Germans had completely alienated its inhabitants. The ruthless cruelty and destruction that were systematically pursued inevitably caused a partisan movement, which was encouraged and built up by the Soviet government. It sent arms and instructors to the partisan groups, and this led to an almost continuous campaign by the Germans against the partisans in their rear areas, which was a significant drain on their resources.

To support Operation *Bagration*, the Soviets organized actions against the occupiers on an unprecedented scale. There were approximately 240,000 partisans in the rear of Army Group Centre, and these undertook 10,500 demolition and sabotage actions against the German railway system and other communications, effectively isolating the German Front line and making the transfer of forces an extremely difficult and time-consuming operation.[8]

The existence of the partisans was another example of the effect of Hitler's racial policies which can only be regarded as the most idiotic manifestation of his nightmarish 'vision' for the eastern empire of the Reich.

Soviet strategy

Far from attacking south of the Pripet Marshes, the Red Army offensive was conceived to strike at an area where the Germans were not expecting to be assaulted, and the obvious place to do so was Army Group Centre because of its weakened state.

Once the attacks had achieved their aim of destroying Army Group Centre, the Red Army forces would have the opportunity to outflank Army Group North, which was still occupying Latvia, Lithuania and Estonia and in position around Leningrad. They could also complete the eviction of the army groups south of the Pripet Marshes by exploiting the gaps in the German defences north of the marshes. Despite their advantages in men and materiel, STAVKA – the Soviet High Command – expected that the fighting against Army Group Centre would be intense and that progress would be slow.

Red Army forces

The forces that had been assembled for this great offensive were overpowering, comprising 5,000 aircraft, 5,200 tanks and 1.4 million men.[9] They had been assembled with such skill that the German intelligence services were completely fooled as to their intentions. The armies involved were organized into the following Red Army 'fronts', which were equivalent to a German army group, although the Soviet division establishments were smaller:[10]

First Baltic Front

Fourth Shock Army, Sixth Guards Army, 1st Tank Corps and Third Air Army.

Third Belorussian Front

Thirty-ninth Army, Fifth Army, Eleventh Guards Army, 2nd Guards Tank Corps, 3rd Guards Cavalry Corps, 3rd Guards Mechanized Corps, Fifth Guards Tank Army, 3rd Guards Tank Corps, 29th Tank Corps and First Air Army.

Second Belorussian Front

Thirty-third Army, Forthy-ninth Army, Fiftieth Army and Fourth Air Army.

First Belorussian Front

Third Army, 9th Tank Corps, Forty-eighth Army, Sixty-fifth Army, 1st Guards Tank Corps, Twenty-eighth Army, Sixty-first Army, Seventieth Army, 4th Guards Cavalry Corps, 1st Mechanized Corps, Sixteenth Air Army and Dnieper Flotilla

German Forces

Against these forces, Army Group Centre comprised:[11]

> six Panzer or Panzergrenadier divisions;
> twenty-four infantry divisions;
> two Luftwaffe field divisions;
> five security divisions;
> one training division.

Luftwaffe forces in Army Group Centre's area were commanded by Luftwaffe General Ritter von Greim. They had a total of 775 aircraft, but only 100 ground-attack types and 100 fighters. The rest were bombers, mainly Heinkel 111s. When the Normandy invasion began, this total was reduced by the despatch of fifty fighters to the West. The Luftwaffe was thus significantly outnumbered in the types that mattered most in defence.[12]

These numbers show that it was very unlikely that the Germans would be able to maintain their positions against such an overwhelming attacking force, and they were not helped by how they were deployed. The Luftwaffe field divisions and the security divisions were of questionable fighting value, and the training division could not be compared to a fully operational army unit, so the army group's effective force should be counted as thirty-two divisions. Moreover, while the Germans had enjoyed an operational and qualitative advantage over the Soviet forces when they invaded in 1941, their opponents had caught up in both respects and the gap was now no longer enough to offset the numerical superiority of the Red Army.

The Germans had suffered terrible losses and reverses during the three years of their invasion of the USSR, which Hitler had embarked upon with such scorn for the Red Army and the supposedly inferior Slavic *untermensch*. It has been estimated that some 1.8 million Germans had been killed[13] by the time that Operation *Bagration* commenced.

The diaries of Joseph Goebbels recorded a conversation he had with Hitler when *Barbarossa* was launched:[14]

> 'The enemy will be driven back in one smooth movement. The Fuehrer estimates that the operation will take four months. I reckon on fewer. Bolshevism will collapse like a pack of cards.'

Rarely has the proclaimer of a prediction been made to look so foolish.

German dispositions

In addition to the problems caused by their inferiority in numbers, the Germans faced various other disadvantages resulting from the deployment of their forces. As can be seen from the accompanying map, Army Group Centre covered a front line of some 488 miles.[15] Its forces also occupied Vitebsk,

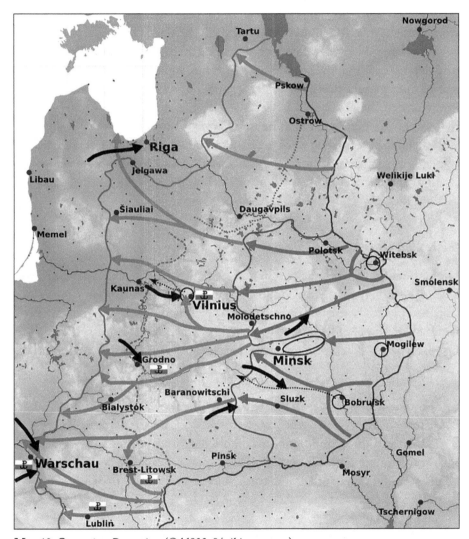

Map 10: Operation *Bagration*. (© kl833x9/wikicommons)
This map clearly shows the disastrous development of the Soviet offensive that capitalised on the deployment of the German forces in Army Group Centre which had been drained of its armoured forces by Hitler to send to the Southern Army Groups in anticipation of an offensive there. In doing so, he ignored the repeated warnings of Field Marshal Busch who warned that an attack was about to occur on the front of Army Group Centre, and who he sacked when the offensive occurred in the manner he told Hitler it would.

which was in an exposed salient that invited being surrounded, and is in fact what happened.

These dispositions had been ordered by Hitler, contrary to the advice of his commanders. Field Marshal Busch, who had been appointed Commander-in-Chief of Army Group Centre after Field Marshal von Kluge had suffered injuries in a motor vehicle accident, and other senior officers of the army group realized how narrowly they had clung on to their positions against the Soviet winter offensive and doubted that they could be held against an offensive in better weather. They therefore recommended that the army group reorganize its defence along the line of the Berezina River, approximately 90 miles in the rear of their present positions, where strong defences taking advantage of the geography of the area could be established on a shorter line. Busch advised that this be done in time to ensure that his troops could take their equipment with them rather than be forced to abandon or lose it during a retreat in battle. Hitler, however, forbad such a step backwards,[16] as he did other attempts to strengthen the defences of Army Group Centre through the rationalization of its front line.

'Feste Platze'

On 8 March 1944, Hitler issued Fuhrer Directive No. 53, which governed the defensive strategy for Army Group Centre. His concept was that 'Feste Platze' (fortified places) be created, which would form the most important centres of German resistance. These were to 'fulfil the function of fortresses in former historical times'. The Fuhrer explained their role as follows:[17]

> 'They will ensure that the enemy does not occupy those areas of decisive operational importance. They will allow themselves to be surrounded, thereby holding down the largest possible number of enemy forces and establishing conditions favourable for successful counter-attacks. Local strongpoints will be tenaciously defended in the event of enemy penetration. ... Fortified area commanders will pledge their honour as soldiers to carry out their duties to the last.'

This order is proof that Hitler had learned nothing from his time in command of the German Army, especially from the disaster at Stalingrad. This strategy may have been apposite if there were adequate reserves to parry any attacking force within a short time of the attackers surrounding these positions. However, in the position of inferiority that the Germans now occupied it was a recipe for disaster. At an even more basic level, the order shows that the Fuhrer had not properly understood the most important element in his own successes in the early stages of the war, and how these could be countered in defensive warfare. The order reduced German formations to a series of static targets and allowed the Red Army to maximize the effect of its superiority in numbers. Field Marshal von Manstein had shown what was possible through the use of manoeuvre to contain advances made by significantly stronger Soviet forces during Army Group South's 1943–44 defensive battles following the failed Operation *Citadel* offensive. At the end of March 1944, however, Manstein was sacked, showing once again that Hitler did not properly appreciate the use of subtlety in strategy and the command of armed forces, or indeed even who his most important and capable commanders were.

This strategy also took little account of the effect that deliberately isolating units had on the morale of troops. After the events at Stalingrad, it would only be reasonable to assume that troops would see being isolated as akin to a death sentence. Any delay in relieving them would only confirm their anxieties in this regard, which were understandable. This strategy also encapsulates Hitler's expectation that all his troops would defend until their death every one of the areas which he designated as being critical. Such an expectation is completely out of touch with normal human psychology. Troops, even when experienced and battle-hardened, will not fight to the death where they see no probability of victory, the only exception to this rule in the Second World War being the Japanese.

In addition, the Soviet forces were not the same army they had been in summer 1941. The increased output from their factories in all categories of armaments and the significant aid received from Lend-Lease supplies were now having an impact in meaningful ways, one of the most important being the growth in the Red Army's operational flexibility and ability to sustain its offensives. This was largely due to the use of American trucks which had been received as part of the aid package.[18] By the end of the war, more than 400,000 US trucks of excellent design and endurance had been received by the Red Army, which were a crucial addition to its capabilities. Indeed, the difference in the flexibility and endurance of the Red Army created by this addition to its supply capabilities can hardly be overstated.

The Vitebsk *Feste Platz*

To illustrate what Hitler's strategy meant in practice, it is instructive to see what unfolded at Vitebsk, which was designated as one of the *Feste Platze*, although it was almost entirely surrounded in an exposed salient resulting from the pressure exerted during the Soviet 1943–44 winter campaign. The

German LIII Corps was designated to defend Vitebsk and the *Feste Platz*. General Friedrich Gollwitzer commanded the corps, and upon Vitebsk being designated a *Feste Platz* in April 1944 he had an interview with the Commander-in-Chief of Army Group Centre, Field Marshal Busch, during which the following exchange took place:[19]

'Q [Gollwitzer]: Where does the Commandant get his Staff?
'FM: That's your business. Apply to your Army.
'Q: The strength of the garrison is not sufficient for all round defence.
'FM: More troops are not available. Take them from units withdrawing from the front.
'G. Goll: Who can build the Vitebsk defences as there are no civilians who can do the work, and combat troops cannot be used?
'FM: Staff personnel, administrative troops and Hiwis.
'G. Goll: If an attack is threatened, can the Corps expect any reserves to prevent the encirclement of its flanks?
'FM: No! Put the strongest part of your defences at the junction with your neighbours!
'G. Goll: The junctions of my LIII Corps are with my neighbouring Corps, the VI and IX. Presumably they will halt the first attacks and must build up strong defences at these points.
'FM: Everything will be as I have said! The Fuehrer has ordered it!'

It is obvious from this discussion that the field marshal was extremely wary of straying from Hitler's edict.

The attack on the Vitebsk salient occurred in exactly the expected way, the Soviets assaulting its shoulders on 23 June. It was quickly apparent that the position could not be held, and the LIII Corps commander requested permission to withdraw to a more defensible position. Busch put the request to Hitler, who refused permission but instructed that the corps withdraw to the *Feste Platz*, which because of the difficulties recited earlier by Gollwitzer did not in fact exist. This order ensured that the troops would be surrounded and destroyed in situ. Further requests for the withdrawal of the troops were also refused. On 24 June, Busch again requested that Hitler allow the withdrawal of the troops in order 'to create reserves before 3rd Panzer Army collapsed completely'.[20] This request was refused too, Hitler instead ordering that:[21]

'206 Division is to hold firm under General Hitter. Remaining divisions are to reopen the road from Vitebsk to the west.'

This order was impossible to carry out as the Soviet forces were far too strong for the remnants of the Germans to successfully attack.

LIII Corps tried unsuccessfully to break out of Vitebsk on 25 June. At 2.00 pm that day, the corps reported:[22]

> 'Situation fundamentally changed. Complete encirclement by enemy who is growing steadily stronger. 4th Luftwaffe Field Division now non-existent. 246th Division and 6th Luftwaffe Division heavily engaged on a number of fronts. Several penetrations, bitter fighting.'

Later that day, the LIII Corps reported that it was concentrating all its remaining force to attempt to break out through the surrounding Soviet formations. This report 'caused consternation because the field marshal knew that Hitler wanted Vitebsk held for at least another week'.[23] Nevertheless, General Gollwitzer had decided that the troops had to break out and had no intention of attempting to comply with his orders, which he knew were impossible. Yet the breakout was no easy task because by 26 June, the nearest part of the German lines was over 70km away from Vitebsk. Even then, Field Marshal Busch sent a message that Gollwitzer had no freedom of decision and Vitebsk must be held in accordance with the Fuhrer's order.[24]

Some survivors of LIII Corps did eventually make their way back to the German lines. However, Gollwitzer estimated that of the 28,000 men who attempted to break out, some 22,000–23,000 were taken prisoner and about 5,000 were killed. The Soviet estimate was that 20,000 were killed and 10,000 taken prisoner.[25]

General Gollwitzer survived the war and :[26]

> '[Gollwitzer] remained a prisoner in Russia until 1955. On his return he wrote a full account of the battles and suffering of his LIII Corps, and laid the blame fairly and squarely on the higher leadership and, in particular, on Hitler personally.'

I have dealt with the Vitebsk salient in some detail as it is indicative of the result of Hitler's direct orders, which were the same for all the corps of Army Group Centre.

Needless to say, they had the same effect across the whole front that the army group was attempting to hold.

The wider picture

The disaster suffered by LIII Corps was replicated in the case of the German troops covering Mogilev, Bobruisk and then Minsk, which was the main supply and administrative centre for Army Group Centre and had many thousands of wounded in its hospitals.

On 26 June, Hitler had belatedly authorized the withdrawal to the Berezina, as the army group had requested before the Soviet offensive had begun. But there were no prepared defences and it was thus impossible to conduct a staged, controlled withdrawal, as would have been the case if Field Marshal Busch's recommendation had been accepted when it was put forward.

On the same day, Busch made a desperate attempt to get Hitler to change his obviously failing strategy:[27]

'Busch flew to the Obersalzberg to present the facts of the rapidly deteriorating position to Hitler and try to get some change to his "Hold Firm" policy so that some of the formations of Army Group Centre could be salvaged before it was too late. The Field Marshal was accompanied by General Jordan who had been summoned by Hitler to explain his conduct of the battle, in particular his use of the 20th Panzer Division. Although Army Group Centre had appreciated that the two major Soviet thrusts would join eventually in the area of Minsk, they still had not recognised that the Soviet plan was even more ambitious, and aiming further west. Hitler agreed to Ninth Army retiring into the Bobruisk position, not knowing the move had been afoot since midday. During the morning, Soviet 9th Tank Corps blocked all road and river crossings north and east of Bobruisk, thus cutting off the greater part of the Ninth Army.'

On 29 June, Busch was replaced in charge of Army Group Centre by Field Marshal Model, a dubious honour if ever there was one. Hitler agreed to most of Model's recommendations relating to tactical operations against the Soviet offensive but would not accept the necessity for all German formations to be withdrawn to a line that allowed a concentration of forces to defend the Reich and where some preparations could be made to do so. This would have involved the redeployment of Army Group North, which Hitler would not allow because the Finns would then withdraw from the war (which they did anyway on 19 September 1944). Hitler also alleged that he needed the Gulf of Finland to be controlled so that the U-boats could continue to be trained there. Neither of these reasons was sufficient to halt the Red Army.

Minsk was surrounded and approximately 100,000 German troops – including many wounded – were taken prisoner on 5 July, although some elements of the German forces escaped.

The pain did not stop there for the Germans. The reinforcements Hitler had sent and the remnants of the army group made a temporary stand west of Minsk, but there were no prepared positions because Hitler had specifically forbidden that they be built when there was still time to do so. The forces available were far too weak to hold their positions against the Red Army, which simply bypassed them and continued its westward advance.

Army Group North was separated from the remains of Army Group Centre on 31 July, as Model and Busch had predicted, when Soviet forces of the First Baltic Front reached Riga, the capital of Latvia. The Red Army was thus way behind the front line of both Army Group North and the remnants of Army Group Centre; such were the fruits of Hitler's inspired leadership.

Result of Operation *Bagration*

The German forces on the Eastern Front never recovered from the disaster inflicted on them by the Red Army in Operation *Bagration*:[28]

'[The German Army lost] about 30 divisions. It is difficult to be more precise because some divisions were only partly involved and others were introduced as reinforcements during the course of the fighting. It is impossible to find accurate figures of the losses suffered by Army Group Centre because some divisions disappeared almost without trace, and their survivors were killed after the fighting or died in captivity. The OKW figure gives their version of the losses and quoted them as 300,000. Ziemke gives a breakdown based on 25 divisions, and says that Fourth Army lost 130,000 of its original 165,000-man strength. Third Panzer Army lost 10 divisions, and 10,000 to 15,000 men of the Ninth Army escaped through the intervention of the 12th Panzer Division. Buchner puts the losses as high as 350,000 including 150,000 captured by the Russians. He also states that losses including those killed on their way to assembly camps, deaths due to overcrowding and starvation on their way to prisoner-of-war camps and during their sojourn in those camps are estimated at 75,000, giving a total of 275,000 dead German soldiers. The exact total will never be known.'

The victory that resulted from *Bagration* was partly due to the Allied landings in France, which meant that Hitler could no longer freely transfer reinforcements between theatres of war, but this could also be said with respect to the Allies' success on the Western Front. The truth is that each victory was made greater by the participation of all the Allies attacking at virtually the same time. The scale of the losses resulting from *Bagration* meant that even had the other fronts not existed, it would have been extremely difficult for the Wehrmacht to replace them, although it may have been able to hold onto its positions in European Russia for longer.

The losses were not just in men and materiel. The territory lost during the offensive meant that the Red Army had split the German Front, with Army Group North isolated in the Courland region, from which Hitler would not let it retreat to join the other German armies to achieve some concentration of the forces that remained.

The Red Army's great offensive liberated Minsk (5 July), Vilna (9 July), Grodno (13 July), Lublin (24 July) and Brest-Litovsk (27 July), and on 31 July reached the eastern bank of the Vistula River and Warsaw. As has already been stated, 31 July also saw the Red Army take Riga, thereby isolating Army Group North. The offensive that began on 22 June and destroyed Army Group Centre therefore developed into a catastrophe of the first order for Hitler and the Nazi regime.

Conclusions

1. The operational tactics Hitler used to defend against the Red Army were not the result of any overall strategic plan, unless disputing every square metre of the territory Germany had conquered could be called a plan. The Germans would have been better off employing the concept of elastic defence, which was put to Hitler by Manstein and some of his other most senior commanders and was partially used by Manstein when Hitler agreed to his recommendations in the 1943–44 defensive battles of Army Group South. Manstein here showed that this form of defence could be adapted to achieve results which were best suited to the skills of the German Army and to inflict the most casualties on the Red Army while preserving its own strength. Hitler's failure to adopt this method of defence undoubtedly cost the Germans excessive casualties without any corresponding benefit and hastened the demise of the Third Reich.

2. Hitler's command of the defensive actions employed by Army Group Centre exhibited all the same problems which were apparent in his overall command of the Wehrmacht. Specifically, his decisions were taken against the advice of local commanders, ignored operational limitations and geographic realities, underestimated the strength of the enemy, and took far too long to be made in situations where speed was of the essence.

Chapter 8

The Ardennes Offensive, December 1944

By November 1944, Nazi Germany was being crushed between two gigantic military offensives from east and west, both of which were now on the very borders of the Reich. The air forces of the Western Allies roamed the skies over Germany at will, the once powerful Luftwaffe unable to do anything to prevent the rain of destruction pulverising Germany's cities by day and night. The success of the Allies' invasion of France meant that Germany would now lose the war. Hitler had expressed such a view on a number of occasions, as related by Warlimont,[1] but had also stated that 'anyone who speaks to me of peace without victory will lose his head no matter who he is or what his position'.[2] Whether Hitler did view the war as lost cannot be stated with certainty, but he affected to believe in ultimate victory and for as long as he ordered it, the war would continue.

The strategic situation

Following the virtual destruction of the German forces in Normandy at Falaise, the Western Allies pursued their remnants with great speed, liberating Paris on 25 August. By mid-September they had reached a line that threatened a rapid invasion of Germany, but here limitations of supply meant that they had to consolidate their position. Eisenhower described the situation facing the armies under his command:[3]

'With 36 divisions in action we were faced with the problem of delivering from beaches and ports to the frontlines some 20,000 tons of supply every day. Our spearheads, moreover, were moving swiftly, frequently seventy-five miles per day. The supply service had to catch these with loaded trucks. Every mile of advance doubled the difficulty because the supply truck had always to make a two-way run from the beaches and back, in order to deliver another load to the marching troops. Other thousands of tons had to go into advanced airfields for construction and subsequent maintenance. Still additional amounts were required for repair of bridges and roads, for which heavy equipment was necessary.'

This short statement shows how difficult the position of the Allies was and the magnitude of the achievement of the supply services in keeping the armies moving and fighting.

In order to obviate these supply problems and finish the war before the end of 1944, Field Marshal Montgomery devised a plan to breach the German lines in the Netherlands by taking the bridges across the Rhine, exploiting the breach and invading northern Germany. This ambitious scheme, named Operation *Market Garden*, involved the use of the Allied airborne armies together with armoured units to attack on a very narrow front and take a succession of seven bridges in the Netherlands, culminating in the bridge at Arnhem. The attack was defeated at the last bridge by a combination of bad luck and errors in planning, meaning that the war would go on and the Allies would have to mount another offensive to cross the Rhine, the last barrier into Germany.

Hitler's reaction to defeat in France was characteristic in that he planned to attack the Western Allies, split their armies apart, 'Dunkirk' the British again by cutting them off from their lines of supply and retake Antwerp. Such a reverse would, he believed, force the British to negotiate with him or knock them out of the war. His main problem was to obtain the forces to achieve these aims.

While the Allied advance into France was unfolding, Hitler was frantically creating new divisions and re-forming some panzer divisions which had been destroyed in recent fighting to undertake the offensive, retake the initiative and forestall the invasion of Germany. On 19 August, Jodl's diary stated:[4]

'The Fuhrer discussed the equipment and manpower position in the West with Chief of OKW, Chief Army Staff (General Buhle), and Speer. Prepare to *take the offensive in November* when the enemy air forces can't operate. Main point: some *25 divisions* must be moved to the West in the next one or two months.'

Hitler's intention of striking in November was not possible because of the disruption caused to his plans by the *Market Garden* offensive, the continuous pressure exerted by the other Allied armies and the continuing crisis on the Eastern Front.

Based on the level of losses that had been inflicted on the Germans during the Normandy campaign and the threat from the Soviets in the East, Allied intelligence considered that there was little likelihood of any major attack in the West, although not everyone agreed with this view. Although this was a logical evaluation of the situation, Hitler's view was that if Germany remained on the defensive the war was certain to be lost. Consequently, the Germans had to attack because he was totally unwilling to consider surrender, as he made plain to everyone, as related by Warlimont:[5]

> '[H]e would say over and over again to those around him ... "anyone who speaks to me of peace without victory will lose his head, no matter who he is or what his position".'

The problems associated with working in such an atmosphere can only be imagined.

German attacking forces

The German forces involved in the planned attack – codenamed Operation *Watch on the Rhine* – comprised the three armies of Army Group B, commanded by Field Marshal Model:[6]

Fifth Panzer Army – commanded by General of Panzer Troops Hasso von Manteuffel.

> Four infantry divisions, three Panzer divisions, 460th Heavy Artillery Brigade, 766th Artillery Korps, Fuhrer Begleit Brigade (armoured) and 401st VolksArtillerie Korps.

Sixth SS-Panzer Army – commanded by SS-Colonel General Josef ('Sepp') Dietrich.

> Four SS-Panzer divisions, one SS-Panzergrenadier division, one Fallschirmjager (paratroop) division, five infantry divisions, one heavy tank battalion, two flak divisions, three artillery korps, one SS heavy artillery battalion, two VolksWerfer brigades and an independent panzer brigade.

Seventh Army – commanded by General of Panzer Troops Erich Brandenberger.

> Comprised of nine infantry divisions.

The German forces included the new King Tiger tanks in some of the armoured formations, which were the best such units in the Wehrmacht. However, the infantry divisions were nearly all new formations, 'Volksgrenadier', which had not been in battle before and were based on a smaller establishment than normal German divisions. This reflected Hitler's preference for creating new formations rather than keeping existing ones up to establishment. Because of this system, experience gained in battle was not retained within integrated formations. Hitler refused to change this despite strenuous objections from almost every one of his senior commanders, who saw this method as being wasteful and inefficient.

The Luftwaffe – Hitler's intention was to use every available aircraft, including the new jet-powered ME262, to disrupt the Allied air forces on the ground and protect the attacking formations. According to *The Luftwaffe Diaries*, a reserve of 3,000 fighter aircraft had been accumulated to challenge Allied air supremacy over Germany, the aim being to launch an all-out attack on the bomber fleets using all available aircraft in a single operation. However, Hitler ordered these aircraft to support the Ardennes offensive, although the pilots had not been trained in ground-support operations. The reserve was therefore 'sacrificed in a brief and futile attempt to support the army'.[7]

Allied forces in the Ardennes

The United States forces deployed in the Ardennes region on 16 December were as follows:[8]

American 12th Army Group – commanded by Lieutenant General Omar Bradley.

US First Army – under Lieutenant General Courtney Hodges.
B Troop, 125th Cavalry Recon Sqn
5th Belgian Fusilier Bn, 99th Infantry Bn (Norwegian Americans)
526th Armored Infantry Bn, 143rd and 413th Anti-Aircraft Artillery Bns
825th Tank Destroyer Bn, 9th Canadian Forestry Co
61st, 158th, 299th, 300th and 1278th Engineer Combat Bns

V Corps – Major General Leonard T. Gerow.
51st, 112th, 146th, 202nd, 254th, 291st and 296th Engineer Combat Bns
186th and 941st Field Artillery Bns, 62nd Armored Field Artillery Bn
102nd Cavalry Group (mechanized)

78th Infantry Division
95th Armored Field Artillery Bn, 709th Tank Bn, 893rd Tank Destroyer Bn
2nd Infantry Division
16th Armored Field Artillery Bn, 18th, 200th, 955th and 987th Field Artillery Bns
741st Tank Bn, 612th and 644th Tank Destroyer Bns
Combat Command B 9th Armored Division

VIII Corps – Major General Troy Middleton.
35th, 44th, 159th and 168th Engineer Combat Bns
333rd, 559th, 561st, 578th, 740th, 770th, 771st, 965th and 969th Field Artillery Bns
274th Armored Field Artillery Bn
14th Cavalry Group (mechanized)
106th Infantry Division
28th Infantry Division
630th Tank Destroyer Bn, 687th Field Artillery Bn, 707th Tank Bn
4th Infantry Division
81st and 174th Field Artillery Bns
802nd and 803rd Tank Destroyer Bns, 70th Tank Bn
Combat Command A and Combat Command R 9th Armored Division
52nd and 60th Armored Inf Bns, 2nd and 19th Tank Bns, 3rd and 73rd Armored Field Artillery Bns

While the American forces were comparatively weak given the length of the line they were holding, among them were strong elements of mobile troops, artillery, and anti-tank weaponry. As the terrain favoured the defence, this force would not be easy prey for the Germans, with or without Allied air cover.

Allied air forces

The battleground was accessible to all Allied aircraft in mainland Europe and Britain. Therefore, the whole of the Allied air forces were available for use by SHAEF. During the fighting in the Ardennes, better known as the Battle of the Bulge, both the Allied tactical and strategic air forces were used to defeat the German attack. These included 8,000 aircraft in the tactical air forces, 4,000 heavy bombers in the strategic air forces and the 2,000 aircraft of the transport services. Against such a force, the Luftwaffe was powerless.

Hitler's plan of attack

The overall commander of the offensive was Field Marshal von Rundstedt, the re-instated Commander-in-Chief West, under whom Field Marshal Model commanded the attacking forces of Army Group B. In reality, however, the attack was conceived and commanded by Hitler himself, who was involved at every stage and in every decision.

General von Manteuffel, who commanded the Fifth Panzer Army in the offensive, stated:[9]

'The plan for the Ardennes offensive was drawn up completely by OKW [Hitler's HQ] and sent to us as a cut and dried "Fuhrer order".'

This order included the timing of the attack, the preceding artillery barrage and all other details concerning its execution. Liddell Hart remarked:[10]

'Hitler had worked out the plan at his headquarters in detail, with Jodl, and seemed to think that this would suffice for its fulfilment. He paid no attention to local conditions or the individual problems of his executants.'

In other words, he acted as he always had. It was the same approach as his plan for the 1942 summer campaign in the USSR which ended in the Stalingrad disaster, when he had omitted the practice of testing any plan of attack, and which the General Staff had invariably included in their preparations. He had learned nothing. However, on this occasion when Manteuffel made suggestions relating to various aspects of the tactics used in the attack and to changing the timing to improve the prospects of success for the infantry, Hitler agreed to them.

The territory Hitler chose for the attack was in the same general area of Belgium and Luxembourg through which the panzers had attacked in 1940. However, Namur and Liege, which were the points where he now aimed to split the Allied armies, are approximately 60 miles north of Sedan, where the 1940 offensive broke through the French defences. The concept of the December 1944 plan was very similar to one that Hitler had postulated in 1940 before adopting Manstein's strategy. The circumstances also seemed to be strikingly similar to 1940 in that the section of the Allied line to be attacked was the weakest one held by defending (in this case US) forces. However, while there thus seemed to be quite strong similarities, these were deceptive.

The actual situation was that the area in which the battle was to be fought in 1944 was easily accessible to the mobile forces in Montgomery's 21st Army

Group reserve, XXX Corps. This formation had been taken out of the line to prepare for the next offensive across the Rhine and was powerful enough to frustrate any attempt to cut off the British forces in the Netherlands, as Hitler planned. Similarly, Patton's Third Army to the south of the battleground had very strong, highly mobile forces which could be used to defeat the offensive or to mount an attack of their own. In addition to these forces, SHAEF had powerful mobile reserves available to commit to the battle immediately the need became apparent. In 1940, there had been no Allied reserves of any strength that were able to intervene in that campaign.

Furthermore, the German Army's supply position bore no resemblance to that in 1940, the Wehrmacht now suffering from acute shortages resulting from the dislocation of the German transport system and destruction of the factories producing the materiel they needed. The most acute problems with supplies of fuel and ammunition occurred during critical periods of the offensive. Manteuffel noted that in the operations to surround Bastogne, the 2nd Panzer Division was short of fuel, and that there was a shortage of ammunition to such a degree that the Germans could not put down a heavy bombardment on the town. This was contrary to OKW's assurances that there would be sufficient fuel and ammunition:[11]

Additionally, the Allied air forces in 1944 in no way resembled those of 1940, when the Luftwaffe was much more powerful. All these factors combined to make the similarities between the circumstances in the Ardennes in 1940 and 1944 more superficial than real.

Hitler's plan was that the Sixth SS-Panzer Army would attack the US forces slightly to the north of the important road junction of St Vith and cross the Meuse River near Liege. The Fifth Panzer Army would attack slightly south of the Sixth SS-Panzer Army, taking St Vith and the area's other vital road junction at Bastogne in the centre of the battle zone. Once Bastogne had been taken, the Fifth Panzer Army too would cross the Meuse in the vicinity of Namur and exploit its success, manoeuvring in conformity with the Sixth SS-Panzer Army to cut off the British 21st Army Group in the Netherlands and capture the port of Antwerp. The Seventh Army was to act as a defensive block for the left flank of the Fifth Panzer Army's attack and ensure that the enemy could not disrupt the operations of the formations on its right flank. The plan relied heavily on surprise on the ground and the overcast seasonal weather to obviate the ubiquitous support of the Allied air forces.

Hitler sent the plan to Rundstedt in late October who:[12]

'was staggered. Hitler had not troubled to consult me .... It was obvious to me that the available forces were far too small for such an extremely ambitious plan.'

Similarly, when Model saw Hitler's plan for the operation he commented:[13]

'This plan hasn't got a damned leg to stand on.'

SS-Colonel General 'Sepp' Dietrich,[14] who was in command of the Sixth SS-Panzer Army which Hitler had assigned the main role in the offensive, stated shortly after the war:[15]

'All I had to do was cross a river, capture Brussels and then go on and take the port of Antwerp. And all this in December, January and February, the worst three months of the year; through the Ardennes where snow was waist deep and there wasn't room to deploy four tanks abreast, let alone six armoured divisions; when it didn't get light until eight in the morning and was dark again at four in the afternoon and my tanks can't fight at night; with divisions that had just been reformed and were composed chiefly of raw untrained recruits.'

The alternate plan proposed to Hitler by Rundstedt and Model, with the more modest aim of destroying the US salient around Aachen, would probably have been achievable with the available forces. Implementing it could have caused the Western Allies significant damage, but Hitler rejected this alternative out of hand because it would not have caused a critical problem for the Allies, as his plan – realistic or not – aimed to achieve.

Warlimont recalled the opposition to the Fuhrer's plan from the senior German commanders:[16]

'On 3 November, barely three weeks before the date set for the attack, Colonel-General Jodl appeared at Army Group B Headquarters to brief the assembled senior commanders in the West on the plans for the offensive. He stated that the enemy situation and the terrain in the Eiffel area offered a certainty of a successful breakthrough. **The armoured formations which would follow up immediately would, within two days, cut the communications of the American First Army and Montgomery's Army Group and thereby set the stage for the subsequent destruction of twenty-five to thirty enemy divisions [Author's emphasis].** Vast quantities of material of all types which the enemy had assembled in this area for his attack across the Rhine would be captured or destroyed.

'... From the outset Jodl left no doubt that these directions came from Hitler and were therefore unalterable. Nevertheless, as one man, the assembled commanders protested, primarily against the distance of the objective – over one hundred and twenty-five miles away. The forces proposed, they said, even if they could be concentrated and more or less adequately equipped in time, which recent experience showed was improbable, were nothing like adequate, particularly under winter conditions.

'... Jodl remained totally unyielding in the face of these and all other objections. He replied that he knew the way that Hitler's mind ran and that **the "limited solution" would "merely postpone the day of reckoning and would not make the western powers ready to negotiate", thereby revealing that the Supreme Command's real objective was political [Author's emphasis].'**

Hitler addressed his senior commanders on 11 and 12 December, half at a time. Manteuffel recalled:[17]

'The assembly presented a striking contrast. On one side of the room were the commanding generals, responsible and experienced soldiers, many of whom had made great names for themselves on past battlefields, experts at their trade, respected by their troops. Facing them was the Supreme Commander of the Armed Forces, a stooped figure with a pale and puffy face, hunched in his chair, his hands trembling, his left arm subject to a violent twitching which he did his best to conceal, a sick man apparently borne down by the burden of responsibility. His physical condition had deteriorated noticeably since our last meeting in Berlin only nine days before. When he walked he dragged one leg behind him.

'At his side was Jodl, an old man now, overworked and overtired. His expression used to be taut and his bearing rigid, but this was no longer so. He was mentally and physically exhausted.'

And these were the two key planners of the Ardennes offensive just prior to it being launched. The plan bore all the indications of delusion and reflected the physical and mental condition of those who planned it. Whether Hitler was the main planner, as seems likely, or Jodl, it did not bear any relationship with the factual context then existing and can only be described as a fantasy, concocted by desperate men.

According to Warlimont, Hitler stated during his speech:[18]

'The following must also be considered, gentlemen. In all history there has never been a coalition composed of such heterogeneous partners with such totally divergent objectives as that of our enemies. The states which are now our enemies are the greatest opposites which exist on earth: ultra-capitalist states on one side and ultra-Marxist states on the other. ... These are states whose objectives diverge daily. And anyone who, if I may use the phrase, sits like a spider in his web and follows these developments can see how hour by hour these antitheses are increasing. **If we deal it a couple of heavy blows, this artificially constructed common front may collapse with a mighty thunderclap at any moment [Author's emphasis].'**

It is clear that Hitler was intending to inflict a major defeat on the Western Allies to force them to negotiate with him so that he could achieve a compromise peace and then turn his full force against the Soviet Union. Hitler obviously did not grasp the intense loathing which he and the Nazi regime evoked in the Western governments and people of whom he had so gratuitously and recklessly made enemies and who had already stated that they would not negotiate with him. The chances of any positive diplomatic outcome for the Germans were even more remote than hopes for any military success, showing the depth of Hitler's delusion.

Speer noted that Hitler told him the following about the offensive:[19]

'A single break-through on the western front! You'll see! It will lead to collapse and panic among the Americans. We'll drive right through their middle and take Antwerp [Author's emphasis].' Then they'll have lost their supply port. And a tremendous pocket will encircle the entire English Army, with hundreds of thousands of prisoners. As we used to do in Russia.'

Although Hitler's last offensive was based on such fantasies, the lives lost because of them were real enough.

The Germans attack

The Germans launched their attack at 5.30 am on 16 December. The initial artillery barrage disrupted normal landline communications between many of the front-line American units and their headquarters, but the radio net was still operative, although the terrain of the Ardennes made reception uneven.

For the offensive to have any hope of success, it was vital that the Germans kept to the timeline Jodl had outlined to the senior commanders of crossing the Meuse River within forty-eight hours to forestall any redeployment of Allied forces. During the 1940 campaign, Guderian had taken three days to reach the Meuse, so this timetable was extremely optimistic.

Although the Americans were heavily outnumbered at all the German objectives, the attack did not achieve the planned timetable. The main reason was that the US troops defended vigorously and did not 'collapse and panic', as Hitler told Speer they would. The terrain in the Ardennes favours the defender and the configuration of the road network channels attacking forces into small road junctions which can be held by relatively few troops, hindering the exploitation of any gains made. Manteuffel commented upon the effect of the terrain on the attackers:[20]

'The main roads contained many hairpin bends, and were frequently built into steep hillsides. To get the guns of the artillery and flak units as well as the pontoons and beams of the bridging engineers around these sharp corners was a lengthy and difficult business. The guns and trailers had to be disconnected and then dragged around the corner by a capstan mechanism, naturally one at a time. Vehicles could not pass one another on these roads. In the event of air attack there could be no question of taking cover in the scrub or forests that flanked the roads, since the sides of the hills into which they were built were far too steep.'

These problems had also occurred in 1940, but then the Luftwaffe covered the advance, and the defending forces were second-line French troops without armoured support, in contrast to the position in 1944.

Although the attack of the Sixth SS-Panzer Army seemed to make a good start and the covering American units suffered heavy casualties, the panzers were channelled by the road network, which prevented the exploitation envisaged by Hitler's plan. During the afternoon of 17 December, the 1st SS-Panzer Division missed an opportunity to capture a huge fuel dump around the town of Malmedy, which would have been invaluable to the continuance of the attack. During a lull in the fighting while they were going through Malmedy, SS-Colonel Joachim Peiper's battle group murdered eighty-six Americans who had surrendered, further blackening the reputation of the Waffen-SS, if it was still possible to do so.

Units of the Fifth Panzer Army soon ran up against American troops in and around St Vith, who frustrated the German attack, although once again at the cost of heavy casualties.

In the centre of the front, around Clervaux, the attackers were also held up but made the most gains of any of the German units. Late on 17 December, they had advanced to within 5 miles south-west of Bastogne, which was the most important road junction and the shortest route to the Meuse in that section of the front.

Warlimont claimed that just two days into the offensive, on 18 December, Hitler was quick to herald the attack's success, with delusion piling upon delusion:[21]

'Supreme Headquarters was carried away by these partial successes and was completely the prisoner of its own wishful thinking; it therefore entirely failed to realise that with every day which the enemy was allowed for the movement of his considerable reserves, the prospects of a major victory, getting anywhere near the planned objectives, were becoming more improbable. Jodl's diary of 18 December gives a good idea of the attitude of mind: **They must be cut off from the rear so that they cannot be supplied; they will then surrender [Author's emphasis].**' Shortly thereafter, however, the focal point of Bastogne, instead of surrendering, began to absorb an even greater proportion of the attacking forces; the weather cleared and in spite of all the efforts of the Luftwaffe the Allied air superiority began to make itself felt.'

In addition to being behind their timetable, the German attacks had also been costly. The Volksgrenadier infantry did not have sufficient combat experience; although they were full of fight, they suffered higher rates of casualties than would veteran formations. Manteuffel commented upon the dearth of trained units:[22]

'The standard of training was no longer sufficiently high in all the divisions to allow any confidence in their performance when pitted against an enemy, superior in numbers and equipment, who had recently been rested and who were extremely well fed. Every senior commander was aware of these shortcomings on the part of our troops. What is more, the army had undertaken no large-scale offensive operations since 1942. To make good this lack of experience in offence, it would have been necessary to withdraw the divisions from the front, rest them, and give them a thorough training in favourable conditions. Hitler saw to it that the majority of his SS divisions did have such rest and training, but this was not the lot of the army divisions. The infantry divisions that were to play so decisive a part in the assault could only give their replacements partial and, it must be admitted, inadequate training for the task that lay ahead of them.'

This was a major problem because there were comparatively few infantry divisions in the attack. The offensive's impetus could not be maintained for any length of time using infantry with low training levels and high casualty rates.

Allied reaction

On 16 December, the Commander-in-Chief of the US 12th Army Group, Lieutenant General Bradley, was with the Supreme Commander of SHAEF, General Eisenhower, at his headquarters when they heard of events in the Ardennes. Eisenhower recalled:[23]

'I was immediately convinced that this was no local attack; it was not logical for the enemy to attempt merely a minor offensive in the Ardennes.... The operational maps before us showed that on each flank of the Ardennes the bulk of a United States armored division was out of the front lines and could be moved quickly. On the north was the 7th Armored ... on the south was the 10th Armored ... . We agreed that these two divisions should immediately begin to close the threatened area, the exact destination of each to be determined later by Bradley.

'... we carefully went over the list of reserves then available to us. Among those most readily accessible was the XVIII Airborne Corps under General Ridgway, located near Reims. It included the 82nd and 101st Airborne Divisions, both battle-tested formations of the highest order.

'... The US 11th Armored Division had recently arrived and the 17th Airborne Division was in the United Kingdom ready to come to the Continent. The 87th Infantry Division could also be brought into the area within a reasonable time.

'... In the British sector, far to the north, Montgomery was preparing for a new offensive. At the moment he had one complete corps, the 30, out of the line. With the resources available to us, we were confident that any attack the German might launch could eventually be effectively countered.'

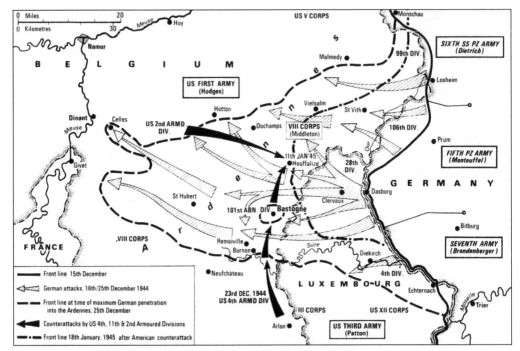

Map 11: The 1944 Ardennes Offensive.
The second Ardennes Offensive was a forlorn operation from its inception. The forces were too weak, the timetable for success was hopelessly optimistic and the Allies were too strong on the ground and in the air for it to have any realistic chance of achieving its aims. The Germans never came close to succeeding and the losses suffered were, this time, and finally, irreplaceable.

On 17 December, the 82nd and 101st Airborne Divisions were indeed released to Bradley, being sent to Bastogne and Stavelot, a little to its north. The 11th Armored Division was also allocated to Bradley and sent to the battle area, and the 17th Airborne Division was hurried to France from the UK. Thus, by the end of the second day of the German counterattack, Allied forces had already been allocated to the battle, which made it virtually certain that Hitler's fantasy would not become reality. The main questions now were how far the Germans would be able to progress and what degree of damage and disruption the attack would cause.

Eisenhower's early appreciation of the enemy's likely strategy and his speedy action in releasing reserves to Bradley are clear evidence of his grasp of the situation and his command abilities, for which he is given scant regard by some commentators and historians.

Changes to the Allied command structure

Soon after the scale of the German attack in the Ardennes became clear, Eisenhower took a very important decision relating to the Allied command structure. He later stated:[24]

'The depth of the German advances on the eighteenth and nineteenth had broken all normal communications between Bradley's headquarters at Luxembourg and the headquarters of the Ninth and First Armies. For this reason it was completely impossible for Bradley to give the attack on the southern shoulder the attention that I desired and at the same time to keep properly in touch with the troops in the north who were called upon to meet the heaviest German blows.

'To this whole situation only one solution seemed applicable. This was to place all troops in our northern salient under one commander. The only way to achieve the necessary unity was to place Montgomery temporarily in command of all northern forces and direct Bradley to give his full attention to affairs on the south. ... I telephoned Bradley to inform him of this decision and then phoned Field Marshal Montgomery to give him his orders.'

This was the logical step to take, as the most powerful reserves available on the northern flank of the battlefield were British; placing Montgomery in charge of all the forces there would ensure that the Allied response from this direction would be completely integrated. In practice, the arrangement worked well, and the responses from the north and south of the German penetration were well co-ordinated. However, Montgomery could not resist making some characteristically tactless remarks relating to the battle and command changes, which seemed to imply that he had saved the US forces from a situation they couldn't handle. This caused deep and lasting resentment against him in the higher echelons of the US Army.

Once again, this practical and effective decision by Eisenhower showed the strength of the Allied command structure and Eisenhower's decisive ability, for which he deserves great credit.

The failure of the offensive

In the northern sector of the front, the Americans were defending the vital road junction of St Vith with increasing strength. Elements of the US 7th and 9th Armored Divisions, together with infantry from the various units which had originally been defending the area, fought aggressively and fended off the German attacks during 18 and 19 December. Without St Vith, the Germans could not fully develop their offensive. On 21 December, the Germans made an all-out effort to take the town, which finally fell to them that night. On 22 December, the US forces re-formed to the west of St Vith in a position that still blocked the Germans, but the 1st SS-Panzer Division managed to press on westward using minor roads. However, the foremost element, consisting of the battle group commanded by SS-Colonel Peiper, finally became isolated near Stoumont, where it ran out of fuel and was surrounded by Allied forces. Cut off and unable to advance further, the battle group disabled and abandoned its vehicles before retreating to the German lines on 24 December, having suffered 75 per cent casualties.

In the centre of the attack front at Bastogne, elements of the US 10th Armored Division arrived on 17 December, and the defences were further strengthened when the 101st Airborne Division began arriving on the morning of 19 December. Both divisions had been released to Bradley by Eisenhower on 16 December. The Bastogne position was supplied by air drops, which the Germans could do nothing to prevent. Nevertheless, the Germans managed to by-pass Bastogne by 20 December, having manoeuvred around it during the previous day, and engaged the covering forces. Manteuffel appreciated the decisive nature of the clashes at Bastogne:[25]

'Bastogne became a maelstrom into which the German forces, including the attacking forces intended for the Meuse, were sucked. Bastogne had at one time drawn nine German divisions, with two corps commands, into the battle. It necessitated the transfer of units form the Sixth SS-Panzer Army to the Fifth Panzer Army, and thereby nullified all offensive intentions of the Supreme Command. **The defense of Bastogne, undertaken in apparently hopeless circumstances, was thus decisive in foiling our offensive plans [Author's emphasis].'**

'... A unified attack on Bastogne might have had a chance of succeeding even now, provided that it had been possible to collect all the reinforcements within a few days and send them into the assault together. This was not the case. Units were delayed on the roads and arrived only piecemeal and below strength. **The Supreme Command, however, insisted on rigid adherence to its plans: despite the changed situation, it ordered one uncoordinated attached after the other, none which was successful [Author's emphasis].'**

As usual, the German commanders on the ground were not allowed any discretion to adapt operations to suit actual circumstances, with predictable results.

Support for the Allied ground troops from their air forces came into full operation on 23 December when the weather cleared, causing great difficulties for the German troops from then on. Manteuffel stated:[26]

'From the 23rd and 24th December on the Allied Air Forces were able to operate freely: they found worthwhile targets throughout the whole area of our offensive. ... The mobility of our forces decreased steadily and rapidly. ... Movement by daylight became for all intents and purposes impossible behind our front.'

Speer noted that the Fuhrer refused to accept the operation had failed:[27]

'On December 23 Model told me that the offensive had definitely failed – but that Hitler ordered it to continue.'

Despite abundant evidence that the offensive had stalled and could not succeed, Hitler ordered further attacks on 26 December.

The pattern was the same as had been exhibited everywhere else. Hitler's 'generalship' consisted merely of ordering 'no withdrawal', with consequent higher losses to no advantage for the Germans.

On 26 December, Patton's relieving force, attacking from the south, reached the US garrison at Bastogne, and from then on, although there was continuing hard fighting, there was no prospect of the offensive succeeding.

On 31 December, Speer visited Dietrich, the commander of the Sixth SS-Panzer Army:[28]

'He had set up headquarters in the vicinity of the Belgian border town of Houffalize. One of the old fighters in the early days of the party, in his own plain fashion he too had parted ways psychologically with Hitler. Our conversation soon turned to the latest batch of commands. Hitler had decreed with increasing insistence that encircled Bastogne be taken "at any cost." He refused to understand, Sepp Dietrich grumbled, that even the elite divisions of the SS could not effortlessly overrun the Americans. It was impossible to convince Hitler that these were tough opponents, soldiers as good as our own men. "Besides," he added, "we are receiving no ammunition. The supply routes have been cut by their air attacks."'

Dietrich had been a follower of Hitler since the 1920s. For him to recognize that the position was hopeless surely meant that Hitler's offensive was doomed.

Ultimately, in addition to the problems faced on the field, the supply situation became an insuperable headache for the Germans, a fact confirmed by Speer:[29]

'I arranged with Field Marshal Model, the commander of Army Group B, to keep him supplied with improvised armaments aid during the offensive. On December 16, the day of the attack, I set out from Berlin, bound for a small headquarters in a hunting lodge near Bonn. Riding through the night in a Reichsbahn diesel car, I saw the switching yards east of the Rhine jammed with freight cars. The enemy bombers had prevented the movement of supplies for the offensive.

'... by the second day of the offensive, transportation had already reached a chaotic state. Motor vehicles could move only a foot at a time along the three lane highway. My car took an hour on average to move two miles, wedged in as it was by ammunition trucks. I kept fearing that the weather might improve.

'Model offered all sorts of reasons for this confusion – lack of discipline in newly formed units, for example, or the chaos in the hinterland. But whatever the reasons, the whole scene showed that the army had lost its erstwhile famous talent for organization – surely one of the effects of Hitler's three years of command.'

Hitler finally admitted that the attack had failed, and on 3 January 1945 agreed to a withdrawal which took the Germans back to their original positions.

Manteuffel offered an overview of the offensive:[30]

'Within a few days of its opening, it seemed likely that it would fail, because of the objectives assigned. The target was too remote and the strength of the attacking force quite disproportionate to this distant aim. Our forces lacked the necessary "depth" in men and material alike to exploit rapidly and powerfully the break-through, once it had been achieved.

'... The general lack of strength had as [a] result another and greater failure. No definite point of main effort was established. **There can be no question that the rigid adherence to the original objective was a mistake, as was the organisation and commitment of our forces. The Supreme Command, out of touch with conditions at the front and displaying an increased and misplaced obstinacy in its insistence that**

orders be carried out to the letter, no longer displayed the necessary flexibility in adjusting operations to the situation as it developed [Author's emphasis].'

Manteuffel was something of a favourite of Hitler's and the youngest army group commander in the Wehrmacht. His verdict on the offensive and the role of the Supreme Command can only be regarded as completely damning, confirming the futility and utter waste of it ever having been attempted. In his speech to the senior commanders before the offensive, the Fuhrer had maintained that there was, in effect, no choice but to attack because Germany would be defeated if it remained on the defensive. Yet if he had harboured the slightest regard for his countrymen's lives, as he so often professed to do, he would have relieved them and the rest of the world of having to go through this further trial and surrendered before wasting more lives in a hopeless attempt to keep himself in power. That he didn't do so reveals his utter contempt for the German people who had placed so much trust in him.

Hitler proclaimed many times to have an intimate knowledge of the works of the noted Prussian strategist Carl von Clausewitz, but if he had read them he obviously had not absorbed the following passage from his most famous work, *On War*:[31]

'However highly we must esteem courage and firmness in War, and however little prospect there is of victory to him who cannot resolve to seek it by the exertion of all his powers, still there is a point beyond which perseverance can only be termed desperate folly, and therefore can meet with no approbation from any critic.'

Hitler's Ardennes offensive must surely be equal to any such situation in the history of warfare.

Conclusions

1. Hitler's plan has been called 'brilliant' by some commentators, who go on to state something along the lines of 'except for the fact that he didn't have the forces necessary to carry it out'. Yet no plan that fails to take this fundamental element into account can be termed as such. Hitler's plan of the Ardennes offensive was, in fact, a desperate gamble by a sick and delusional tyrant whose only priority was to perpetuate his own rule. It was not the product of a militarily rational or completely sane mind.

2. The dispositions made, giving the emphasis to the role of the Sixth SS–Panzer Army, was obviously done for the political prestige that would accrue to the Nazi regime. Equally obviously, the dispositions were faulty and amateurish in that the terrain through which the Army had to advance was decidedly in favour of the defence, and in the event led to delays which rendered the development of the attack as envisaged impossible. This was entirely predictable.

3. Hitler's dismissal of the defensive capabilities of the US forces were shown to be completely delusional, reflecting his utterly mistaken evaluation of their combat abilities. Not even Sepp Dietrich could convince him otherwise. Once again, the Fuhrer showed the same underestimation of his opponents as he had with respect to the Red Army.

4. Hitler's assurances relating to the provision of supplies – particularly petrol – were proven to be completely wrong. He expected that the attackers would overrun American supply bases and that these would enable the success of the offensive, an assumption that proved utterly unfounded. In essence, it was negated by the fighting ability of the US troops who prevented the development of the German attack.

5. The Waffen-SS showed itself in its true colours during the offensive, killing unarmed US troops who had surrendered. SS-Colonel Pieper escaped the death sentence of a military court, only to be killed after being released from prison when he was identified. The outrage committed by the SS only served to make the Allied soldiers more determined to defeat Germany, the opposite to the desired effect.

Any objective examination of the Ardennes offensive shows beyond doubt that Hitler had not changed any of the basic elements of his mode of command. Underestimation of the enemy, amateurish planning and objectives beyond the power of the attacking forces were all present, proving that he had learned nothing from being Supreme Commander of the Wehrmacht and much less from assuming the role of Commander-in-Chief of the Army.

Appendix 1

Comparative Production of Weapons

Aircraft	1939	1940	1941	1942	1943	1944	1945	Total
Britain	7,940	15,049	20,094	23,672	26,263	26,461	12,070	131,549
USA	5,856	12,804	26,277	47,826	85,998	96,318	49,761	324,840
USSR	10,382	10,565	15,735	25,436	34,900	40,300	20,900	158,218
Germany	8,295	10,247	11,776	15,409	24,807	39,807	7,540	117,881

Tanks	1939	1940	1941	1942	1943	1944	1945	Total
Britain	969	1,399	4,841	8,611	7,476	5,000	2,100	30,396
USA	–	400	4,052	24,997	29,497	17,565	11,968	88,479
USSR	2,950	2,794	6,590	24,446	24,089	28,963	15,400	105,232
Germany	1,300	2,200	5,200	9,200	17,300	22,100	4,400	61,700

Artillery	1939	1940	1941	1942	1943	1944	1945	Total
Britain	1,400	1,900	5,300	6,600	12,200	12,400	–	39,800
USA	–	1,800	29,615	72,658	67,544	33,558	19,699	224,874
USSR	17,348	15,300	42,300	127,000	130,300	122,400	31,000	485,648
Germany	2,000	5,000	7,000	12,000	27,000	41,000	–	94,000

These figures are extracted from Richard Overy's book *Why The Allies Won* (Random House, London, 1995), pp. 331–32. There are differences in the dates of each country's total production from year to year. Some figures that are not reliable have not been included.

Notes

Introduction

1. See 'Hossbach Memorandum', a record of a meeting that Hitler held on 12 November 1937 and was regarded as being so important that he stated that his views should be taken as his testament. It was presented by US Counsel on 20 December 1945, as Exhibit USA 25, and read into the record of the 'Trial of the Major War Criminals' at Nuremberg, p.262 of Vol 2.
2. The concept was that the German territory in Europe was too small to guarantee the space that the German 'volk' needed to properly develop. Therefore, because it was the superior race in Europe, Germany should take the territory it needed from the states of the East. This is a central theme of Hitler's book *Mein Kampf.*
3. One of Hitler's favourite descriptions of what would happen to his enemies, meaning 'annihilated'.
4. For example, prescribing the method of cooking lobsters. R.G.L. Waite, *The Psychopathic God* (Da Capo, New York, 1993), p.3.
5. This was the 'Leader principal' which vested all authority in the Fuhrer and required unquestioning obedience to Hitler's orders.
6. Walter Warlimont, *Inside Hitler's Headquarters, 1939–1945*, Presidio Press, California, 1991, p.500.
7. Kurt Zeitzler, in William Richardson & Seymour Freidlin (eds), *The Fatal Decisions* (Pen & Sword, Barnsley, 2012), p.145.
8. Field Marshal Erich von Manstein, *Lost Victories* (Presidio Press, California, 1994), p.547.
9. I.S. Playfair, *History of the Second World War* (HMSO, London, 1966), p.460.
10. Warlimont, p.457.
11. Omar Bradley, *A General's Life* (Simon and Schuster, New York, 1983), p.255.
12. Richard Overy, *Why The Allies Won* (Johnathon Cape, London, 1995), p.176.
13. S. Westphal, in *The Fatal Decisions*, p.211.

Chapter 1

1. Speech of 14 March 1936, Munich, see Waite, *The Psychopathic God*, p.28.
2. Adolf Hitler, *Mein Kampf* (Reynal & Hitchcock Edition, New York, 1941), pp.947–50.
3. Spencer Tucker, *The Encyclopedia of World War I: A Political, Social, and Military History*, Vol 1 (California), p.225.
4. In a speech on 31 May 1921, see Eberhard Jackel and Axel Kuhn, *Hitler, Samtichle Aufzeichnugen* 1905–1924 (Stuttgart, 1980), p.426.
5. Martin Bormann controlled the Nazi Party Secretariat and eventually became the most powerful person in Germany apart from Hitler.
6. Hugh Trevor Roper, *Hitler's Table Talk* (Enigma Books, New York, 2000), p.40.

7. Trevor Roper, p.5.
8. Albert Speer, *Inside the Third Reich* (The MacMillan Company, New York, 2003), p.234.
9. Charles Burdick and Hans-Adolf Jacobsen (eds), *The Halder War Diary, 1939–1942* (Presidio Press, California, 1988), p.227.
10. Burdick and Jacobsen, p.231.
11. Burdick and Jacobsen, p.244.
12. *The Trial of the Major War Criminals at Nuremberg*, Volume XV, 5 June 1946, p.390.
13. *Nazi-Soviet Relations 1939–41* (Didier, New York, 1948).
14. Geoffrey Roberts, *Stalin's Wars* (Yale University Press, New Haven and London, 2008), p.63.
15. Richard Overy, *The Dictators* (Penguin Books, London, 2005), p.492.
16. Walter Gorlitz (ed.), *The Memoirs of Field Marshal Wilhelm Keitel* (Cooper Square Press, New York, 2000), p.98.
17. Speer, p.244.
18. Paul Schmidt, *Hitler's Interpre*ter (The History Press, Gloucestershire, 2016), p.204.
19. Schmidt, p.208.
20. Schmidt, p,210.
21. Schmidt, p.210.
22. Gerhard Engel, *At The Heart of The Reich* (Greenhill Books, London, 2005), p.100.
23. Warlimont, p.136.
24. Nuremberg, Vol IX, 15 March 1946, p.344.
25. Nuremberg, Vol IX, 21 March 1946, p.604.
26. Speer, pp.249–50.
27. Guenther Blumentritt, *Von Rundstedt: the Soldier and the Man* (Odhams Press, London, 1952), p.98.
28. Nuremberg, Vol XX, 9 August 1946, p.577.
29. Basil Liddell Hart, *The Other Side of the Hill* (MacMillan London Limited, 1993), pp.255–56.
30. Liddell Hart, p.257.
31. Manstein, p.181.
32. Burdick and Jacobsen, p.314.
33. Gorlitz, p.122.
34. Nuremberg, Vol IX, 8 March 1946, p.49.
35. Burdick and Jacobsen, see note 9 above.
36. Burdick and Jacobsen, p.231.
37. Burdick and Jacobsen, p.233.
38. Burdick and Jacobsen, p.235.
39. Burdick and Jacobsen, p.244.
40. Burdick and Jacobsen, p.246.
41. Warlimont, p.135.
42. David Stone, *Twilight of the Gods* (Conway Books, London, 2011), p.191.
43. Franz Kurowski, *'Panzerkrieg'* (J.J. Fedorowicz Publishing, Winnipeg, 2005), p.124.
44. Warlimont, p.137.
45. Warlimont, p.138.
46. Warlimont, p.139.
47. Burdick and Jacobsen, p.314.
48. Nuremberg, Vol XXVI, p.361, Exhibit USA-134, OKW Conference Minutes, 3

February, 1941.
49. Manstein, p.175.
50. Manstein, p.176.
51. Blumentritt, pp.103–04.
52. Burdick and Jacobsen, p.352.
53. These army strength figures are collated from *Operation Barbarossa: The Complete Organisational and Statistical Analysis, and Military Simulation*, Vol II B (Lulu Publishing, US), and Alan Clark, *Barbarossa* (William Morrow, New York, 1965), pp.12, 13.
54. Cajus Bekker, *The Luftwaffe Diaries* (Ballantine Books, New York, 1973), Appendix 10, p.552.
55. Alan CLark, '*Barbarossa, The Russian German Conflict, 1941–45*', Hutchinson & Co, London, 1965, pp.38–9.
56. Heinz Guderian, *Panzer Leader* (Da Capo Press, Cambridge, MA, 2002), p.138.
57. See Basil Liddell-Hart, 'A History of the Second World War', p.197; David Stahel, 'Operation Barbarossa and Germany's Defeat in the East', pp.114–16, and Guderian, 'Panzer Leader' p.139.
58. David Stahel, *Operation Barbarossa and Germany's Defeat in the East* (Cambridge University Press, Cambridge, 2009), p.116.
59. The full story of Sorge's incredible activities is set out in Owen Matthews' *An Impeccable Spy* (Bloomsbury Publishing PLC, London, 2019).
60. Warlimont, p.145.
61. Warlimont, p.211.

Chapter 2
1. Nuremberg, Vol XXVI, p.396, Exhibit USA-134, OKW Conference Minutes, 3 February 1941.
2. Gabriel Gorodetsky, *The Maisky Diaries* (Yale University Press, New Haven and London, 2015).
3. Gorodetsky, p.361.
4. Gorodetsky, p.362.
5. Gorodetsky, p.364.
6. Overy, *The Dictators*, p.491.
7. Overy, *The Dictators*, p.491.
8. Blumentritt, in *The Fatal Decisions*, p.31.
9. Blumentritt, in *The Fatal Decisions*, p.47.
10. Burdick and Jacobsen, p.446.
11. Warlimont, p.179.
12. Warlimont, p.180.
13. Burdick and Jacobsen, p.457.
14. Clark, p.43.
15. Warlimont, p.180.
16. Clark, p.49.
17. Blumentritt, in *The Fatal Decisions*, p.48.
18. Burdick and Jacobsen, p.474.
19. Charles Messenger, 'The Last Prussian', p.144.
20. Klaus Gerbet, *Generalfeldmarschall Fedor von Bock, The War Diary, 1939–1945* (Schiffer Military History, Atglen, PA, 1996), p.247.

21. Warlimont, p.183.
22. Warlimont, p.184.
23. Gerbet, p.262.
24. Burdick and Jacobsen, p.487.
25. Burdick and Jacobsen, p.263.
26. Blumentritt, in *The Fatal Decisions*, p.50.
27. Warlimont, p.185.
28. Gorlitz, p.148.
29. Gorlitz, p.150.
30. Burdick and Jacobsen, p.495.
31. Engel, p.115.
32. Burdick and Jacobsen, p.506.
33. Gorlitz, p.145.
34. Engel, p.117.
35. Burdick and Jacobsen, p.515.
36. Gorlitz, pp.69–70.
37. Guderian, p.190.
38. Guderian, p.198.
39. Guderian, p.98.
40. Guderian, p.199.
41. Guderian, p.199.
42. Guderian, p.200.
43. Guderian, p.225.
44. Charles Messenger, 'The Last Prussian', pp.153–4.
45. Burdick and Jacobsen, p.544.
46. Guderian, p.230.
47. Burdick and Jacobsen, p.545.
48. Burdick and Jacobsen, p.546.
49. Guderian, p.232.
50. Burdick and Jacobsen, p.546.
51. Guderian, p.233.
52. Blumentritt, in *The Fatal Decisions*, p.56.
53. Guderian, p.234.
54. Burdick & Jacobsen, p.549.
55. Guderian, p.234.
56. Burdick and Jacobsen, p.551.
57. Gerbet, p.327.
58. Burdick and Jacobsen, p.552.
59. Guderian, p.237.
60. Guderian, p.239.
61. Gerbet, p.333.
62. Gerbet, p.336.
63. Gerbet, p.336.
64. Gerbet, p.340.
65. Guderian, p.242.
66. Guderian, p.245.
67. Gerbet, p.354.
68. Gerbet, p.355.

69. Gerbet, p.357.
70. Engel, p.120.
71. Guderian, p.248.
72. Stuart Goldman, *Nomonhan 1939: The Red Army's Victory that Shaped World War II* (Naval Institute Press, Annapolis, 2012), p.177.
73. Gerbet, p.365.
74. Engel, p.121.
75. Burdick and Jacobsen, p.561.
76. Burdick and Jacobsen, p.563.
77. Burdick and Jacobsen, p.564.
78. Engel, p.122.
79. Burdick and Jacobsen, p.571.
80. Guderian, p.247.
81. Guderian, p.259.
82. Field Marshal Albert Kesselring, *A Soldiers Record* (William Morrow and Company, New York, 1954), p.108.
83. Engel, p.123.
84. Burdick and Jacobsen, p.584.
85. Gorlitz, p.163.

Chapter 3
1. Burdick and Jacobsen, p.573.
2. Burdick and Jacobsen, p.574.
3. Burdick and Jacobsen, p.576.
4. Gerbet, p.381.
5. Gerbet, p.382.
6. Burdick and Jacobsen, p.579.
7. Burdick and Jacobsen, p.582.
8. Burdick and Jacobsen, p.584.
9. Gerbet, p.386.
10. Engel, p.124.
11. Warlimont, p.206.
12. Warlimont, p.206.
13. Warlimont, p.207.
14. Burdick and Jacobsen, p.585.
15. Burdick and Jacobsen, p.584.
16. Burdick and Jacobsen, p.584.
17. Gerbet, p.391.
18. Gerbet, p.392.
19. Gerbet, p.394.
20. Roberts, p.112.
21. Roberts, p.112.
22. Roberts, p.114.
23. Burdick and Jacobsen, p.590.
24. Burdick and Jacobsen, p.590.
25. Blumentritt, in *The Fatal Decisions*, p.64.
26. Burdick and Jacobsen, p.592.
27. Warlimont, p.214.

28. Burdick and Jacobsen, p.596.
29. Blumentritt, in *The Fatal Decisions*, p.67.
30. Burdick and Jacobsen, pp.597–98.
31. Burdick and Jacobsen, p.598.
32. Burdick and Jacobsen, p.600.
33. Burdick and Jacobsen, p.600.
34. Burdick and Jacobsen, p.604.
35. Gerbet, p.404.
36. Gerbet, p.405.
37. Gerbet, p.407.
38. Guderian, p.265.
39. Guderian, p.265.
40. Warlimont, p.223.

Chapter 4
 1. Hugh Trevor Roper, *Hitler's Table Talk* (Enigma Books, New York, 2000).
 2. Trevor Roper, p.340.
 3. Burdick and Jacobsen, p.613.
 4. Speer, p.331.
 5. Warlimont, p.243.
 6. Warlimont, p.243.
 7. Guderian, p.274.
 8. Zeitzler, p.115.
 9. Manstein, p.293.
10. Stone, p.238.
11. See Westphal, 'The Fatal Decisions', p.77 and Liddell-Hart, 'The Other Side of The Hill', p.301.
12. Speer, p.328.
13. Burdick and Jacobsen, p.633.
14. Burdick and Jacobsen, p.635.
15. Burdick and Jacobsen, p.635.
16. Burdick and Jacobsen, p.637.
17. Burdick and Jacobsen, p.638.
18. Gerbet, p.524.
19. Gerbet, p.525.
20. Burdick and Jacobsen, p.639.
21. Gerbet, p.526.
22. Warlimont, p.246.
23. Burdick and Jacobsen, p.641.
24. Burdick and Jacobsen, p.641.
25. Stone, p.235.
26. Burdick and Jacobsen, p.646.
27. Burdick and Jacobsen, p.647.
28. Burdick and Jacobsen, p.647.
29. Burdick and Jacobsen, p.648.
30. Burdick and Jacobsen, p.649.
31. Burdick and Jacobsen, p.649.
32. Alan Clark, 'Barbarossa', pp.210–11..

33. Burdick and Jacobsen, p.650.
34. Burdick and Jacobsen, p.650.
35. Warlimont, p.255.
36. Kurowski, p.337.
37. See Burdick and Jacobsen, 'The Halder War Diary, 1939–1942' p.662, and Liddell-Hart, 'The Other Side of the Hill' p.309.
38. Burdick and Jacobsen, p.661.
39. Warlimont, p.251.
40. Leon Goldensohn, *The Nuremberg Interviews* (Pimlico, London, 2006), p.294.
41. Burdick and Jacobsen, p.662.
42. Burdick and Jacobsen, p.664.
43. Burdick and Jacobsen, p.664.
44. Warlimont, p.256.
45. Trevor Roper, p.694.
46. Warlimont, p.256.
47. Engel, p.131.
48. Burdick and Jacobsen, p.668.
49. Burdick and Jacobsen, p.669.
50. Engel, p.133.
51. Burdick and Jacobsen, p.670.
52. Warlimont, p.258.
53. 'Zeitzler, in the '*The fatal Decisions*', p.117.
54. Zeitzler, p.117.
55. See *The Fatal Decisions*, p.120.
56. Zeitzler, p.120.
57. Zeitzler, p.121.
58. Zeitzler, p.124.
59. Zeitzler, p.126.
60. Manstein, p.291.
61. Manstein, p.293.
62. Speer, p.343.
63. Zeitzler, p.128.
64. Zeitzler, p.131.
65. Zeitzler, p.131.
66. Zeitzler, pp.132–33.
67. Speer, p.344.
68. Speer, p.345.
69. Zeitzler, p.145.
70. Zeitzler, p.146.
71. Manstein, p.297.
72. Manstein, p.294.
73. Manstein, p.295.
74. Manstein, p.304.
75. Manstein, p.296.
76. Manstein, p.319.
77. Zeitzler, p.149.
78. Zeitzler, p.153.
79. Manstein, p.304.

80. Nuremberg, Vol XV, 5 June 1946, p.371.
81. Gorlitz, pp.185–86.
82. Zeitzler, p.143.
83. Zeitzler, p.154.
84. Zeitzler, p.155.
85. Manstein, '*Defensive Operations in southern Russia*', Marine Corps Gazette (April 1957), p.53.
86. Warlimont, p.243.
87. Siegfried Westphal, '*The Fatal Decisions*', Pen & Sword Military, Yorkshire, 2012, p.77.
88. David Stone, '*Twilight of the Gods*', Conway Books, London, 2011, p.238.
89. Zeitzler, '*The Fatal Decisions*', p.126.
90. Zeitzler, p.149.
91. Speer, p.345.

Chapter 5
1. Manstein, p.438.
2. Joachim Fest, *Hitler* (Harcourt Books, Florida, 1974), p.693.
3. Joachim Fest, *Hitler* (Harcourt Books, Florida, 1974), p.693.
4. Manstein, p.445.
5. Roberts, p.159.
6. Warlimont, p.245.
7. Robin Cross, *The Battle of Kursk: Operation Citadel 1943* (Penguin Books, London, 2002), pp.101–03.
8. Cross, p.110.
9. Cross, p.112.
10. Mungo Melvin, *Manstein: Hitler's Greatest General* (Weidenfeld & Nicolson, London, 2010), p.356.
11. Richard W. Harrison, *The Battle of Kursk*, Helion & Company, Warwick, England, 2016, p.31.
12. Harrison, p.15.
13. W.V. Madej, *Red Army Order of Battle, 1941–1943* (Game Publishing Co, Allentown, PA, 1983).
14. Melvin, pp.353–54.
15. Guderian, p.306.
16. Manstein, p.447.
17. Guderian, p.309.
18. Kurowski, p.447.
19. Max Pemsel, 'Fighting the Invasion' pp.62–63.
20. Bekker, p.432.
21. Manstein, p.448.
22. Melvin, p.377.
23. Manstein, pp.448–49.

Chapter 6
1. Lord Ismay, *The Memoirs of General Lord Ismay* (Viking Press, London, 1960), p.343.
2. Ismay, p.345.
3. Dwight D Eisenhower, *Crusade in Europe* (Doubleday & Company, New York 1948), p.230.

4. Adolf Heusinger, *Befel im Widerstreit* (Tübingen und Stuttgart, Rainer Wunderlich Verlag Hermann Leins, 1950), p.155.
5. That is, all responsibility for decisions was borne by the Fuhrer and therefore everyone else had to obey his orders.
6. Lieutenant General Max Pemsel, in David C. Isby (ed.), *Fighting the Invasion* (Frontline Books, Yorkshire, 2016), p.54.
7. Lieutenant General Hans Speidel, in *Fighting the Invasion*, p.41.
8. Geyr von Schweppenburg, in *Fighting the Invasion*, p.73.
9. Bodo Zimmerman, in *The Fatal Decisions*, p.175.
10. Max Pemsel, in *Fighting the Invasion*, p.53.
11. Zimmerman, p.177.
12. Zimmerman, p.178.
13. Warlimont, p.400.
14. Blumentritt, 'von Rundstedt, The Soldier and the Man', p.185.
15. Guderian, p.328.
16. Schweppenburg, p.75.
17. Pemsel, p.65.
18. B.H. Liddell Hart, *The Rommel Papers* (Da Capo Press, New York, 1953), p.453.
19. Kesselring, pp.199–200.
20. Speidel, p.43.
21. See for example, Pemsel, 'Fighting the Invasion' pp.63–4; David Fraser, 'Knight's Cross', p.432; and Liddell-Hart, 'The Rommel Papers' p.453.
22. Blumentritt, 'Von Runsdtedt', p.219.
23. Guderian, p.331.
24. Warlimont, p.423.
25. Karl von Schlieben, in *Fighting the Invasion*, p.98.
26. Fritz Ziegelmann, in *Fighting the Invasion*, p.122.
27. Manstein, p.319.
28. Melvin, p.215.
29. Schweppenburg, p.96.
30. Schweppenburg, p.97.
31. Edgar Feuchtinger, in *Fighting the Invasion*, p.115.
32. Albert Speer, *Spandau: The Secret Diaries* (Collins, London, 1976), p.51.
33. Pemsel, p.66.
34. Liddell Hart, The Rommel Papers, p.457.
35. See Pemsel, 'Fighting the Invasion' p.63 and Blumentritt, 'Von Rundstedt, p.206.
36. See Blumentritt, 'von Rundstedt, the Soldier and the Man', p.205 and Fraser, 'Knight's Cross' p.455.
37. Warlimont, p.424.
38. Pemsel, p.68.
39. Pemsel, p.71.
40. Warlimont, p.424.
41. Warlimont, p.427.
42. Warlimont, p.428.
43. Bradley, p.255.
44. Speer, *Inside the Third Reich*, p.480.
45. Kurowski, p.579.
46. Blumentritt, in *Fighting the Invasion*, p.174.

47. Friederich von Criegern, in *Fighting the Invasion*, p.185.
48. Ziegelmann, p.193.
49. Ziegelmann, p.201.
50. Zimmerman, p.190.
51. Lord Ismay, p.290.
52. Speer, *Inside the Third Reich*, p.482.
53. Zimmerman, p.190.
54. See Zimmerman, 'The Fatal Decisions,' p.190, and Liddell-Hart, 'The Rommel Papers,' p.480.
55. Zimmerman, p.193.
56. Zimmerman, p.193.
57. David Fraser, 'Knight's Cross,' p.491 and Liddell-Hart, 'The Rommel Papers', p.481.
58. James Wood, '*Army of the West*', Stackpole Books, Pennsylvania, 1978, pp.144–145.
59. Liddell Hart, *The Rommel Papers*, p.487.
60. See 'Knight's Cross' David Fraser and Liddell-Hart, 'The Rommel Papers,' p.495.
61. Warlimont, p.434.
62. B.L. Montgomery, *The Memoirs of Field Marshal Montgomery* (Da Capo Press Inc, New York, 1958), p.232.
63. See Woods, 'Army of the West' p.147, and Liddell-Hart 'The Rommel Papers', p.489.
64. Eisenhower, p.221.
65. Richard Freiherr von Rosen, *Panzer Ace* (Greenhill Books, 2018), p.247.
66. Warlimont, p.447.
67. Zimmerman, p.196.
68. Warlimont, p.449.
69. Eisenhower, p.274.
70. Eisenhower, p.288.
71. Warlimont, p.449.
72. Warlimont, p.455.
73. Zimmerman, p.198.
74. Zimmerman, p.202.
75. Eisenhower, p.279.
76. Bradley, p.285.

Chapter 7
1. Grigori Krivosheev, *Soviet Casualties and Combat Losses in the Twentieth Century* (Greenhill Books, 1997), pp.85–97.
2. Melvin, p.410.
3. Manstein, p.279.
4. Manstein, p.280.
5. Kurowski, p.535.
6. Overy, *The Dictators*, p.529.
7. Kurowski, p.536.
8. Kurowski, p.535.
9. Overy, *The Dictators* p.529.
10. Paul Adair, *Hitler's Greatest Defeat: The Collapse of Army Group Centre, June 1944* (Arms and Armour Press, London, 1996), p.175.
11. Adair, p.173.
12. Jonathan Trigg, *The Defeat of the Luftwaffe* (Amberley Publishing, Gloucestershire,

2018), p.224.

13. Rudiger Overmans, *German Military Losses in World War II* (De Gruyter, Oldenbourg, 2016).

14. Fred Taylor (ed.), *The Goebbels Diaries* (Penguin, London, 1984), p.414.

15. Adair, p.62.

16. Liddell Hart, *A History of the Second Word War*, p.739.

17. Stewart Binns, *Barbarossa* (Wildfire, London, 2021), p.228.

18. Alexander Werth, *Russia at War, 1941–45* (Pan Books, London, 1965), p.771.

19. Adair, p.91.

20. Adair, p.95.

21. Adair, p.95.

22. Adair, p.95.

23. Adair, p.95.

24. Adair, p.97.

25. Adair, p.99.

26. Adair, p.99.

27. Adair, p.118.

28. Adair, p.171.

Chapter 8

1. Warlimont, p.455.

2. Warlimont, p.462.

3. Eisenhower, p.290.

4. Warlimont, p.457.

5. Warlimont, p.462.

6. Peter Caddick-Adams, *Snow and Steel* (Arrow Books, London, 2015), pp.xxxv–xxxviii.

7. Kajun, p.533.

8. Caddick-Adams, pp.xxxiii–xxxiv.

9. Liddell Hart, *A History of the Second World War*, p.824.

10. Liddell Hart, *The Other Side of the Hill*, p.450.

11. Manteuffel 'The Fatal Decisions' p.244.

12. Donald Brownlow, 'Panzer Baron', The Christopher Publishing House, Massachusetts, 1975, p.125.

13. C.B. MacDonald, *A Time for Trumpets* (William Morrow and Company, New York, 1985), p.35.

14. Josef 'Sepp' Dietrich was a comrade of Hitler's from the First World War. He was a sergeant then and had no further officer training. He was, however, one of the few people whom Hitler apparently trusted.

15. Caddick-Adams, p.239.

16. Warlimont, p.481.

17. Hasso von Manteuffel, in *The Fatal Decisions*, p.231.

18. Warlimont, p.487.

19. Speer, *Inside the Third Reich*, p.556.

20. Manteuffel, p.226.

21. Warlimont, p.490.

22. Manteuffel, p.226.

23. Eisenhower, p.342.

24. Eisenhower, p.355.

25. Manteuffel, p.250.
26. Manteuffel, p.249.
27. Speer, p.559.
28. Speer, p.559.
29. Speer, p.557.
30. Manteuffel, p.252.
31. Carl von Clausewitz, *On War* (Leonard & Howard, Putnam and Sons, New York, 1967), p.148.

Index